THE STRAIGHT DOPE
TELLS ALL

Also by Cecil Adams
The Straight Dope
More of the Straight Dope
Return of the Straight Dope

Also by Ed Zotti
Know It All!

THE STRAIGHT DOPE
TELLS ALL

Cecil Adams

Edited and with an Introduction by
Ed Zotti

Illustrated by Slug Signorino

Ballantine Books • New York

A Ballantine Book
Published by The Ballantine Publishing Group

Copyright © 1998 by Chicago Reader, Incorporated

"The Straight Dope by Cecil Adams" is a trademark of Chicago Reader, Incorporated

http://www.randomhouse.com

Library of Congress Cataloging-in-Publication Data

Adams, Cecil.
The straight dope tells all / Cecil Adams ; edited and with an introduction by Ed Zotti ; illustrated by Slug Signorino. — 1st ed.
        p.   cm.
Includes index.
ISBN 0-345-42007-1 (alk. paper)
1. Questions and answers.   I. Zotti, Ed.   II. Title.
                AG195.A393   1998
031'.02—dc21   97-38612
                                                                CIP

Cover and interior illustrations by Slug Signorino

Manufactured in the United States of America

First Edition: February 1998

10   9   8   7   6   5   4   3   2   1

To Jane and Jenny and the rest of the Straight Dope's far-flung online staff, on whose tireless efforts Cecil has come to depend, and whose loyalty is doubtless sustained in large part by the fact that they don't actually have to be in the same room with him.

Contents

Twenty-five years!
   Hmm. Too understated. Let's try again.
   TWENTY-FIVE YEARS!
   Still not happening. Once more.

¡¡¡T*W*E*N*T*Y* *F*I*V*E* Y*E*A*R*S!!!

Well, it's not holograms and lasers, but it'll have to do. Yes, it's been *twenty-five years* since Cecil began his noble work. The Straight Dope column first began appearing in February 1973, and Ballantine promised us this book would come out in February 1998.

What have we accomplished in twenty-five years? Looking around us, realistically, it's not like the world intelligence situation has noticeably improved. We had these T-shirts made up saying:

THE STRAIGHT DOPE
Fighting Ignorance Since 1973
[It's taking longer than we thought.]

. . . and people thought this was funny! Ha. It was a cold assessment of the facts. Perhaps just the sort of cold assessment you'd like to have decorating your body. This can be arranged. Visit our America Online or Web sites, about which more later. Sorry to have these mercantile concerns intrude into the literary sphere, but the Straight Dope has become a vast media empire, and we have many mouths to feed.

Where were we? Right, progress on the antistupidity front. Granted we haven't made as much of a dent as we'd like, but it's amazing how often you meet somebody these days and you think, "Wow, this person isn't *completely* comatose." Naturally we figure this is our doing.

For example, awhile back we were addressing a Mensa convention. You know, the smart people's society. (Cecil couldn't join. He was above the cutoff.) We were talking about the expiration date somebody sent us from a package of M&M's—you know, the one where it says:

12 DEC 88
805 AM

. . . and of course the question was, what happens at 8:06? No sooner had we said this than somebody sang out from the back of the room with the obvious answer: "They melt in your hand!" Clearly this person had been regularly exposed to "The Straight Dope" as a child.

A few years later the Mensa people had us back to address another convention. Naturally we told the M&M joke, because we felt this is the kind of quality humor that everyone should have a chance to hear again and again. And naturally somebody in the audience figured she could top it. So she got up and said she used to work for veterinarians, and they had bottles of euthanasia solution, which were labeled:

WARNING
Euthanasia Solution
Known to be habit-forming

What can I tell you? It gives one the strength to go on.

And now to business.

First: the size of the present volume. It is, we admit, smaller than the three earlier Straight Dope collections. Some people feel the process of downsizing began with the previous volume, *Return of the Straight Dope*. One sighs. *Return* was thinner than the first two books,

but that's because it was *printed on thinner paper, you freaking mor—*
excuse us. It's been a long 25 years. Anyway, the book had more or less
the same number of pages as the earlier ones.

Not this time. You are perhaps wondering why. You are perhaps
thinking, these Straight Dope guys, they want to put in half the work
for the same dough! Well, it's not like we're not trying to maximize our
investment. But this method has advantages for the Teeming Millions,
too. When was the last time a Straight Dope book came out? Nineteen
ninety-four, that's when—four years ago. The book before that came
out in 1988, *ten* years ago. One can only imagine the life of desperate
unhappiness that Cecil's admirers have led during this time. We have
vowed to bring books out every two years henceforth. Trouble is, in
contrast to many of our competitors, whose work is generated by machine, Cecil's wisdom is handcrafted. He produces only 30,000 words
per year. Thirty thousand words that sparkle like diamonds in a world
of darkness, it is true. But still, even if we pack in a lot more of Slug's
drawings plus the usual accumulation of updates, ephemera, and amus-
ing rubbish from the Teeming Millions, they are unavoidably the makings of a thinner book. Can't be helped. Trust us, it's all for the best.

The years since Cecil's last book have seen many changes. The most
notable is the great expansion of Straight Dope World Media Enter-
prises to which we have previously alluded. In addition to the books
and weekly column, we now operate a site on America Online
(keyword: Straight Dope) and a site on the World Wide Web
(www.straightdope.com). More information about these sites may be
found at the end of this book. If you have to choose one site over the
other, pick AOL. We say this because we make money on AOL. Cecil
may be the world's smartest human, but even he hasn't figured out
how to make a buck on the Web.

We also briefly had our own TV show, which aired—well, was dif-
fused through the coax—in fall of 1996 on the Arts & Entertainment
cable network. Fearing that the world was not ready for direct exposure to Cecil himself, we had his wisdom filtered through the medium
of host Mike Lukas. We thought Mike was pretty cool. Also he was
willing to walk barefoot through beds of hot coals for us (really), and a
guy like that you want to hang on to. Unfortunately, despite pleas to
the TV moguls from 3,000 viewers (not making this up, either), the
show did not get renewed. Maybe next year. We hope so. When you

get to tie up traffic in New York City for 90 minutes on the pretext that you are filming alligators in the sewers, you definitely feel you have chosen a rewarding career path.

Maybe you're thinking: but guys, it's been 25 years! Haven't all the good questions been answered?

Sure. And all the good songs have been written. You seeing a lot of scientists quitting because all the good knowledge has been discovered?

But, you say, we live in the electronic age! People nowadays have vast data resources at their fingertips! Why do they need you?

No question, the Web is an amazing thing. Allows you to propagate total horse manure across the planet at the speed of light. We figure we've got the most secure job on earth.

We'll level with you. We didn't expect to be doing this so long. But here we are. It's still fun. They pay us to do it. How can you beat a gig like that?

—ED ZOTTI

As always, questions, compliments, and large cash grants cheerfully accepted by:

Cecil Adams
c/o Chicago Reader
11 E. Illinois
Chicago, IL 60611
E-mail: cecil@chireader.com
Web site: www.straightdope.com
America Online site at keyword: Straight Dope

Technically Speaking

If the "black boxes" used on aircraft to record cockpit conversation and flight data are so indestructible, why can't they make the whole airplane out of the same material?—Terry Surowy, Kenosha, Wisconsin

They must get this question all the time at the National Transportation Safety Board. The guy I talked to didn't miss a beat with the answer: because the interstates aren't wide enough. His point, in case you're new to sarcasm, was that a plane built to black box standards would be so heavy you'd have to drive it rather than fly.

Unlike the rest of the aircraft, which is mostly made of light materials such as aluminum and plastic, the cockpit voice recorder and the flight data recorder are encased in stainless-steel boxes roughly 10 inches by 10 inches by 5. The steel is maybe a quarter-inch thick, and the boxes are so heavy in consequence that the designers don't even bother enclosing the accompanying electronics, which in a crash generally meet the same fate as the passengers. As an added precaution, the boxes are lined with a liquid-filled foam bladder encased in plastic that's supposed to protect against the intense heat of a postcrash fire.

Over the years these precautions have proven pretty effective. Investigators got useful data off one recorder that had been immersed in the ocean for seven years. But in another crash in Thailand the recorder landed in a pool of flaming fuel and basically got cooked.

One thing the NTSB learned from experience: be careful where you put these things. Recorders used to be located near the point where the wings joined the fuselage, the theory being that this was the most heavily constructed part of the plane. Problem was, being heavily constructed, the parts of the plane falling on the recorders often crushed them. Now the recorders are put in the tail section so that, assuming your typical crashing plane goes in nose first, the forward part of the airframe absorbs most of the impact.

Sitting back there won't help *you*, though. When you mix stuff in the Cuisinart, you think it matters which end of the banana went in last?

I have been searching for the answer to this question for some time now. I hope you can solve my dilemma. What was the Leaning Tower of Pisa originally designed to house? Such as, apartments, shops, observatory, monument, etc. Thank you in advance for any help.— Rebecca Smith, via the Internet

You get questions in this business that give you pause. The other day someone writes in and says, "If making a robot limb is so hard but other types of machines are easy, how come no animals species has ever evolved wheels?" Had to think about that for a while. Same with the purpose of the Leaning Tower of Pisa. Since, unlike the wheel thing, the answer isn't likely to come to you by process of introspec-

tion, I'll just come out and tell you: it's a *campanile*. This perhaps raises additional questions in your mind, e.g.:

Q: What's a *campanile*?

A: A bell tower.

Q: Why a bell tower?

A: Why not? Guys, being guys, always want to build towers. In fact, the region around Pisa was famous for them. But the best excuse for a tower they could come up with in the twelfth century was: We could put bells on it! Whereas we twentieth-century sophisticates, with our mature grasp of the architectonic possibilities, would be more likely to say: What a great place for a satellite dish.

Q: Seriously.

A: "The bell tower [was] begun in 1174 as the third and final structure of [Pisa's] cathedral complex," the *Encyclopaedia Britannica* says. *Scientific American*, however, says construction started in 1173. I'm not saying *EB* screwed up. But you remember what they said about drawing and quartering. (See page 240.)

Q: So what's the deal with the slant?

A: You've heard the expression "building on sand"? The Leaning Tower of Pisa is exhibit A. All of the Piazza dei Miracoli, the square in which the tower stands, is subsiding, but the spot under the LT seems particularly unstable. The tower began to lean while it was still under construction.

Q: So why'd they keep going?

A: Obviously you've never dealt with contractors. During the first phase of construction, from 1173 to 1178, the tower began to lean slightly north. When they got to the third level the builders made the walls higher on the north side and shorter on the south side to level out the top.

Q: Why didn't they just start over again from scratch?

A: Maybe they figured nobody would notice (another thing contractors do a lot). An alternative explanation comes to mind when you look at a cross section of the tower. The thing is massive, with masonry walls maybe eight or nine feet thick at the base. All told, the tower weighs 14,700 metric tons. The guys may have figured, no way we're doing *this* sucker over.

In 1178 construction halted due to "political unrest." (Probable translation: the unions went on strike.) By the time construction resumed in 1272, the building was leaning the opposite way, toward the south. A reasonable crew would have concluded: this project is doomed. Let's see if we can unload it on somebody with astigmatism. Not the Pisans. They added stories four through seven. At level five, having previously zigged south, they decided to zag north, making the walls noticeably taller on the south side in an attempt to square things up. This gives the building the squashed-layer-cake look it has today.

Construction halted again in 1278 (more unrest) and resumed in 1360. Bear in mind that it was now 187 years after the first stone was laid, the tower was dangerously out of true, and there were still no bells in it. What the hell, said the Pisans, let's put in some bells. They added the eighth and final story—the bell chamber—which zagged even further north, and at some point installed the first of seven bells. The largest of these, cast in 1655, weighed nearly three and a half tons.

Q: These people had no clue.

A: Maybe not, Ms. 20–20 Hindsight, but the thing is still standing today, more than 800 years after it was started. How long do you think that aluminum siding on your garage is going to last?

That said, the fact that something has lasted 800 years is no guarantee it's going to last 900. Despite, and in a couple cases because of, various ameliorative efforts, the tower's tilt steadily increased over the centuries, so that today it's about 17 feet out of true (pretty steep tilt for a building that's only 185 feet high). Remarkably, the bells were still rung, and the public was still allowed to climb to the top. Then in 1989 a similar bell tower in Italy collapsed. Oops, said the Pisans. They promptly closed the Leaning Tower and began some serious rehab. The most visible signs of this are 750 metric tons of lead weights piled around the north side of the base, and steel straps around the second level to keep it from collapsing under the weight of the unevenly loaded masonry above. Results to date: It's still standing, but I wouldn't want to have a picnic under it. With apologies to the guy on Usenet whose sig I ripped off the following from, the latest plan is to take out the bells and put in a clock.

Q: Why a clock?

A: Because it's no use having the inclination if you haven't got the time.

What purpose do the "fins" on a fountain pen serve?—La Mantia, Washington, D.C.

I tell you, you don't appreciate the vast edifice of modern technology until you start looking into stuff like fountain pens. I mean, geniuses sweated over these things! And all so you wouldn't get ink on your fingers.

Lest the Teeming Millions visualize a fountain pen equipped like a 1950s Buick, let me clarify that the fins we're talking about are those inky ribs or vanes just back of the writing tip. Pen engineers (no joke—one guy I talked to at Sheaffer Pen used to be in aerospace) call this the "comb feed." Basically it acts as a sponge to keep excess ink from dribbling out of the tip.

Suppose your ink cartridge is half full. When you pick up the pen, your hand's warmth makes the air in the cartridge expand, forcing more ink into the tip. Rather than get all over your page, the ink flows into the thin slots between the fins ("combs"), remaining there by capillary attraction. As ink flows out the tip during writing, the slots empty out, air manages to get up the fill tube into the cartridge, and more ink flows down to replenish the supply. Meanwhile you just scribble away, blissfully unaware of the technology that makes it all possible. On the scale of inventions that have enhanced the quality of life, I'm not saying it ranks up there with perforated toilet paper. But I'd still rather have it than not.

In a world of A, AA, AAA, C, and D, are there any B-sized batteries?—Paul Guss and Bill Rauchholz, Arlington, Virginia

A batteries? In what alternative universe did you guys find A batteries? Virtually no one makes them today, or B batteries either. The letters are part of a standard for single-cell batteries devised by the American National Standards Institute, or ANSI, beginning in the 1920s. (I realize that, strictly speaking, a battery consists of two or more cells, but let's not get picky.) Today the standard sizes range from AAAA to G, and for some reason there are also J, N, and 6. AAA, AA, C, and D were the only sizes that caught on in a big way commercially, but the others haven't totally disappeared. If you pry apart one of those big 6-volt lantern batteries, you'll find four F cells inside.

Why are residential toilet seats always round, and public toilet seats always "U" shaped? Who started this practice?—R.G., Jacksonville, Florida

Three times readers have sent me this question in the space of four months. You people really have to start getting out of the house.

Public toilets are designed the way they are for the obvious reason: men are pigs. In particular, they splash, and when they're out of the house and away from the restraining influence of their families, they splash even more—and they don't wipe up. The relevant male apparatus being in the front, this makes the front of the toilet seat (particularly the underside) pretty gross—or rather, it *would* make it gross, if toilet-seat makers hadn't been shrewd enough to head the problem off at the pass.

Who the unsung genius was who started this practice we may never know, but it's now embodied in industry standards. Cecil was chatting with Shabbir Rawalpindiwala, chairman of the toilet-seat committee for the American National Standards Institute, and he told me that after months of solemn deliberation, he and his fellow intellectuals had definitively set the design of public (and private) toilet seats for all time, ensuring that our grandchildren will have U-shaped public potty seats, too. (Actually, Shabbir heads the Committee on Synthetic Organic Materials in Plumbing Fixtures, but it'll always be the toilet-seat committee to me.) One small step for man, another giant leap for mankind.

Since when do CDs skip? Since last week, in my case. What gives? I thought CDs were immune to the failings of mere vinyl.—John Bagdonas, Jersey City, New Jersey

Alas, another bit of audio hype. Dirty CDs will skip just like dirty records. A complicated system of beam splitters and servomechanisms keeps the laser centered on the CD "groove," but an opaque glob stuck to the disc may throw the system off and cause a skip. The cure, usually, is to clean the disc with a clean dry cloth, always by wiping from the center of the disc to the edge. That way an accidental scratch won't obliterate so much consecutive musical data that the error-correcting circuitry gives up in disgust.

What do you know about those plastic ion laundry balls that supposedly replace detergent?—RosenClan, via AOL

Here's what I know:

1. People are charging as much as $75 for a set of little gizmos that look like they came as a prize in a Happy Meal.

2. Fifty bucks a set is more typical, but even that has to be an outrageous markup inasmuch as there's an outfit in Hong Kong that will sell them to you for $3.60 a pair. (Minor drawback: you have to go to Hong Kong to pick them up.)

3. If you believe *Consumer Reports*, even $3.60 is a rip because you can get equally good results tossing your kid's Koosh ball in the washing machine, i.e., none.

Taking all this into consideration, I figure laundry balls aren't just the name of the product, they're what you need to sell it.

But we believe in fairness around here. So I'll say this. We tested a set of laundry thingies (laundry disks rather than laundry balls, actually, but what's the diff?) with unexpected results. But more about that in a sec.

Laundry balls and such are mostly sold via direct marketing—e.g., catalog firms and "multilevel marketing" concerns. An MLM basically is a network of individuals who sell a product and at the same time try to recruit other sellers, in whose profits they share. I'm not saying every MLM is a racket. There are probably a few people who thought

their time-share condos were a good deal, too. But MLMs do seem to hawk more than their share of junk.

Laundry balls/disks allegedly eliminate or greatly reduce the need for conventional laundry detergents. You get different stories on how they're supposed to work, including a lot of hokum about "structured water" and "nanotricity" and whatnot, none of which makes much sense. The most coherent account comes from a catalog firm called Real Goods:

"1. Metallic elements (including copper and silver) in the activated ceramics [inside the device] release electrons which in turn produce ionized oxygen. This form of oxygen is a totally natural cleanser which breaks up dirt and organic compounds."

Sure, it's possible, says the Straight Dope Science Advisory Board. A metal could produce a peroxide, better known as bleach. But probably not enough to accomplish anything.

"2. The activated ceramics also emit 'far infrared electromagnetic waves' which cause water molecule clusters to disassociate, allowing much smaller individual water molecules to penetrate into the innermost part of the fabric and remove dirt."

SDSAB: All objects at room temp emit "far infrared"; this is known as "being warm." (Well, OK, "radiating heat energy.") No appreciable effect on water molecules.

"3. When water contacts the activated ceramics, an abundance of OH ions is produced, reducing the surface tension of the water and greatly increasing its penetrating power. Ordinary detergents make use of this same principle, but do so by using harsh chemicals."

SDSAB: Possibly OH- ions, also known as hydroxide, could be created in this way, although not in large quantity. These would lower the water's pH. Substantially the same thing happens with lye soap and sodium hydroxide, the main component of Drano. What was that about no harsh chemicals?

But now to the practical test, which was conducted by my assistant Jane. (You may think it sexist that she got stuck doing the laundry, but she volunteered.) She stained various items of clothing with ketchup, chocolate, ink, grass, and "some of the purple dye I use for my hair." That Jane! She washed three batches: one with three laundry disks from Real Goods; one with Tide; one in plain water. As advised, she used a prewash stain treatment on all the batches. Result: little difference among the three except that the disks did better getting rid of the grass stain. "Hmm," said Jane.

Round two. The disks got the wash "a tad" cleaner. Hmm-HMM.

OK, the slightly better showing by the disks may be a fluke. Other investigations (e.g., the aforementioned *CR* test, reported in the February 1995 issue) found no difference. The real surprise is that Tide didn't perform much better than plain water. I'm not saying you need laundry balls or disks. But the soap makers' dirty little secret, you should pardon the expression, is that you might not need conventional detergent, either.

Laundry Balls: Taking Folks To The Cleaners?

Got some interesting mail about laundry balls. First, reader David Harris reported his satisfaction with the Laundry Solution, a laundry ball sold by TradeNet. "It has performed well even on the smelly dog blankets we keep on the furniture to ward off hair and dirt from a greasy Airedale," he wrote. "Without the detergent residue, cottons are noticeably fluffier without using softener or dryer sheets (great for towels)." He went on to tout the company that developed the Laundry Solution for TradeNet, American Technologies Group, which "created a coolant that is both safe and 20 percent more efficient than Freon, and is working on a particle beam device to neutralize nuclear waste." Laundry balls *and* particle beams! Are these guys brilliant or what?

Shortly afterward, another reader sent us some newspaper articles reporting that the Utah state division of consumer protection had sent a couple of TradeNet's laundry balls out for tests and found they contained, not crystal technology as claimed, but dyed water! A TradeNet spokesman said the state was testing an "earlier model." Meaning what—TradeNet at one point thought dyed water would actually work?

Other readers pointed out numerous explanations for the fact that, in our tests, laundry balls seemed to work as well as regular detergent: 1) laundry often contains a lot of residual detergent from earlier washings; 2) the stain remover often recommended for use with laundry balls itself contains detergent; and 3) the laundry ball may work by mechanical action—the equivalent of beating clothes on a rock. And of course you can't discount the influence of good old wishful thinking, which one suspects was a factor in the glowing evaluation by David Harris above.

One more thing. Amway listed a ceramic washing disk in a 1997 catalog, but decided not to sell the thing after tests showed it had "no measurable impact on overall cleaning." Figured you'd want to know.

A question gnaws at me. We've all used those drive-up teller machines at banks. Why are the buttons identified with braille?—Vox Populi, Baltimore

Congratulations, Vox, you are the one millionth person to ask this question! Please send us your address so we can burn down your house.

Hey, just kidding! Although if you ever ask why we park on the driveway and drive on the parkway, you won't get lucky twice.

Anyway, you asked a question, and by God you are going to get an

answer. Drive-up ATM buttons are marked with braille because federal regulations require it. To be specific, section 4.34.4 of the *ADA Accessibility Guidelines for Buildings and Facilities* (Appendix to Part 1191, 36 CFR Chapter XI, issued pursuant to the Americans with Disabilities Act of 1990) says, "Instructions and all information for use [of an automated teller machine] shall be made accessible to and independently usable by persons with vision impairments." Drive-up ATMs, unlike the walk-up variety, don't need to be wheelchair accessible, but the rules make no exception regarding accessibility by the blind.

You're now thinking: boy, those federal bureaucrats sure are stupid. Don't they realize a blind person isn't going to be able to drive to a drive-up ATM? Cecil reserves judgment on the stupidity question, but even if the feds weren't smart enough to notice this little problem on their own, there were plenty of people who pointed it out for them before the rule was finalized. The American Bankers Association, for one, asked that drive-up machines be exempt from the visually impaired requirement, arguing that a blind person using a drive-up ATM would have to be a passenger and that the driver of the vehicle could help with the transaction.

No dice, said the Architectural and Transportation Barriers Compliance Board, reasoning that driver assistance "would not allow the [blind] individual to use the ATM independently." This may sound like one of those absurd points of principle, but ATM manufacturers say a fair number of blind people do take cabs to drive-up ATMs, and nobody wants to ask a total stranger to help with a financial transaction.

Your question does point to a more serious problem, which other readers have also raised: how the hell is a blind person supposed to use any kind of ATM? Whether the keypad numbers are identified with braille or not, there isn't any braille translation of the on-screen instructions, without which the machine is useless. Maybe, you're thinking, the problem isn't the brainless bureaucrats, it's the brainless (or cynical) bankers and ATM builders, who figure a pretense of accessibility will get them off the hook.

But that isn't it, either. At the time the accessibility rules were written, and to a great extent still today, there was no agreement on the best way to make ATMs accessible to the blind. More than 50 ideas have been proposed, including a "talking machine," detailed braille instructions, an automated "bank-by-phone" setup with a telephone handset and a keypad, and so on. (Sample problem: if you use a "voice guided" ATM, how do you keep others from overhearing?) Another difficulty was retrofitting the thousands of machines already installed.

The bankers and ATM builders argued that the best thing to do was leave the federal rules vague until the industry figured out a practical approach. The not-entirely-satisfactory solution in the interim has been to 1) mark ATM keypads, input and output slots, etc., with braille, and 2) send braille ATM instruction brochures or audiocassettes to blind bank patrons requesting them. The theory is that while ATM operation varies from machine to machine, people conduct most of their transactions at just a few locations, the operating sequences for which they can memorize. The drawback of this approach is that you have to know that the special instructions are available and you can only use the machines you have instructions for.

Happily, the banks and ATM builders have been reasonably diligent in trying to come up with more accessible equipment, some of which is starting to show up in the marketplace now. About time, say some advocacy groups. "We don't want to see information technology [e.g., ATMs] become the new curb," says Elga Joffee of the American Foundation for the Blind. "There's certainly no reason to squelch evolving technology. I just wish they'd hurry up and evolve it."

And Now For The Funny Version

The question of why they have braille on drive-up ATMs once showed up in the Internet Oracle a couple years back (you could probably search the Oracle archives for it), and the answer was something like: "Because the dog can't be expected to drive and use the ATM machine!"—Rishi Fish, via AOL

That's right up there with: "Why don't blind people bungee jump? Because it scares the heck out of the dogs."—Seal TX, via AOL

You gotta love the Internet Oracle (www.pcnet.com/~stenor/oracle/). It proves that if the Teeming Millions combine their resources and answer each other's questions, they can be just as funny as me.

A few years ago there was a lot of noise about the United States finally going metric. We saw road signs with mile and kilometer equivalents and soda bottles containing peculiar fractions of liters that corresponded to quarts and ounces. Then what happened? No one talks about metric anymore. How come? Is there any serious metric movement? Is not going metric part of the decline of U.S. industry in world markets?—Eric Gordon, New York

Like hell. Had U.S. industry suffered a real (as opposed to relative) decline, Americans would have quit screwing around and converted to metric long ago, just as the United Kingdom did—and remember, the British are the ones who invented this dram-bushel-inch stuff. As it is, U.S. industry is sufficiently prosperous and the domestic market is so large that the country can afford the luxury of supporting two separate systems of measurement. Which is basically what it has. Most big multinational firms use metric for goods they sell abroad, and some (e.g., the automakers) have abandoned the inch-pound system altogether. Smaller companies serving primarily the U.S. market and of course most ordinary folks have clung to the old system, mainly for lack of a compelling reason to change. If significant numbers of midsize firms routinely had to convert from millimeters to inches (how fast can you multiply by .03937?), opposition to metrication would evaporate. But in the United States they don't, and it hasn't.

One of the reasons the United States will probably never fully convert to metric is the country's genius for compromise—its saving grace in politics, maybe, but not so useful when it comes to weights and measures. The first round of attempted metrication, which took place following passage of the Metric Conversion Act of 1975, is now remembered as the time when "we made a mistake . . . trying to force metrics down people's throats," one advocate says. Baloney. It was a typical let's-please-everybody muddle. Dual posting of highway signs in miles and kilometers cost money without any compensating advantage and, by calling attention to the fact that one kilometer equalled .621 miles, made the metric system seem needlessly complicated. The folly of dual measurements persists to this day. Rather than baffle consumers by pointing out that a gallon of milk equals 3.78 liters, it would be better simply to replace gallons with four-liter containers. The two-liter pop bottle no doubt succeeded because it was just that simple.

Opponents of metrication have succeeded in painting it as a one-world plot, with the introduction of an alien system of weights and measures the obvious prelude to a takeover by the Bolsheviks. To this day you'll hear media commentators moaning that recalculating football fields and baseball diamonds in meters threatens the integrity of American sport. Converting to metric will cost money, the critics say, and unless you're involved in foreign trade it confers no benefit.

These arguments are specious. If people still calculate horse races in furlongs, a medieval measure, there's nothing to prevent them from using feet and yards in sports indefinitely (although the Olympics have gotten people used to meters). And while converting to metric costs something, much of the money has already been spent. Rare is the auto mechanic, for example, who doesn't have metric wrenches.

As for the metric system conferring no benefit—come on. For many everyday purposes the inch-pound system is useless. How many people understand fluid ounces, bushels, pecks, rods, and grains? How many can visualize an acre? (A hectare, the comparable metric unit, is 100 meters on a side.) Two centuries ago the United States adopted a decimal system of currency, and today everybody's happy they did. A decimal system of measurement would be at least equally useful.

Officially the United States is still trying to convert to metric. In 1988 Congress reiterated that the metric system was the "preferred system of measurement." Federal agencies, which procure more than $300 billion in goods and services annually, are supposed to require their vendors to supply metric products. Most still don't. But who knows? In an age when every dieter can quote you "fat grams," the metric system may sneak up on us yet.

Do you need a key to start an F-16?—Dave Johnson, Chicago

No. It is important to make the public aware of this. If you take your F-16 into a bad neighborhood, make sure you don't leave it on the street overnight.

How do "night" rearview mirrors work? One flick of the button and it seemingly dims all.—Chris Gaffney, Toronto

Here at Straight Dope University, we have explanations suited to all levels of intellectual attainment. We offer the intro-level course first.

In a dimming rearview mirror you've got two reflecting surfaces— one with high reflectance, one with low. During the day you use the high reflector. At night the dimmer button swings the low reflector into place, dimming glare from headlights behind you.

Satisfied? Then cut to the funnies, wimp. Still thirsting for more? Coming right up.

The trick is that the two reflecting surfaces are the front and back of the *same piece of glass*. Said glass is specially ground so that the back surface is slightly tilted relative to the front one. In other words, the glass looks wedge-shaped from the side. The back surface is coated with silver like a bathroom mirror, making it highly reflective. The front surface isn't coated, but it's still slightly reflective, like all glass.

Because the two surfaces are out of parallel, anytime you look at the rearview mirror, you're seeing two different reflections simultaneously. During the day with the mirror tilted into the normal position, the silvered surface shows you the road behind you. The nonsilvered surface, meanwhile, shows you the backseat of the car—but it's so dim you don't notice it.

At night the situation is reversed. When you flip the dim button, the silvered surface tilts so it's showing you the car's ceiling, which is so dark you don't notice it. But now the nonsilvered surface is showing you the road.

Because the headlights of the cars behind you are so bright, the nonsilvered surface reflects enough light to let you see what's behind you. But it's not so bright that you're blinded.

The folks at GM tell me that on Cadillacs you can now get a high-tech "electrochromic" mirror that dims at night automatically, without having to flip a switch. The Caddy mirror has only one reflective surface, but there's a special film in front of it that gradually darkens at night through the magic of electronics.

Very impressive. But for sheer low-tech genius the tilting surfaces are hard to beat.

Questions We're Still Thinking About

I just got back from the auto shop where I bought four new tires for my car. They said to come back every 7,500 miles to have the tires rotated. That seemed strange, since the tires rotate every time I drive the car. What's the deal?—Will Fitzhugh, via the Internet

I play chess with my brother by mail. We send our moves and a short note to each other on a computer disk that shuttles between southern California and Massachusetts. We'd been using a 32-cent stamp to send the disk for the first six or seven moves. On the eighth move I became uncertain whether 32 cents would be sufficient as the number of moves increased. Is the computer disk growing heavier as more data accumulates on it? My experiment weighing a blank and a full disk failed to detect any difference, but maybe you have a more accurate scale.—Richard Briones-Colman, Irvine, California

My physics teacher in high school explained how motion is relative to a person's frame of reference. When you look through the window of a train and see another train moving, you can't be certain whether your train is moving forward and the other train is sitting still or whether your train is sitting still and the other train is moving backward. Recently I've been wondering whether the same principle applies to VCRs. When I fast-forward my video player, how can I be certain my life isn't moving backward very fast? Last night when I rented Apocalypse Now *and fast-forwarded through large parts of it, I had the sensation of losing two hours of my life. Is this just my imagination?—Paul Farwell, Boston*

Hard to say. Lotta people figured they lost two hours after they got *Apocalypse Now* and pressed "play."

From The Straight Dope Message Board

Subj: LITTLE RED BALLS
From: DrGiardina

In my travels I have seen red balls (spheres) on power lines—sometimes on high tension lines in the middle of nowhere, at other times on regular power lines in a local area. I have asked numerous people what they are for and no one seems to know. Any ideas?

From: Hyperlinks

I was told these were weights to hold the lines down in bad weather like windstorms. I am not sure, but maybe they are on the lower lines to hold them down from touching the middle lines, that is just a guess.

From: WilsonSA
On military bases at least, they are there so pilots can see the wires better (lots of low flying helicopters).

From: XYZ1PDQ
I was worried for a moment. I thought this post was about a sexually transmitted disease.

From: BatGrrrl
ROFLMGDBAOSTC!!! :D

From: Juliet McA
<<ROFLMGDBAOSTC!!!>>
I am sorry for this. I haven't heard this one! Please spell it out for newbies like me.

From: BatGrrrl
Well, Juliet, since you asked so nicely, it is:
"Rolling on [the] floor laughing my GD bloody arse off, scaring the cat."

2

Looking Back

What's the straight dope on Jimmy Carter's once being attacked by a killer rabbit? I heard there were actually photos of Carter swinging for his life at this rabbit, but his people refused to release them because "some facts about the president must remain forever wrapped in obscurity." What the hell is going on?—Donald Lilly, North Hollywood, California

Well, right now I'd say it's pretty quiet, which is about what you'd figure, seeing as how the killer rabbit thing happened in 1979. Not that stories about feckless good ol' boy presidents don't have their pertinence these days. Say what you will about Bill Clinton's PR problems, though, Jimmy Carter was in a class by himself. Nice man, but

he was one president whose image a couple accusations from bimbos would have probably improved.

The rabbit incident happened on April 20 while Carter was taking a few days off in Plains, Georgia. He was fishing from a canoe in a pond when he spotted the fateful rabbit swimming toward him. It was never precisely determined what the rabbit's problem was. Carter, always trying to look at things from the other guy's point of view, later speculated that it was fleeing a predator. Whatever the case, it was definitely a troubled rabbit. "It was hissing menacingly, its teeth flashing and nostrils flared and making straight for the president," a press account said.

The Secret Service having been caught flatfooted—I'll grant you an amphibious rabbit assault is a tough thing to defend against—the president did what he could to protect himself. Initially it was reported that he had hit the rabbit with his paddle. Realizing this would not play well with the Rabbit Lovers Guild, Carter later clarified that he had merely splashed water at the rabbit, which then swam off toward shore. A White House photographer, ever alert to history's pivotal moments, snapped a picture of the encounter for posterity.

Good thing, too. Carter's own staff was skeptical when he told the rabbit story back at the White House. Some ventured the opinion that rabbits couldn't swim, didn't attack people, and sure weren't about to take on a sitting president, even if it was Jimmy Carter. Miffed, Jimmy ordered up a print of the aforementioned photo, but this failed to resolve the issue. The picture showed the president with his paddle raised, and something in the water, "but you couldn't tell what that something was," an anonymous staffer was quoted as saying. The average politician would have said, goddamit, I'm president of the United States and I say it was a rabbit. But Carter was not that kind of guy. He ordered a blowup made, establishing at last that his attacker was, well, a bunny, or "swamp rabbit," to use press secretary Jody Powell's somewhat fiercer sounding term.

OK, not one of the shining moments of Carter's career, but so far not a major train wreck, inasmuch as nobody outside the White House knew anything about it. Jody Powell took care of that problem the following August when he told the rabbit story to Associated Press reporter Brooks Jackson over a cup of tea. Powell ought to have known that you cannot tell anything to reporters in August because there is nothing else to write about and they will make any fool thing into a front-page scandal. Which is exactly what happened. The *Washington Post* put the bunny story on page one complete with a cartoon takeoff of the famous *Jaws* movie poster entitled "Paws." The media ran with the story for a week, the worst aspect from Carter's perspective undoubtedly being the columnists, who basically all said, yeah, it's just a rabbit, but it shows you the kind of president we've got here. The administration refused to release the photos, although I seem to recall that Reagan's people later found and leaked them. Carter's subsequent drubbing at the polls was a foregone conclusion, hostage crisis or not. Lesson for life #1: if it moves, kill it. Lesson for life #2: if you can't kill it, for God's sake don't talk about it to the Associated Press.

Rabbit Redux

I have a theory that should put to rest this President Carter/killer rabbit thing once and for all. I propose that the president's antagonist was not a rabbit but a nutria (Myocastor coypus). *The world's largest rodent, the nutria is semiaquatic with webbed hind feet and is very aggressive. Native to South America and valued for its durable fur, the nutria was introduced into the southern United States in the last century and quickly became a well-established pest species. A partially submerged nutria (a lightning-fast swimmer) would look very similar to a rabbit. Its lack of long, rabbitlike ears could easily be overlooked in the fog of battle.*

I hope this serves to partially rehabilitate the much-maligned 39th president.—Thomas Canaday, San Francisco, California

You think being attacked by the "world's largest rodent" is an improvement? Then again, it had to give Carter a taste of what it would be like fending off Alfonse D'Amato.

Incidentally, the nutria isn't the world's largest rodent. The honor, such as it is, goes to the capybara, 110 pounds of pure ugly. Jimmy should count his blessings.

We all know that America was named for Amerigo Vespucci. What does "Amerigo" mean in Italian?—Dave Curwin, Newton, Massachusetts

What do you mean, what does it mean in Italian? What does Dave mean in English? Amerigo by Vespucci's day was an established if not especially common name whose original meaning, it is safe to say, had long been forgotten. AV apparently got it for no more profound reason than that it was his grandfather's name.

Since you asked, there are a couple of theories on the name's origin. One is that it is a variant of "Enrico," the Italian form of Henry, and derives from the Old German "Haimirich," in later German, "Emmerich," in English, "Americus", from *haimi*, home, plus *ric*, power, ruler. Alternatively, it may come from the Old German "Amalricus," from *amal*, work, plus *ric*, ruler. (Amalricus the foreman? Beats me.) Amerigo shows up in Italian writing from around the twelfth century and may have been introduced by the Ostrogoths six centuries earlier (this from *Dictionary of First Names*, Hanks and Hodges, 1990).

A more interesting question is why the cartographer Martin Waldseemueller in 1507 named the New World (actually, just South America) America rather than Vespucciland—although I guess to ask the question is to answer it. Amerigo's first name was a lot more euphonious than his last name, and (no small matter) could be latinized into a word that started and ended with the letter A, just like Asia and Africa before it. Also, unlike Christopher Columbus, invariably referred to by his last name, Vespucci was one of those people known in his own lifetime mostly by his first.

The most interesting question of all is why America was named after a guy who was otherwise so obscure. For centuries it was argued that Amerigo Vespucci was a fraud who had never traveled to the continent that bore his name and did not deserve to have either of his names applied to anything. But it is now fairly well established that he made at least two voyages to the Americas, not as leader of an expedition but possibly as navigator, the first time in 1499. He was not the first European of his era to set foot on the mainland, as was once thought, but probably was the first to realize that the land he helped explore was a separate continent and not merely the coast of Asia, as Columbus and others believed.

Vespucci came to the world's attention chiefly through the publication in 1503 and 1504 of two brief letters he purportedly wrote to Lorenzo de Medici about a voyage undertaken for the king of Portugal. Obviously the work of an educated man (the Vespuccis were a prosperous family in Florence), the letters managed to be both scholarly and entertaining, combining a sober discussion of navigational issues with the news that the natives of the New World would have sex with anybody, including Mom. Vespucci, or perhaps his anonymous publisher, also had the wit to entitle the first letter *Novus Mundus*, the New World, an audacious and, as it turned out, accurate claim.

The letters were by far the most interesting account of explorations in the Americas that had appeared up to that time and caused a sensation that, if anything, exceeded that created by Columbus's description of his first voyage ten years earlier. The letters were reprinted in every European language and soon came to the attention of Waldseemueller and his friends, who were members of a think tank of sorts in the town of Saint-Die, Lorraine, now part of France. The Waldseemueller group published *Cosmographiae Introductio* (Introduction to Cosmography), the first attempt to update the geography texts of the ancients. They were quite taken with Vespucci's idea that the Americas were a new land, since it meant they had gone beyond the knowledge of the ancients, in whose shadow they had long toiled. They thought it only appropriate that AV's name grace the new land, of whose extent they had at that point only the vaguest inkling. The naming of America after Amerigo Vespucci was thus a bit capricious but not entirely undeserved.

A friend and I are having an, uh, open exchange of views on the topic of John Tyler. My friend says, "The United States never had a president named Tyler," and pulled out some reference that said Tyler had no constitutional authority to assume the presidency when William Henry Harrison died but was only the vice president performing the duties of the president. I pulled out the Encyclopaedia Britannica, *where John Tyler is listed as "10th president of the United States." My friend, and at this point I am using the term loosely, disputes this but has agreed to abide by Cecil's opinion, which is hereby requested. NB: There is a fairly expensive meal riding on providing the correct information. Not that you need any incentive.—Fania, via the Internet*

Of course not. But while Cecil's soul hungers only for knowledge, his body wouldn't mind a nice steak. Your friend is being obnoxious. Tyler was the first vice president to assume the powers of the presidency upon the death of the incumbent. There was some question at the time whether he was president or merely acting president, the Constitution being ambiguous on this point. Tyler's detractors in fact referred to him as "His Accidency." What practical consequence the matter had is debatable, but in the interest of clarity both houses of Congress passed resolutions declaring that Tyler was president, period. That settled things for all but a few nitpickers, of whom your friend regrettably is one. When do we eat?

What happened to the astronauts after the Challenger *explosion? Everyone assumes they were blown to pieces, but about six months after the accident I saw an article saying the emergency oxygen systems for the astronauts had been manually activated, meaning some or all of them had survived the explosion. I also remember the tanks had three to five minutes of usage, meaning they were breathing for at least as long as it took to fall. I recall something about government interference with the autopsy results and (this is the X-Files-type detail) warnings to fishermen to stay away from some mysterious green vials that might be floating in the wreckage. Is there more to the story?—Fox M., Oakland, California*

More facts? No. More weirdness? You bet. Recently what purports to be a radio transcript of the *Challenger* crew's last minutes has been

showing up on computer bulletin boards. Here are some of the more melodramatic lines, with M or F indicating the sex of the speaker:

M: What happened? What happened? Oh God, no—no!

M: I told them, I told them . . . Dammit! Resnik don't . . .

F: Don't let me die like this. Not now. Not here . . .

F: I'm . . . passing . . . out.

M: If you ever wanted (unintelligible) me a miracle (unintelligible). (Screams.)

M: Can't breathe . . .

M: God. The water . . . we're dead! (Screams.)

F: Good-bye (sobs) . . . I love you, I love you . . .

M: Our Father (unintelligible) hallowed be thy name (unintelligible) . . .

This is said to have originated in the supermarket tabloid *Weekly World News*. NASA says it's a hoax, but the agency's credibility in this regard is about zero. After insisting for months that the astronauts never knew what hit them, NASA conceded that they not only survived the explosion but tried to save themselves and may even have been alive when the cabin smashed into the sea at 200 mph. A 1988 exposé by the *Miami Herald* also revealed that NASA preempted local officials' efforts to do an autopsy, no doubt to avoid having gory pictures (or at least embarrassing quotes) splashed in the newspapers at a time when the agency's prestige was already in the toilet. But the "green vial" stuff seems to be the product of an overactive imagination. Boaters were merely warned to avoid debris lest they mess up evidence or be messed up themselves by fuel or other dangerous chemicals.

Contrary to common belief, the *Challenger* did not explode into a million pieces in midair. What we all saw on TV was the external tank breaking open and its contents erupting in a fireball that enveloped the shuttle. Pilot Michael Smith said "uh-oh!" and a fraction of a second later the shuttle broke into several large pieces. "Separate sections that can be identified on film include the main engine/tail section with the engines still burning, one wing of the orbiter, and the forward fuselage [including sealed crew cabin] trailing a mass of umbilical lines pulled loose from the payload bay," the official report on the disaster said.

"The forces on the orbiter at breakup were probably too low to cause death or serious injury," NASA medical honcho Joseph Kerwin wrote in a separate report. "The crew possibly, but not certainly, lost consciousness in the seconds following orbiter breakup." Some of the astronauts managed to get their emergency air packs switched on; of the four units later recovered, three had been manually activated. The fact that the fourth was not may indicate it was only a short time before everybody blacked out, but nobody knows for sure.

If the cabin depressurized immediately, the crew would have survived 6 to 15 seconds; if not, they might have lived two and a half minutes as their ruined vessel arced through the upper atmosphere, reaching a height of 65,000 feet before falling to earth. If the astronauts were still alive when they struck the water, they weren't afterward. The impact pulverized both cabin and crew, and that plus long immersion in salt water made it impossible to tell what really happened. Millions of eyes and billions of dollars in technology were trained on them, yet nobody was watching when they died.

Some time ago I came upon this little tidbit of info: that during the debates over the U.S. Constitution in the 1780s, disgust for the British was so intense that a proposal advanced was to ditch English and adopt some nice pseudo-dead dialect as the new nation's official language. Is this true? If so, can you confirm that Hebrew was seriously considered as a replacement but came one vote shy of being adopted?—Terrence Levine, Mount Royal, Quebec

Hebrew the national language? *Oy*, such *meshuggas* you talk. (And yes, Cecil knows the difference between Hebrew and Yiddish.) There was some discussion just after the Revolution about switching to a language other than English, but it's not known how serious this was—probably not very.

Nonetheless there's a 150-year-old legend that English was almost replaced, not by Hebrew but by German. Supposedly it lost by one vote, cast by a German-speaking Lutheran minister named Frederick Muhlenberg. Some say the vote took place in the Pennsylvania legislature and that Muhlenberg voted against it because he didn't want Pennsylvania to be isolated from the rest of the nation. Another version, commonly heard in Germany, says the proposal would have passed except that a German-speaking legislator went to the toilet at the crucial moment.

It never happened, of course. In the eighteenth century German speakers constituted a significant fraction of the population only in Pennsylvania (remember the Pennsylvania Dutch?), and even the most fanatical British haters weren't crazy enough to think they could change the national language by legislative fiat. But the story isn't pure invention. Here's what really happened, courtesy of Dennis Baron, professor of English at the University of Illinois at Urbana-Champaign:

In 1794 a group of German speakers in Virginia petitioned Congress to publish federal laws in German as well as English. The intention was not to supplant English but simply to supplement it. A House committee recommended publishing German translations of the laws, but on January 13, 1795, "a vote to adjourn and sit again on the recommendation" (apparently an attempt to keep the measure alive rather than kill it immediately) failed by a vote of 42–41. Frederick Muhlenberg (1750–1801) was in fact Speaker of the House at the time, but how he voted is unknown. Tradition has it that he stepped down to cast a negative vote, apparently being the German-speaking equivalent of an Oreo. Not that it mattered. The vote was merely procedural; its success would not have guaranteed passage of the measure, and in any case German translations of federal statutes are a far cry from making German the official language of the United States. A similar measure came up a month later and was also voted down, as were subsequent attempts in later years.

The Muhlenberg story was widely publicized by Franz Loher in his 1847 *History and Achievements of the Germans in America*. He wrongly set the event in the Pennsylvania legislature, over which Muhlenberg had previously presided, and also wrongly claimed that Muhlenberg was reviled by his fellow German speakers for selling them out. Germans did get on Muhlenberg's case for later casting the deciding vote in favor of the Jay Treaty, which was viewed as anti-German; his brother-in-law stabbed him and he lost the next election in 1796. Loher conflated this genuine controversy with the trivial language debate and the legend has survived ever since.

The truth is that the United States has never had an official language. Several states have declared English official at one time or another, most recently in response to the influx of Spanish speakers. The so-called English Language Amendment (ELA) to the U.S. Constitution, which would give English official status, has been before Congress since 1981, and given the country's sour mood it may yet pass. But even if one concedes the usefulness of a common language in unifying the country, one might as well attempt to legislate the weather.

In a discussion of product liability in Restatement of Torts *I came upon this passage: "Many products cannot possibly be made entirely safe for all consumption. . . . Ordinary sugar is a deadly poison to dia-*

betics, and castor oil found use under Mussolini as an instrument of tor-
ture." My question: what did Mussolini do with the castor oil? My boss
doesn't know. My parents don't know. All the WWII-vintage people I've
asked don't know. Please, Cecil, help the world remember and keep this
heinous event from being repeated.—Gabrielle, Madison, Wisconsin

No danger, kid—for starters, where would a would-be torturer get the castor oil? Besides, castor oil wasn't really in the same league as the iron maiden and the rack. It was more an instrument of mob violence, sort of like tar and feathers. A gang of Fascisti would grab one of their opponents, beat him up, and pour castor oil down his throat. Why? To give him the world's worst case of diarrhea, that's why. Sometimes the hoods would squirt a quart (OK, liter) or more into the guy; sometimes they'd mix it with gasoline; and sometimes, as a consequence, the victim died. But I gather most people lived through the experience, which was meant mainly to put the fear of *il Duce* in them and in the populace at large.

Castor oil treatment is said to have been invented by Gabriele d'Annunzio, a flamboyant poet/revolutionary who in 1919 seized the disputed port city of Fiume in what used to be Yugoslavia with 1,000 *arditi* (disgruntled Italian army veterans). D'Annunzio's moment of glory lasted little more than a year, but in that time he introduced many of the later trappings of Fascism, including the raised-arm salute and the tasseled black fez and black shirt that became the Fascist uniform. Where he got the idea for castor oil is unclear, but the stuff was

in common use at the time as a cure for constipation, then thought to be the cause of half the world's ailments. It was often administered to kids, who hated it. Possibly after one such dose little Gabe vowed that someday he'd pay his oppressors back big time.

Apparently he wasn't the only one. Castor oil caught on in a big way with Fascist mobs in the early 1920s. In one town, a historian notes, "the Fascists stamped out alcoholism by forcing every wine-seller to display a pint bottle of castor oil in his window—a warning of the fate awaiting any man found drunk." Mussolini's opponents in the Italian parliament charged that his power was built on the *manganello* (bludgeon) and castor oil.

Sounds almost quaint, and well it might. The Fascists had few qualms about killing people when it suited their purpose but did not do so often for fear of turning the masses against them. When Mussolini's thugs exceeded their orders (or so some historians think) and murdered an opposition leader in 1924, the Italian public was outraged and for a time the Duce thought the jig was up. In an era when mobs, bombers, and death squads randomly slaughter thousands, one almost longs for a time when the worst the bad guys dared do to somebody was to give him a case of the runs.

While reading your first book I came across a reference to President Zachary Taylor dying of eating strawberries on a warm day. The only other reference I have heard to something like this was in the Book of Lists, *which mentions someone having eaten cherries with milk on a warm day and dying. Everything else I have ever read to find out why this is has been mysteriously mute, though my mother, when I mentioned it (out of fear, because I love cherries), warned me against the practice. I cornered her on it, but all she could say was she had a vague memory of her mother warning her, and she had classed the information with such dubious practices as putting butter on a burn. Cecil, I appeal to you. You say a president died of this—what's the story?—Dan Shick, San Francisco*

Zachary Taylor was diagnosed with "cholera morbus," a catchall term that included diarrhea and dysentery but not true cholera. Exactly what he had and how he got it is not known. It had been steamy in Washington and Taylor, against popular advice, had eaten raw foods

such as milk, green apples, and cherries (although maybe not straw-berries, my assertion notwithstanding). Sanitation at the time stunk and food contamination was common. Dysentery, for example, was commonly spread by eating food tainted with infected human feces. Taylor's demise may have been hastened by the moronic medical treatments of the day, e.g., bleeding and dosing with mercury com-pounds. Hygienic standards allegedly having improved, today you can eat your cherries without fear. But I'd wash them just the same.

Who invented the smiley face, that obnoxious little design you see plastered on stickers everywhere? Some anonymous hero lost in the quagmire of Commercial Art History? A team of dedicated iconogra-phers hoping to devise the perfect expression of mindless optimism? Will we ever know? Hey, this is what we pay you big money for.—Ivan Brunetti, Lansing, Illinois

Oh? Guess your check got lost in the mail. A few weeks ago, my usual sources having come up dry, I convinced a reporter to post this question in *USA Today*. Overcome by wickedness, however, I phrased it, "Who invented the smiley face, and did he do time for it?" Not that I actually thought the responsible party should be imprisoned, of course; I'd settle for 20 years' house arrest in a room wallpapered with smileys. Be that as it may, I got a few calls, made a few more, and now can confidently assign credit and/or blame.

The smiley face craze, if not necessarily the smiley face itself, was

the work of two brothers in Philadelphia, Bernard and Murray Spain, who were in the business of making would-be fad items. In September of 1970 (Bernard says 1969, but I suspect he's misremembering), they heard destiny calling. Casting about for some peace symbol–like item with more general appeal, they recalled the smiley faces that had been floating around for years in the advertising business. By George, they cried, or would have cried if I'd been around to write the dialogue, we're in the midst of a ghastly war, we're surrounded by protests and hate, what the country needs is a nickel-size depiction of a guy who's just had a prefrontal lobotomy. Whoa, just kidding! Actually, what they wanted was for all mankind to be happy and live in harmony . . . OK, I confess, that wasn't it, either. Bernie, with admirable frankness, says they did it to make a buck.

Anyway, Bernard dashed off a smiley face, Murray added the slogan "Have a happy day," and soon they and their many imitators were cranking out buttons, posters, greeting cards, shirts, bumper stickers, cookie jars, earrings, bracelets, key chains, corneal implants . . . OK, maybe not corneal implants, but wouldn't they have been cool? The fad lasted about a year and half; the number of smiley buttons produced by 1972 was estimated at 50 million.

But who invented the *original* smiley face? The best bet is that the smiley Bernard and Murray had seen floating around was created circa December 1963 for a subsidiary of the State Mutual insurance company by Harvey Ball, a graphic artist in Worcester, Massachusetts.

Harvey got the assignment from the company's promotions director, Joy Young, who wanted a smile button for a morale-boosting campaign ordered up by her boss. Harvey, not a man to waste ink, initially drew just the smile. Pondering the result, he realized that if you turned the button upside down, it became . . . a frown! To head incipient wise-arsedness off at the pass, he added two eyes, which of course you could also turn upside down, but then it meant . . . I'm standing on my head!—a more ambiguous sociopolitical message. He made the thing yellow to give it a sunshiny look, and State Mutual, whom nobody would accuse of rashness, printed up 100. The buttons were a big hit, the company began handing them out by the thousands, and the rest you know. Mr. Ball's total take: his $45 art fee. State Mutual, not very quick on the uptake, didn't make any money, either.

Fine, but how do we know Harvey wasn't just copying some still earlier unsung genius? It's not as though nobody had ever drawn a smiley face before. Bernard Spain says he's heard Sunkist oranges used smileys in a 1930s ad campaign, and we find smileys in Munro Leaf's 1936 kid's book *Manners Can Be Fun*. But the Leaf smileys are crude black-and-white stick drawings bearing little resemblance to the finished work of art cranked out by Harvey Ball. Speaking as the voice of history, we declare Harv the author of this classic piece of Americana—and if anybody wants to take the honor away, they'll have to talk to us. Bidding starts at a hundred bucks.

Unca Cecil: Not Smiling Anymore

Cecil's minions were crowing on a local radio show the other day about having finally found the people responsible for the smiley face, only to get two alarming calls from listeners. Both had worked for the same Los Angeles ad agency, Carson Roberts (now apparently defunct), and both distinctly recalled seeing a smiley face on the firm's notepads, complete with the slogan, "Have a happy day." The year: 1961. The year we said the smiley face was invented: 1963.

Naturally we were concerned. If the callers were right, there were only two explanations: either 1) some bizarre kink in the space-time continuum had enabled the people in LA to know about something that would not be created in Worcester, Massachusetts, until two years later, or 2) we were wrong. Sadly, we resigned ourselves to giving the heave to our previous views about chronological cause and effect.

First, however, we wanted proof. We asked Phil Renaud, a Chicago illustrator and former Carson Roberts employee, to send us a sheet of C-R's notepaper-cum-smiley, which, amazingly, he still had. When we got it we immediately tore up the letter we were about to send to the physics society. The notepaper in fact did have a smiley face, but it was not the classic full-frontal two-dots-and-a-curve-on-a-yellow-circle that we all know and love/loathe. Rather, it was a three-quarters view of a not-quite-so-brain-dead-looking little guy with hair, nose, etc. No yellow, either, just B&W. Clearly a distant cousin at best to the smiley Harvey R. Ball drew in 1963.

One thing, though. The notepaper did have the slogan "Have a happy day" on it, which we had been previously led to believe had been composed by Murray Spain, one-half of the team of Philadelphia brothers that started the smiley fad in 1970. Murray's claim of originality now clearly lies in the dust. His only consolation is that he made a gazillion bucks.

Regarding the origin of the once ubiquitous smiley face, I've enclosed the version I'm most familiar with for your entertainment and information.—Jeff Kurtti, Los Angeles

Ah, the David Stern story. Several people have sent me this, including someone who must be either Stern's press agent or his mom, since it includes a whole packet of stuff about the guy. Stern, the Seattle adman who gave Egghead Software its name, came up with a smiley face for a campaign for Seattle's University Federal Savings and Loan. Trouble was, he did this in 1967. We have already clearly established that Harvey R. Ball drew a smiley face in 1963.

A more potent claim is that the smiley face first appeared in 1962 on sweatshirts given away by WMCA radio in New York. I have not been able to track down one of these shirts yet (although I would be pleased to accept a donation), and so cannot be sure we are talking about the canonical smiley, i.e., two eyes and a mouth on a yellow background, and not merely some proto-smiley having a vague resemblance. We will interrupt your normally scheduled program with a bulletin if we learn more.

One more thing. We had been crediting the launching of the smiley craze (though not the creation of the smiley) to Bernard and Murray Spain, brothers who ran a Philly novelty company. Now some say credit must be shared with New York button manufacturer N.G. Slater. Cecil despairs of getting to the bottom of this—what am I going to do, take depositions?—but if further info emerges I'll let you know.

The Story Of The Smiley: The Saga Continues

Readers breathlessly awaiting further word from this department on Harvey R. Ball's beleaguered claim to have drawn the original smiley face in 1963 will be pleased to know that one of the smiley sweatshirts given away by WMCA radio in New York in 1962/1963 has turned up—and it's *not* the canonical smiley. (We love the word canonical, incidentally, and the chance to continue using it is the principal reason we are pursuing this interminable quest.) The WMCA smiley is, however, close, having perhaps a Bill Clinton half-brotheresque relationship to the genuine article. The smiley is printed in black on yellow cloth and consists of two eye-dots and a mouth-curve in a circle. But it appears to have been drawn with a thick paintbrush and consequently is more irregular (and frankly has more personality) than the Ballic (Balltic? Ballistic?) smiley. Harv, as far as I'm concerned, is still da man.

Also . . . I am not sure what to make of this, but looking at the smiley buttons that are accumulating on my desk, I notice that the Harvey Ball smiley and the David Stern smiley . . . you remember David Stern . . . are *exact duplicates*, down to a minor variation in the size of the right vs. left eyes. I make no accusations, but it seems clear to me that somebody has been up to something.

Enough Already With The WMCA Sweatshirts

Cecil has been showered lately with Polaroids, photocopies, etc., of WMCA smiley-face sweatshirts, along with numerous other examples of the smiley in history. I am awestruck at the enterprise the Teeming Millions have shown in this regard, but feel obliged to remark that IF

I SEE ONE MORE FREAKING SMILEY FACE I AM GOING TO
THROW UP. Thank you, and have a nice day.

The Origin Of The Smiley Face:
The Scandal Deepens

I don't care if you're tired of this. I'm writing this column, and I find
this topic a source of never-ending fascination. Just the other day I was
thinking to myself, you know, there is the stuff of tragedy in this smiley
face thing. As usual, I was right. Word comes that the city of Seattle
has been rocked (well, jiggled) by a smiley face scandal.

For many years Seattle ad man David Stern has been taking (or at
least not refusing) credit for inventing the smiley face, saying he
cooked it up for a local savings and loan in 1967.

Now we learn that the citizens of Seattle, figuring that the inventor
of the symbol for brain-dead optimism was the ideal candidate to lead
them into the brave new world of the '90s, voted for Stern in sufficient
numbers to make him one of the two contenders in that city's 1993
mayoral runoff.

But the sordid truth was not long in coming out. Our column re-
vealing the smiley's actual origins (Harvey R. Ball, if you recall) circulated in samizdat in the Pacific Northwest, eventually coming to the
attention of reporter Bruce Barcott of the *Seattle Weekly*.

Seeing a Pulitzer in it, Barcott jumped on the story with both feet.
In a searing exposé, he revealed to shocked Seattleites not only that:

- David Stern did not originate the smiley face, but that:
- The smiley campaign Stern came up with for University Federal
  Savings & Loan in 1967 did not single-handedly boost the institu-
  tion from one office and $40 million in assets to 23 offices and $1
  billion in assets, as a Stern campaign ad somewhat disingenuously
  suggested. Furthermore:
- Stern did not personally invent the name and concept for the
  Egghead Software retail chain. (He invented the name and Professor Egghead; somebody else came up with the idea for a chain
  of software stores.)

Needless to say, these revelations rocked The City That Bill Gates Lives Not Far Away From. Stern wrote an affronted letter to the *Seattle Weekly*. (He asks: What about "my plans to manage crime, the homeless, graffiti and litter, revitalize downtown," etc.? Don't distract us with side issues, Dave.)

Will Stern be hounded from office, or platform, or whatever it is that mayoral candidates are houndable from? Will the Seattle Election Commission award the mayoral runoff spot to Harvey R. Ball, who has promised to name me Commissar of Human Knowledge? You better believe you'll read about it here.

One more thing. (What, you thought we were done?)

Cecil has learned that a smiley museum, of all things, has been established by Mark Sachs of Silver Spring, Maryland. The theme park and gardens not having been completed yet, right now the museum is housed in Mark's house. Mark has had the temerity to ask if I will donate my collection of smileys to his museum, saying he is "more than happy to reimburse you for postage and handling."

Postage and handling! Mark, you cur, these things have incalculable sentimental value. But throw in a box of cigars and I'll give it some thought.

Seattle's Honor Preserved

In the general election, incumbent Seattle Mayor Norm Rice defeated happy face noninventor David Stern. Thank God. I was prepared to swear off latte for good.

From The Straight Dope Message Board

Subj: spit spray
From: BLauraclar

How come sometimes when we open our mouth a spray of spit comes out? How does it do that? How come we can't do it at will? It's pretty embarrassing to open my mouth to talk and I become a fountain.

From: GFHH

If you ever join us in a live chat, please sit at the rear and face the back.

From: Sonne Flwr

You can do it at will. It is called gleeking.

From: WhoMeYeahU

Never knew there was an actual term for this, but yes, it can be done at will as well as accidentally. It happens when there's a good bit of saliva in a recess of the mouth that is pushed out forcefully by the tongue, most notably when talking.

I'm one of those who can do it at will. Just pool a bunch of spit on your tongue (eating some gum or hard candy helps, since it seems like plain old spit spit doesn't work every time) and then fold the front quarter of your tongue backward using the roof of your mouth. *Voilà*—instant spitting cobra effect . . . Good gleekers can get a spit stream of several feet.

Strange but true.

From: Ezotti

You may be a wonderful person, Who, but you are never getting invited to a party at MY house.

From: GFHH

You know, my ex-husband used to be able to do that, too. And that's about the only positive thing I can think of to say about him.

From: BMaffitt

Actually, I've always believed you're inducing the salivary glands beneath the tongue to forcibly eject their contents, that's all. Lodge the tip of your tongue on the roof of your mouth and push your tongue forward . . . presto! An all-natural squirt gun! (I've given it up—promise—but I was a master of this technique from childhood through college.) It has the advantage of being completely silent, and as the results are body-temperature someone may not notice they've been "gleeked" for several seconds, plenty of time to beat a retreat.

The phenomenon can show up involuntarily when something stimulates the salivary glands—I suppose "pooling" your spit on top of your tongue could qualify—but I always induced it by lightly biting the side of my tongue, just enough to get things flowing.° Force the tongue forward and "gleek"! (I never heard that label before, but it fits.)

A close examination of the underside of your tongue in a mirror will reveal a slight bump where the saliva is, um, "released." Learn to "gleek" and you can see for yourself.

° Sounds masochistic, but I promise it isn't . . . no more so than turning one's eyelids inside out, which was the hit of every postpuberty party I attended.

Chapter 3

Out There

As an X-Files *junkie and conspiracy freak, I was watching the blockbuster* Independence Day, *and I got to the part where everybody goes to Area 51 and there's a big spaceship and Brent Spiner says they've been studying aliens there since Roswell. I thought, what's the deal? Area 51 was on an episode of the X-Files, it's got a video game, a band—what the hell do they have in there? Biological weapons? Plutonium? Cold fusion? The body of Jimmy Hoffa? Or the bodies of hundreds of dead aliens? I'm starved for info.—Andy Ryder, via the Internet*

Oh, yeah, if it's on *X-Files* and there's a video game you know it's

ST HWY 375
ET HWY
AREA 51

gotta be legit. The Pentagon always notifies the entertainment industry when it gets in some fresh aliens.

In fact, what we've got here is a showcase example of the American genius for hype. Officially, at least, there's no such place as "Area 51." The name refers to a six-by-ten-mile section numbered 51 on an old grid-type map of the Nevada A-bomb test site.

Now part of the Nellis Air Force Range, Area 51 is the home of a used-to-be-secret-but-everybody-and-his-dentist-knew-about-it airfield at Groom (dry) Lake. The Pentagon reportedly has used the airfield to test spy planes and more recently the F-117A Stealth fighter.

For years the military didn't acknowledge the existence of the Groom Lake facility, and even now it speaks only vaguely of "testing . . . technologies and systems" there. This of course made Area 51 the perfect place for UFO buffs to store hypothetical alien spacecraft.

What really put Area 51 on the map, so to speak, were the revelations of an enigmatic character named Bob Lazar, who operated a photo lab in Las Vegas. In 1989 Lazar told a Las Vegas TV anchorman that he was a physicist who'd been hired to "reverse engineer" one of nine alien spacecraft stored at a facility supposedly near Groom Lake that Lazar called "Area S-4."

Lazar claimed he had a top-secret security clearance for this job. So what did Mr. Trustworthy do? After only a few months he took some UFO enthusiasts to a spot near the secret base so they could see the alien spacecraft fly. On the last such visit guards caught them, and Lazar claims that shortly thereafter his employment at S-4 ended.

Lazar's description of the spacecraft was filled with enough technical mumbo jumbo about antimatter propulsion systems to persuade people he knew what he was talking about. But the key academic credentials he claimed didn't check out, he'd earlier filed for bankruptcy, and he's since been convicted of pandering.

Yeah, I know: presidential material. But even a lot of people in the UFO community now think Lazar's a flake.

Not that it matters. State highway 375, which runs past Nellis Air Force Range, has now become a sightseeing stop for UFO buffs hoping for a glimpse of a flying saucer. (Supposedly the primo viewing spot is a certain "black mailbox." Where the aliens get their welfare checks, I bet.)

Some nights you can see lights. Glenn Campbell, a well-known researcher of Area 51 mysteries who's skeptical about flying-saucer sightings, says they're "meteors, flares, aircraft lights, and many manifestations of the bombing runs and war games" at Nellis. But sure, they *could* be emissaries from beyond the stars.

Now the state of Nevada has declared the road "Extraterrestrial Highway" and promotes it as a tourist destination. Larry King's been out there. So have the networks, Hollywood, the *New York Times*. In case you missed any of the coverage, Campbell keeps copies on his wonderfully informative Web site (www.ufomind.com/area51). Just shows you the impenetrable veil of secrecy the Pentagon has been able to draw over the whole affair.

Legal action may eventually pry a few more facts loose. Some workers at Groom Lake have sued the U.S. Air Force, saying they were injured by toxic waste burning at the site. Site? What site? the feds said initially. (They finally caved on that point.) Dismissed on national-security grounds, the case is now being appealed.

But why wait? You want to see beings from another planet, go out to the black mailbox. There are bunches of 'em, looking up.

About 200 years ago Sir Edmund Halley discovered an anomaly in space around the stars of the Pleiades. A hundred years later Friedrich Wilhelm Bessel confirmed Halley's findings. In 1961 Paul Otto Hesse defined and measured this anomaly. It's an energy ring of incredible size, 760 thousand billion miles wide, and is due to intersect the earth just about any minute now. He also calculated that this is part of a 25,000-year-long cycle that our solar system goes through.

It's expected that once we're into the Photon Belt, electricity won't function and there will be three to five days of total darkness. All indigenous cultures and religions prophesy three days of darkness to mark the "end times."

Scientists discussing the Photon Belt have been fired, moved, or denied access to the equipment used to study it. If you cast around on, say, the Internet for information, folks with CIA or NSA credentials likely will show up and say it would be in the best interest of your family if you gave up the quest.

So my question is, what can you tell us about the Photon Belt? Any hard data?—N. A., Rio Rancho, New Mexico

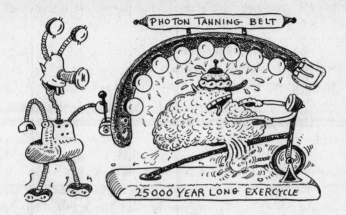

Get off it. Nobody wants hard data. If hard data were the filtering criterion you could fit the entire contents of the Internet on a floppy disk. My mission in life is a little different: you provide the bubble, I provide the pin.

The "Photon Belt" has been a hot topic in New Age circles since 1991, when a story about it appeared in Australia's *Nexus* magazine. In 1994 it received a book-length treatment in *You Are Becoming a Galactic Human* by Virginia Essene and Sheldon Nidle. Essene and Nidle claimed to be "channeling" members of the "Sirian Council," beings from a distant planet.

Exactly when we're going to enter the Photon Belt is a matter of debate. Originally it was thought that the arrival of the belt would lead to a vast transformation of society starting in 1992. So what did we get instead? Bill Clinton. Not to be critical in any way, but I for one would have expected something a little grander than a hike in the minimum wage.

The next target date was May 5, 1997, though there was to be a long buildup. "Apparently, by the end of summer [1996]," one newsletter noted, "most of us will be having conversations with Masters, the spiritual hierarchy, and space commanders of all kinds." Don't know about you, but all I've been seeing is more Bill Clinton. As a fallback, some New Agers are saying the Photon Belt won't get here until 2011.

The question is not whether it's nuts to believe in the Photon Belt.

Of course it's nuts. How many great scientific discoveries do you know of that were channeled from aliens? For the record, however, I feel obliged to say that:

1. No photon belt or other such region of increased energy has been discovered. Photons in any case are merely particles of electromagnetic energy, which we commonly experience as light. Upon exposure to excess photons the most common transformation of your being is sunburn.
2. There's no "anomaly" near the Pleiades star cluster. The Pleiades are surrounded by a nebula, or gas cloud. This cloud is composed not of photons but of dust and hydrogen gas.
3. The Earth isn't heading toward the Pleiades but away from them. In the 1850s it was conjectured that the Earth orbited the Pleiades, but this has long since been discredited.
4. Paul Otto Hesse is unknown to astronomers. Someone dug up a reference to a 1986 book by him in German whose title translates as "Judgment Day: A Book to Mankind That Speaks of Things to Come." 'Nuff said.

What puzzled me was where the Photon Belt story came from. The 1991 *Nexus* article was based on a 1981 article in an Australian UFO mag. I spoke to Colin Norris, head of the Australian UFO society that publishes the magazine, and he said it was coauthored by a "middle-aged mother" and a college undergraduate. Norris denied it was a prank, but it seems clear these folks didn't have detailed technical knowledge, unless of course they were on the horn with the guys from Sirius.

So it's a crock. But don't worry. I'm sure your five-day supply of candles will come in handy for something.

Still Waiting

My family and I just came back out of hiding, and boy are we embarrassed. How was Cinco de Mayo?—Susan Gleason, via the Internet

Pretty quiet, and it's been pretty quiet since—although now that you mention it, the power *did* go out for a couple minutes Saturday night. However, to my way of thinking, the arrival of the Photon Belt ought to be heralded by something a little more impressive than a message saying "RESET" on the microwave. As of this writing (early July 1997), the New Age crowd had not given up on the Photon Belt, but it sounds like they're getting a little fidgety. PB promoter Sheldon Nidle, trying to buck up the troops in a recent communiqué, notes that "time is extremely elastic in its properties." Whatever you say, Shel. But to me that sounds an awful lot like, "The check is in the mail."

I'm interested to know whether electronic technology is available for controlling a) a person's state of mind, such as for brainwashing, making a person commit a crime, commit suicide, and so on; b) a person's inner thoughts or voices by planting an electronic implant in a person's eyes or skull. If such a technology is available, would it be used only by state agencies or would private labs have access to it for their own research? Also, if a person feels he or she was implanted, how can the implants be detected and removed?—Mary B., Plano, Texas

The editor who forwarded your question to me added the note "Watch out, Cecil. This Mary sounds like trouble." But I figure, who needs my help more than the nuts? A surprisingly large number of

people figure they've been implanted with a microchip that controls their thoughts and actions. Related conspiracy theories: they're irradiating my body with microwaves! They're reading my mind by remote control! Voices are coming out of my television set telling me to buy products for which I have no earthly need! Whoops, that isn't a conspiracy theory, that's reality. Sometimes these days it's hard to tell the difference.

This being the '90s, alleged implant victims don't just talk to themselves on the bus; they have their own Web pages. Many of the best are associated with the Freedom of Thought Foundation, which lends "aid and protection to survivors of mind control." (Search for "Freedom of Thought Foundation" and you'll turn up a raft of classic links.) One FTF advisory board member is Paul Krassner, editor of *The Realist*, the '60s-era satire sheet that has now resumed publication. (Address: Box 1230, Venice, CA 90294.) Krassner is a good guy—he sends me free copies, doesn't he? But he's also an indefatigable put-on artist, and his association with the FTF doesn't do much for its credibility. Then again, when your home page says stuff like "Hi! I'm Ed Light, one of many captives of the mind-control cabal's microwave antipersonnel projects. As I type this I'm being forcibly zapped," you're obviously not too concerned about what the outside world thinks.

Among the many delights I found on the Web were two "MRI scans of psychotronic implants" provided by one Brian Bard. In the middle of somebody's skull, presumably Bard's, we see . . . well, it looks like an IUD. Bard, however, says it's "a transducer relay designed to absorb electromagnetic radiation in one frequency range and retransmit that energy in another frequency range." Supposedly it's in the mastoid sinus.

Is it possible? I doubt it. The technology just isn't there yet. Neural implants of various kinds have become common, notably the cochlear implants used to restore some hearing in the deaf. But today's neural implants still have to be connected to an external signal processor. If you wake up with unexplained wires trailing out of your body or find a little computer strapped to your waist, you would be right to be suspicious. Otherwise don't fret.

But who knows what wonders the future holds? Researchers have developed a rice-grain-size microchip designed to be implanted under the skin with a syringe. Zap it with radio-frequency energy, and it beams out a 10-digit ID number. Right now it's used to identify pets and farm animals, but technology paranoids foresee a day when they'll start sticking ID microchips into people.

Horrified? Worse things await. Soon they'll want to stick them into your car. A while back I spoke to a couple transportation experts who figured you could use remote-control microchips to implement "road pricing." As you drove around, sensors in the pavement would detect a microchip built into your vehicle. A central computer would tally your mileage and bill you annually for road usage, with maybe a surcharge tacked on if you traveled the most congested roads during rush hour. Sound crazy? A lot of things sound crazy. Next thing you know they're elected to Congress.

Another View

I was amused at your whimsical attitude toward mind control devices. I am not writing to tell you that I was taken to "AREA 51" for tests, nor was I implanted with what in some circles is referred to as the "DOMINATOR," but I am requesting more information on this Mary B. in Plano, Texas. By the way, the chips are implanted into humans through the nose and as far as cars, LOJACK is only the beginning, and how about Ameritech with its phone lines bugging your whole house while you think they are "protecting" you? Are these all not examples of the power authority watching you and I? I did find your work stimulating, although a bit short on available facts and figures, but then again, who reads this thing? People who have an open mind to conspiracy theory or Euro-slut trash who are only interested in the here and now?—T. Swanson, Downers Grove, Illinois

Well, at least now we know all the nuts aren't in Texas.

I hope you can help me with this one—most of my friends think I'm crazy. I am convinced my physical presence has the ability to make streetlights burn out. On an average night, walking through a parking lot, at least one or two streetlights will go out when I approach, then regain their luminous state after I have passed. Could there be some sort of electrochemical imbalance in my body that causes this to happen? Am I surrounded by some strange magnetic field? This happens

only with streetlights, not with lights in my home or public buildings. Is there a scientific explanation, am I looney, or do I just pay too much attention to streetlights?—Matthew Davis, San Jose, California; similarly from Neal Duncan, Washington, D.C.

Nothing personal, Matthew, but our default explanation for things like this is that you are looney. However, on investigation (we had little Ed bring it up on talk radio), we are wondering if there is more to this than meets the eye.

When the sodium vapor bulbs commonly used in streetlights start to go bad, they "cycle"—go on and off repeatedly. Cecil is having a hard time getting the Straight Dope Science Advisory Board to agree on what happens, but apparently the bulb overheats, goes out, cools down, then relights. If you're walking past when this happens and you're the neurotic type, you think it's your fault. This surely accounts for most of the reports we have gotten about this over the years.

But maybe not all. While making one of his periodic reports to the nation on the Mara Tapp show on WBEZ radio in Chicago, little Ed mentioned your letter, figuring he might get a few calls from, as he indelicately put it, "the looney-tune quadrant of the listening audience." As usual he got no help from Mara Tapp, who thought he was making the whole thing up. Also as usual, though, the lines lit up with listeners saying the same thing had happened to them. One caller, saying there was a 12-step program for streetlight snuffers, pointedly told Mara it was common for people to be in denial about this. So there.

And then there was a call from Joe. Joe claimed that when he and a friend walked down a street in Chicago once, eight or nine of the dozen or so streetlights they passed went out as they approached, then relit after they had gone by. While subsequent forays into the city have not been so unenlightening, Joe says he will sometimes put out two or three lights in the course of a stroll, although he cannot do so at will. Hmm, said little Ed.

We are not about to say we believe in bodily emanations. No doubt it is all just coincidence. Or maybe Joe is lying, crazy, or under the influence. (He sounded OK, but on the phone you can't tell if your source's eyes are dilated.)

But we never rule anything out, especially if we can get a column out of it. We checked with several electrical engineering types, who professed bafflement. Deficient hypotheses include:

- Joe is somehow triggering the photocell that causes streetlamps to switch on and off. But Chicago streetlamps don't have individual photocells. The photocell is in a master electrical box that controls 25 to 30 lights.
- Joe is causing the bulb to vibrate loose. Supposedly if you hit the pole in the right spot the luminaire (the part with the bulb) will whip back and forth so sharply that the bulb loses contact. But Joe says he doesn't hit the poles, periodically drop a box of anvils, or anything like that.

Seeing as how we're not making much progress, we are faced with several choices:

1. Give up in frustration. We'd sooner die.
2. Conduct six weeks of in-depth investigation. Right, like we get paid by the hour for this.
3. Fob the job off on the Teeming Millions. The very thing. We invite reports from persons who believe they douse more streetlights than can be explained by mere happenstance. We are particularly interested in hearing from people who can do this at will, without the aid of wire cutters, slingshots, etc. Perhaps nothing will come of this. But you never know.

The Delightful Ones: A Report

Here's what I've seen as far as the streetlights thing goes, where they go off as people approach, and come back on as they move away. Senior Week in '93 down at Ocean City, Maryland, my girlfriend and I were hanging out with another couple. This other couple had been having a rocky relationship over the preceding few months, but then about three days into the week they had some incredible love thing happen. Both later said that that was their most memorable time in their relationship. Anyhow, as the day wore into night we went to the boardwalk for a little fun, and as we walked down the boardwalk we noticed that the streetlights would flicker and go off as we approached, then flicker back on as we walked away. After a while the other couple separated and went off to do something. As I watched them walk away I noticed that a ratio of about eight out of ten streetlights would go out as they walked beneath and then come back on as they passed by. It had stopped happening to my girlfriend and me, so obviously it was the other couple who were causing this. They later mentioned that it continued all night. . . . Weird stuff, man.—Mutant, via the Internet

While a student in Boston, I often experienced the streetlights shorting out as I passed under them (sometimes three and four in a row). This was witnessed on several occasions by friends. However, I am unable to make this happen at will. In my case, this phenomenon occurs

when I go hyperactive. During this period, usually brought on by binge drinking or a full moon, I have no choice but to exist for long periods of time without eating or sleeping. This hyperactive state is when the lights go out, in more ways than one.—Michael Burns, also via the net

It used to happen to me, too. Then it began to happen less and less. I'm only 30. Too young for electropause. Then I read your column, and on Saturday night I get this whole bank of streetlights to come on. Not as a group, but one after the other just preceding my path down Ashland Avenue.—Lon Ellenberger, Chicago

If I had a few in me it became clear I had some secret, but uncontrollable, power over the streetlight . . .—Joe Wackerman, Washington, D.C.

This is an example of what we in our lab call "the van is always at the corner" because one only notices the van when it is indeed parked at the corner, not the times when it is gone. How many lamps does one walk under that don't go out? You just notice those that do.—Josh Telser, Chicago

Much as I admire your steely logic, Josh, I'm never letting you sit around the campfire when *I'm* telling ghost stories. I'm charmed by the thought that powerful physio-emotional emanations may be behind HLS (human light switch) syndrome. Lest you think my midlife crisis has put me completely off my nut, I realize it's a crock. But it's a fun crock.

Now, since my contract obliges me to insert at least one fact per column, this word from a top high-pressure sodium engineer at General Electric: "It is a combination of coincidence and wishful thinking. . . . Cycling [on and off] occurs because the [lamp] ballast is only able to sustain an arc with a certain maximum voltage. As high-pressure sodium lamps age, their voltage increases as sodium is lost by various chemical processes. [The lamp starts at a low voltage, which climbs to a steady-state value as the lamp warms up.] It is the steady-state voltage that slowly increases with burning hours due to sodium loss. Eventually, the ballast will only be able to start a cold lamp and warm it up to the dropout voltage." Then it goes out until the lamp is cool enough to restart. The GE guy preceded these comments with the note: "Here's one explanation. Space aliens is another." Hmph.

I saw the movie Roswell *the other day and am quite taken with the revelation that: 1) aliens crash-landed in New Mexico back in the '40s; 2) one or two survived long enough to be observed and analyzed; 3) metal never before seen on Earth, which looked like aluminum but was as strong as titanium, was recovered; and 4) the government is covering this up. Any truth to this?—Anonymous*

What's the straight dope on this "alien autopsy" movie making the rounds? From what I saw of it, the purpose of the filming seemed to be to convince viewers that the event actually occurred rather than to document an autopsy. I've seen and heard of autopsy notes and even photographs being made, but is filming of the procedure ever done? What possible value would it have?—John C. Heckler, via the Internet

Just guessing, but considering that Fox built an entire TV show around it, I'd say the value had to be at least a hundred grand. The chance to cash in big is the only thing that could have kept this lame story alive.

The "Roswell incident" began on June 14, 1947, when rancher Mac Brazel found some debris on the spread he managed about 75 miles northwest of Roswell, New Mexico. The junk included sticks, metallic paper, and tape with mysterious writing on it. Total weight: five pounds.

The makings of an alien spacecraft? More like the makings of an alien kite. Brazel probably wouldn't have given the matter much thought, except that 11 days later the first sighting of a "flying saucer" occurred in Washington state. Brazel decided to report his find to the local sheriff, who called the military intelligence office at the Roswell army airfield.

The military guys didn't know what to make of the stuff they collected from Brazel's ranch. But they'd read about flying saucers like everybody else and, let's face it, after you've been stationed awhile in an isolated outpost you get a little desperate for excitement. They sent out a press release saying they'd found the wreckage of a flying saucer. The army's top brass went nuts. They immediately confiscated the Roswell junk and held a press conference at which they declared it was the remains of a weather balloon.

The truth wouldn't come out till years later. In 1947 the government was conducting Project Mogul, an attempt to use high-altitude balloons to detect expected Soviet atom-bomb tests. Periodically researchers in Alamogordo, New Mexico, sent up a "balloon train," a string of balloons carrying electronics plus a sticks-and-tinfoil radar reflector. The remains of one of these balloon trains was undoubtedly what Brazel found. In fact, contact with one had been lost when it was less than 20 miles away from his ranch.

The clincher: the tape with mysterious writing. According to Charles Moore, a Project Mogul scientist, the radar reflectors had been made during World War II by a company in New York City's garment district. When early models proved too flimsy, the company did a quick fix by reinforcing the reflectors using tape with stylized flower designs on it.

We now fast-forward to the late 1970s. Renewed interest in UFOs has led researchers to reexamine the Roswell case. Various parties obligingly come forward with tales about having seen or heard about alien crash victims 30 years earlier.

Having consulted with Philip Klass, a noted UFO debunker who's written extensively about Roswell, I'd say what we've got here is a bunch of people who spent too much time in the desert without a hat. Nonetheless entrepreneurs have used this unpromising material to create a veritable industry of Roswell books, films, museums, and more.

Now it's 1995. An English TV producer—a TV producer, for God's sake—comes up with what he claims is a film of an autopsy conducted on the aliens' bodies. Doctors, Hollywood special-effects guys, and even many UFO buffs who see it pretty much roll their eyes. The thing obviously depicts a bunch of actors in space suits with no idea how a real autopsy is done fumbling over a reject from a Steven Spielberg flick. One giveaway, reported in the July/August 1997 *Skeptical Inquirer*, was that a standard-issue "danger" sign visible on the wall was in a graphic format not adopted until 1967.

But who cares? The honchos at Fox surely figured: hey, the shroud of Turin fooled 'em for 600 years. All we've got to do is keep 'em watching till the last commercial break.

Late News

In 1997 the U.S. Air Force issued a report attributing the 1947 incident to Project Mogul and in addition ascribing sightings of alien bodies to dummies. Just like I said.

He's A Believer

Regarding your column on the Roswell UFO incident: I was executive producer and co-writer of the movie mentioned in the letter to you, called "Roswell" and starring Kyle MacLachlan and Martin Sheen. I have also produced a commercial video ("Reply to the Air Force Report on the Roswell Incident") which contradicts everything you wrote, most of which you collected from Phil Klass, a now well-past-the-age-of-retirement debunker who has never even passed muster as a dispassionate skeptic and who is reviled by everyone I know as a disingenuous and intellectually dishonest writer on UFOs. Here are the known facts which your readers—and you—deserve to read:

The Government Accounting Office (the GAO) recently reported that the military documents that could have explained the Roswell Incident (outgoing messages from the commanding officer and others at the Roswell Army Air Field 1947) were destroyed without proper authorization decades ago. The Air Force never 'fessed up to that in their 1994 report. . . .

Charles Moore's attempt to explain the "strange writing" on the Roswell debris as being flower designs on tape that held together a flimsy balsa wood radar reflector is disputed by the only living witness who has testified about the writing he saw on the debris: Dr. Jesse Marcel, Jr. He categorically states that the symbols he saw on the debris were embossed on metal, they were not designs on tape. He is a flight surgeon and practicing physician, and has investigated crashes for the military. His father was Jesse Marcel, a Roswell intelligence officer who described the Roswell debris in about 1978, on videotape, as having been "not made on this earth."

The dates of the Mogul launches and the written records of the then-secret program do not indicate any launch with instrument packages that coincides in time with the Roswell Incident. . . .

Three generals have publicly gone on record as supporting key aspects of the fact that there was a major cover-up, and that includes 1) Sen. (and Gen.) Barry Goldwater, former head of the Senate Intelligence Committee, who has stated on TV and has written letters stating that he takes the "crashed spaceship" explanation very seriously, 2) Brig. Gen. Arthur Exon, former base commander of Wright Patterson Air Force Base (where the debris and alien bodies were reportedly taken), who confirms on tape it was an extraterrestrial crash with bodies and that "the cover-up won't end until all those originally involved with the cover-up are deceased," and 3) Brig. Gen. Thomas DuBose, who said the "revised explanation" in 1947 that it was a weather balloon was a cover story concocted on orders that came down from those reporting directly to the Commander in Chief, President Truman, and that false debris that had nothing to do with the Roswell Incident was shown to reporters in General Ramey's office and passed off on the public as the Roswell debris.

I have been personally informed by astronaut Gordon Cooper that Roswell did involve the recovery of a crashed extraterrestrial spaceship; that our movie (which he saw) was largely accurate; that there has been a half century of official denial and official lies about it continuing to this day; and that he has a very close friend who saw the alien bodies. Gordon Cooper was one of the original Mercury Seven astronauts. He filmed a flying saucer that even landed at close range while in the service and said the filmed evidence of the inexplicable and technologically advanced craft was "buried" by the Pentagon and *ignored by Project Blue Book, which said it could find no credible evidence for the existence of flying saucers.*

Astronaut Edgar Mitchell, who walked on the moon, believes the weight of the evidence is that Roswell was an extraterrestrial event and recently he publicly suggested that those who knowingly withheld the facts from the astronauts who went to the moon are "criminally liable" for essentially using astronauts as guinea pigs while not telling them the truth about what is known about alien life forms visiting earth. . . .

Former Command Sgt. Maj. Bob Dean, formerly of SHAPE (Supreme Headquarters Allied Powers Europe) states that as part of his job in the military in Europe he was shown a classified document, "The Assessment," that revealed that the military has evidence and exhibits of numerous extraterrestrial craft conducting a surveillance of the earth, and that this certain knowledge has demoralized those of high rank who are in the know.

Mr. Adams, may I suggest you change the name of your column to "The Dope," unless you're prepared to show some hubris and admit in print that you leaped before you looked.—Paul Davids, executive producer/co-writer of "Roswell"

I think the word you're looking for in your last paragraph is "humility," not "hubris." But let's not nitpick. I've attempted to address some of the contentions in your letter below.

1. *Phil Klass is intellectually dishonest, reviled, etc.*

   Nonsense. I spoke with two prominent UFO researchers, Karl Pflock and Kevin Randle. Both have written books about Roswell and believed there was some basis to the stories about crashed spaceships. Pflock no longer believes these stories but Randle still does and in fact he was a technical consultant for your movie. Although both men had fundamental disagreements with Phil Klass, they spoke well of him and said he was a person of integrity. Both said they found you rather credulous.

2. *The military destroyed key documents relating to the case without authorization.*

   Three years' worth of outgoing messages from Roswell were destroyed during housecleaning, apparently when the military records center was moved from Kansas City to St. Louis. The destruction of records was handled somewhat casually but government archivists doubt this can be attributed to a conspiracy. In any case, indications are that the Roswell affair was handled largely by telephone.

There is no question that the military was genuinely concerned about UFOs during the late 1940s and early 1950s. Secret documents declassified in the mid-1980s reveal anxious discussions on the subject among high-level officials. However, none of these documents indicate that the government had any physical evidence of crashed saucers or the like. On the contrary, a number of documents lament the lack of such evidence.

3. *Jesse Marcel, Jr., says the strange symbols he saw on the debris were embossed on the metal, not printed on tape.*

Jesse Marcel, Jr., was a child at the time of the incident. Nearly 50 years have passed. Marcel's statements regarding the debris have made him a celebrity on the UFO circuit. 'Nuff said.

4. *The dates of the secret Project Mogul balloon launches do not coincide with the Roswell incident.*

Baloney. A 600-foot-long string of two dozen weather balloons and several kitelike radar reflectors was launched from Alamogordo, New Mexico, on June 4, 1947. Contact with the balloons was lost when they were less than 20 miles from the Brazel ranch. Mac Brazel found the mysterious debris June 14. Contemporary descriptions of the debris suggest its appearance was similar to that of a wrecked balloon train.

5. *Barry Goldwater takes the "crashed spaceship" explanation very seriously.*

So? Senator Goldwater has no personal knowledge of Roswell. Neither do any of the other famous names you cite.

6. *General Exon says it was an extraterrestrial crash with bodies.*

General Exon's statements were based on hearsay. He did not become commander at Wright Patterson until many years after the Roswell incident. He never saw any debris.

7. *General Dubose says the "weather balloon" story was concocted on orders from above.*

Of course. The weather balloon story was intended to conceal the Project Mogul experiment, a secret Pentagon project to develop a means of detecting anticipated Russian atom bomb tests.

8. *Former Sergeant Bob Dean says he saw a secret memo saying the military has evidence of extraterrestrial spacecraft.*

Neither Pflock nor Randle found Dean's statements believable.

Although I don't suppose there's much chance of persuading you, Paul, others may be interested in Karl Pflock's story. He describes himself as skeptical about Roswell but says "there's still a chunk of [UFO] data that can't be explained by known science."

Pflock initially was inclined to believe the Roswell UFO stories and spent nearly four years researching them. However, "when I got into it, a whole lot of what had been claimed turned out not to have been true at all," he says.

Pflock says he now doesn't think Roswell had anything to do with aliens. "The congruence between the Project Mogul equipment and what we know about the [Roswell] debris is just too great to be dismissed." He plans to discuss the matter in a book to be published on the 50th anniversary of the incident entitled, *The Roswell UFO Mystery: Legend and Reality.*

Everybody says you know how to make an entertaining movie, though.

Unfinished Business

Please be advised that this office represents Uri Geller, to whom you refer on pages 62–65 of Return of the Straight Dope. *I will not bother to debate the majority of your statements regarding Mr. Geller's abilities. . . . What must be addressed is your incorrect assertions regarding Professor Will Franklin.* [Note to reader: I said Franklin examined a ring Geller had allegedly bent psychically and found "evidence that a paranormal influence function was probably operative." I said he later confessed he'd misinterpreted what he saw, and subsequently committed suicide.] *Professor Franklin never disavowed his findings regarding Uri Geller. He, in fact, remained convinced of Mr. Geller's abilities until the time of his death. . . . The enclosed letter, written by Professor Franklin only a few weeks before his death, will attest to that fact. . . . Moreover, Professor Franklin did not commit suicide. Rather, he died from complications due to diabetes. . . . Last year* [Geller de-

*bunker James] Randi repeated his allegations regarding Professor
Franklin's death in Japan. Mr. Geller sued Mr. Randi and won a judgment against him. It is not our desire to litigate this matter further or
to drag you and Ballantine Books into court, despite the fact that
clearly we would prevail on the merits. [However] the untrue allegations contained in your book . . . must be retracted. . . .—Ruth Liebes-
man, attorney, New York*

I can see this is going to be one of those days. I was misinformed
regarding Professor Franklin's death but never suggested Geller was
responsible for it. On whether Franklin "disavowed his findings" about
Geller, what I wrote was correct. I said, "Five years later Franklin publicly confessed he'd misinterpreted the test results; in fact, the fracture
surfaces were easily explained." I quote from the Franklin letter you
sent me: "I did not retract all that I said regarding the unusual nature
of the metal fractures I examined! The fracture surfaces *of the spoons*
are more ductible, have larger holes, and more 'opening' than the control. However, I did make an error or misinterpretation of the PT [?]
ring. . . . [U]nfortunately, the ring (on a recent thorough reexamina-
tion) appears to have been broken at an incomplete braze. I'm extremely sorry for both your and my sakes that I goofed on this. But it
does not change the facts that the *spoons and needle* [my emphasis]
had unusual fracture surfaces." I said nothing about the spoons and
needle but referred only to the ring, regarding which Franklin admitted he was wrong. I'll be happy to ask Ballantine to add this corre-
spondence to future printings of my book.

Questions We're Still Thinking About

*Several of our patients have told us of their fear that if they burp,
fart, and sneeze simultaneously they will die. Like so many other areas
of concern to the general public, this topic was inadequately covered, if
at all, in our medical education. Furthermore, many of us have experienced the simultaneous occurrence of two of these physiological events.
The law of averages suggests for some of us a triple event (the "Big
One"?) may eventually occur. If it were to be accompanied by sudden*

death, this would be a subject of legitimate anxiety. Thank you for your attention to this question.—Richard Levenson, M.D., Mark Swaim, M.D., Ph.D., Duke University Medical Center, Durham, North Carolina

Don't mention it.

Stop The Presses

I have burped, farted, and sneezed at the same time, and I am still alive.—Dan Povenmire, Los Angeles

Doctors Levinson and Swain's patients are suffering from a trauma caused by National Lampoon in the early '70s, in whose pages there was a High Flying Rumors Contest. First prize was awarded to the following: "If you burp, fart, and sneeze at the same time, you will die." Although I've kept this information in memory with my tongue firmly planted in cheek, I suspect that some other Lampoon readers took it as gospel. I myself have used this information as a way of breaking the ice at parties but never did I dream it would become legend.—Randy S. Lavine, Culver City, California

Chapter 4

Showbiz

If you would return with us to those thrilling days of yesteryear, you might recall that Tonto, the faithful Indian companion to the Lone Ranger, called his boss "kemosabe." I heard somewhere that kemosabe was the word, in some Native American tongue, for chicken sh—uh,

guano. Considering the Lone Ranger's habit of sending Tonto into town to get information, and the townspeople's habit of beating the stuffing out of Tonto while the Lone Ranger was back in camp, this translation could make sense. I suspect, however, that kemosabe was the creation of some scriptwriter or the creator of the Lone Ranger stories. Jay Silverheels is no longer with us to tell, and would Clayton Moore know?

Unca Cece, since you are a fighter for Truth, and for all I know, Justice and the American way, too, please tell us the Straight Dope!—Rngrjeff, via AOL

"A fighter for Truth, Justice, and the American way"—boy, I've really got you guys trained, don't I?

As for Jay Silverheels and Clayton Moore . . . c'mon, Jeff, get with the program. The *radio* program, which is where the Lone Ranger originated. It all began on Detroit's WXYZ in 1932, where owner George W. Trendle was trying to develop a hit show to keep his station afloat during the Depression. According to *Who Was That Masked Man? The Story of the Lone Ranger* by David Rothel (1981), Trendle had the basic idea for a Western with a Zorrolike hero. WXYZ staff brainstormed the key elements of the Lone Ranger's shtick, including the mask, the white horse, the signature line "Hi-yo, Silver, away!" and of course the name "Lone Ranger." Hokey, sure, but it worked. The show quickly became popular and was soon heard nationwide.

The term *kemosabe*—there are lots of spellings, but this one's as good as any—seems to have been the contribution of Jim Jewell, who directed *The Lone Ranger* (and another famous serial, *The Green Hornet*) until 1938. In an interview with Rothel, Jewell said he'd lifted the term from the name of a boys' camp at Mullet Lake just south of Mackinac, Michigan, called Kamp Kee-Mo Sah-Bee. The camp had been established in 1911 by Jewell's father-in-law, Charles Yeager, and operated until about 1940. Translation of kee-mo sah-bee, according to Jewell: "trusty scout."

We know Kamp Kee-Mo Sah-Bee existed because we have photos and newspaper clippings to prove it. (Actually David Rothel has the photos and clippings, but we've taken a proprietary interest in this.) What about the translation, though? No disrespect to Yeager, but just because some wily Amerind told him it meant "trusty scout" doesn't mean we can rule out "chicken guano."

We consulted the nation's Native American language experts. (Yeah, they're mostly white folks, too, but I figured the wily Amerinds couldn't be BSing all of them.) Initial investigations into variations of "trusty" turned up nothing. But then Rob Malouf, a grad student of linguistics at Stanford, had a brainstorm: "According to John Nichols's *Concise Dictionary of Minnesota Ojibwe*, the Ojibwe word 'giimoozaabi' means 'to peek' (it could also mean 'he peeks' or 'he who peeks')."

"He who peeks"? Sounds like something you'd get arraigned for in Perverts' Court. But Rob continued: "There are several words with the same prefix ['giimooj,' secretly] meaning things like 'to sneak up on someone'. . . . It is quite plausible that 'giimoozaabi' means something like 'scout'. . . . 'Giimoozaabi' is pronounced pretty much the same as 'kemosabe' and would have been spelled 'Kee Moh Sah Bee' at the turn of the century." Bingo.

After further consultation with Indian language expert Laura Buszard-Welcher, we've established that Kamp Kee-Mo Sah-Bee was in an area inhabited by the Ottawa, who spoke a dialect of Ojibwe with the same word giimoozaabi. There were also Potawatomi in the region who spoke a closely related language with a similar word. So while the "trusty" part may have been hype, kemosabe probably really was a Native American term for "scout."

Let's see, what else? How about Tonto? According to Jim Jewell, there was an Indian storyteller at Kamp Kee-Mo Sah-Bee who would get rowdy when drunk, leading the other Indians to call him "tonto." The commonly told story is that this means "wild one" in Potawatomi. It doesn't, the experts tell me, but it does mean "stupid" or "fool" in Spanish—maybe that's what those Indians were saying to their drunken friend. An alternative theory is that *Lone Ranger* scriptwriter Fran Striker had transmuted the name of an earlier character, Gobo. Sorry we can't give you the definitive answer, but have patience. We chip away at the unknown one word at a time.

Hey, Cecil, tonto *certainly is Spanish for "stupid" or "fool." And* Tonto, *who was not so* tonto, *responded by calling the Lone Ranger* "qui no sabe" *(with an Indian accent), which roughly translates from*

Spanish as "he who knows nothing" or "clueless."—David Holmstrom, via the Internet

This is funny, David. Very very funny. But WRONG! I must have heard from 50 people claiming that kemosabe comes from a Spanish phrase meaning either "he who knows more" or "he who knows nothing," signifying that Tonto was either sucking up or mouthing off to the Lone Ranger. No proof was offered for these assertions; the writers had simply "heard" or "liked to believe" them. Well, I DON'T CARE WHAT YOU LIKE TO BELIEVE, GODDAMMIT! I DEAL IN THE FACTS! Sorry, but one must be firm.

To review: we have the testimony of the guy who introduced the term to the show, plus that of two experts in Native American languages, that kemosabe means "(trusty) scout." This is as close to a definitive answer as you get in my business, so I say case closed.

As for Tonto, "fool" and "wild one" are sufficiently close in meaning for me to believe that the name was originally a Spanish insult. That said, I have no objection to reviewing various other colorful if implausible theories:

1. In the language of the Yavapai Apaches in central Arizona, *k-nymsav-e* means "white man."

2. In the language of the Tewa Indians, *kema* means "friend" and *sabe* means "Apache." These terms may be found on back-to-back pages in an obscure Tewa dictionary; one scholar speculates that a *Lone Ranger* scriptwriter may have stumbled across this dictionary while doing research for the show. Scriptwriters do research? It is to laugh, lady.

3. The same scholar, clearly somebody who needs to find more constructive things to do with her time, spent an afternoon coming up with possible etymologies of kemosabe in Cree, Southern Paiute, Osage, and Navajo.

4. I'm told that in the Genus III edition of Trivial Pursuit, an answer on one card claims that kemosabe means "soggy bush." Trivial Pursuit, you'll remember, also claims that the Great Wall of China is the only man-made structure you can see from space, which is likewise bereft of factual foundation.

5. In an old Gary Larson cartoon, the Lone Ranger looks in an In-

dian dictionary and discovers that kemosabe is "an Apache expression for a horse's rear end."

Yuk yuk yuk. Now get outta here.

What does "pompatus" mean? There's a movie out now called The Pompatus of Love, *and of course it contains the Steve Miller song as a theme. I can't find "pompatus" in the dictionary. Any clues?—Cane95, via America Online*

Clues? Pfui. We have cracked the freaking case, thanks to some outstanding legwork by Jon Cryer—actor, cowriter, and coproducer of the movie *Pompatus of Love*—and my new assistant, J.K. Fabian. J.K. has what it takes to make a real impact in this business: pluck, luck, and an outstanding record collection.

"Pompatus" mystified millions when Steve Miller used it in his 1973 hit "The Joker": "Some people call me Maurice, / Cause I speak of the Pompatus of love."

Maurice referred to Miller's 1972 tune "Enter Maurice," which appeared on the album *Recall the Beginning . . . A Journey From Eden.* "Enter Maurice" had this lyric: "My dearest darling, come closer to Maurice so I can whisper sweet words of epismetology in your ear and speak to you of the pompitous of love."

Great, now there were *two* mystery words. What's more, it appeared even Miller himself was uncertain how pompatus was spelled. It appeared as "pompatus" in at least two books of sheet music but as "pompitous" in the lyrics included with "Recall the Beginning."

Miller has said little about the P-word over the years. In at least one interview, fans say, he claimed "it doesn't mean anything—it's just jive talk."

Not quite.

Some sharp-eared music fan noticed the "Enter Maurice" lyric above bore a marked resemblance to some lines in a rhythm and blues tune called "The Letter" by the Medallions. The song had been a hit in R & B circles in 1954.

J.K. found the record. It had the lines, "Oh my darling, let me whisper sweet words of [something like epismetology] and discuss the [something like pompatus] of love." J.K. tried to find the sheet music for the song, but came up only with the Box Tops hit ("My baby, she wrote me a letter").

Then came a stroke of luck. Jon Cryer the movie guy had stumbled onto the secret of pompatus. Eager to reveal it to the world, he sent it to—who, *Rolling Stone*? The *New York Times*?

Of course not. He sent it to us.

Speculation about "pompatus" was a recurring motif in the script for *The Pompatus of Love*. While the movie was in postproduction Cryer heard about "The Letter." During a TV interview he said that the song had been written and sung by a member of the Medallions named Vernon Green. Green, still very much alive, was dozing in front of the tube when the mention of his name caught his attention. He immediately contacted Cryer.

Green had never heard "The Joker." Cryer says that when he played it for Green "he laughed his ass off." Green's story:

"You have to remember, I was a very lonely guy at the time. I was only 14 years old, I had just run away from home, and I walked with crutches," Green told Cryer. He scraped by singing songs on the streets of Watts.

One song was "The Letter," Green's attempt to conjure up his dream woman. The mystery words, J.K. ascertained after talking with Green, were "puppetutes" and "pizmotality." (Green wasn't much for writing things down, so the spellings are approximate.)

"Pizmotality described words of such secrecy that they could only be spoken to the one you loved," Green told Cryer. And puppetutes?

"A term I coined to mean a secret paper-doll fantasy figure [thus puppet], who would be my everything and bear my children." Not real PC, but look, it was 1954.

Green went on to record many other songs and is still writing today. He can be reached at P.O. Box 1394, Perris, CA 92572.

Steve Miller must have loved R & B. Another line from "The Joker" goes "I really love your peaches, wanna shake your tree. / Lovey dovey, lovey dovey, lovey dovey all the time." A similar line may be found in the Clovers' 1953 hit "Lovey Dovey": "I really love your peaches wanna shake your tree / Lovey dovey, lovey dovey all the time."

When I spoke to Miller's publicist Jim Welch about these remarkable coincidences, he said Miller's comment was "artistic license." Pressed a bit, Welch said Miller acknowledged that he'd been "influenced" by earlier artists. Not perhaps the most forthcoming statement in the world. But at least we now know it didn't come to him in a dream.

Why do old black-and-white movies and newsreels move so fast? With our modern technology, can't we slow them down to make them look normal?—Karl M., Richardson, Texas

Karl, we need to examine our premise here. You think the Keystone Kops *ever* looked normal? But more on this in a sec.

One thing you need to know about the old silent movies: sure, they were shot at slower speeds than today's movies. But the main thing was that the camera was *hand cranked*. The only form of speed regulation was the cameraman going "one one thousand, two one thousand" as he rotated the handle. As a result, there wasn't any such thing as a standard silent speed. Old flicks ran at anywhere from 12 to 22 frames per second, with 16–20 fps being about average up through the early 1920s.

Many old movie hands, far from being annoyed by this, kind of liked it. They thought of the speed of the movie as being like the tempo in music. Near-normal speed might be OK for your basic dramatic exposition. But during the comedy or chase scenes you wanted things to really rip.

With the advent of sound in the late 1920s the industry switched to a standard speed of 24 frames per second. There were two reasons for this. First, it was the average speed of most silents then being made—there had been a steady increase in projection speeds during the '20s as theater owners tried to cram in more showings per night and movie directors speeded up their cameras to compensate. Second, 24 fps was the minimum necessary to produce decent sound quality. The faster the film's sound track ran through the projector, the more sound information you got per second, and the better the fidelity.

Some movie projectors made right after the switch had two speeds, 16 (or 18) fps and 24 fps, and the operator could use whichever speed best suited the movie being shown. But nowadays many projectors have only one speed, 24 frames per second. Run a 16 fps silent through a 24 fps projector and the action gets speeded up 50 percent.

Today it's possible to produce normal-speed versions of the older silents through a process known as stretch printing, in which roughly every other frame is printed twice. The result is slightly jerky but watchable, and has been used in contemporary films to achieve a period feel. Since it's tedious and expensive and many film labs hate to do it, it's mostly reserved for special projects.

Better results can be achieved with less trouble when transferring silents to videotape. In fact, some of the best versions we have of the old silents (that is, that most closely approximate the way they were meant to be seen) are those specially prepared for TV.

Which brings me back to my original point. The old silents weren't necessarily meant to move at the same speed as today's flicks. In some old silents—comedies in particular—things were *supposed* to be speeded up, the better to enhance the comic effect. Chase scenes in the Keystone Kops flicks, for example, were often shot at 8–12 fps but projected maybe twice as fast. Today the frantic action in these films strikes us as hilarious—but people thought the same thing in 1915.

When I was a small boy I attended a circus that featured a "human cannonball." This amazing fellow was shot out of a large cannon and flew about thirty yards into a giant net. How did they do this without blowing the poor guy to pieces? It seems to me if this was legitimate, the only thing emerging from the barrel of the cannon would be ten thousand human cannonball pieces.—Rob Marchant, Carrollton, Texas

That's what you *wish* would happen, you savage. Happily, the art of human ballistics today has reached such a pitch of perfection that it's no more dangerous than, oh, shaving with a chain saw. Which is to say it's still pretty easy to get yourself injured or killed.

Human cannonballs aren't blasted from the cannon with gunpowder. They're propelled by a catapult. The flash, loud noise, and smoke are supplied by firecrackers and such.

The first human cannonball was a young woman named Zazel, who

made her maiden voyage, so to speak, on April 2, 1877, at the Westminster Aquarium, which I presume is in London. Zazel employed "elastic springs," but human cannoneers soon graduated to more potent technology: the propellant of choice today is compressed air. The human projectile climbs into a hollow topless cylinder that slides inside the cannon barrel. Having been lowered to the bottom of the barrel, the cylinder is blasted forward by compressed air at 150–200 pounds per square inch. The cylinder stops at the cannon's mouth. It's occupant doesn't.

Being shot from a cannon, like jumping out of an airplane, isn't that strenuous; it's the sudden stop at the end that's a bitch. Elvin Bale, the "Human Space Shuttle," was experimenting with air bags to break his fall while on tour in 1986. He overshot the air bags and crashed into a wall, seriously injuring himself. On another occasion two members of the Zacchini family, long famous for its cannonballing exploits, were launched simultaneously from opposite ends of the circus. They collided in midair; one Zacchini broke her back.

Historian A.H. Coxe says that of 50 human cannonballs more than 30 have been killed, mostly by falling outside the net. Even if you avoid mishaps, many human cannonballs black out in flight, which makes me wonder about long-term brain damage. (OK, I lied when I said it wasn't strenuous. Sue me.) Of course you might figure anybody who lets himself get shot from a cannon is a couple eggs short of a dozen to start with. If you must have heavy-caliber kicks, I say join the Marines. At least they let you shoot back.

I attended the Ohio Renaissance Festival recently. One of the acts was Thom Selectomy, a sword swallower. He invited persons from the audience to inspect his props, the swords. From all appearances the weapons seemed to be authentic. He then proceeded to "swallow" rapiers of varying lengths. Once he ingested two at a time, extracting them separately. At another point (no pun), he allowed the weight of the hilt (no hands) to force the blade down. Thom also inflated and swallowed one of those long, skinny balloons. (He did not pull the balloon out.) Please, tell me he used deception; it simply cannot be possible to master control of the esophagus to permit the intake of such objects. (I gag thinking about it.)—Gloria Hodgson, Pardeeville, Wisconsin

If people could swallow Ross Perot for president without gagging, I don't see what's so amazing about a sword. Fact is, professional sword swallowers are totally (well, mostly) legit. Testimony on this score comes from Dan Mannix, a onetime carnival sword and flame swallower who published a book about his experiences in 1951.

Mannix says he learned the stunt by practicing an hour or so a day for several weeks with a blunt sword. The first problem was learning to stifle the gag reflex. Having lost his lunch a few dozen times, he finally conquered that difficulty, only to find his throat choked up tight every time he poked the sword in. Finally one day he got distracted while practicing and found that his throat relaxed enough that the sword sank in up to the hilt.

Mannix retched a few more times but was past the hard part, so to speak. Still, for a long time afterward he was obliged to bend forward when the sword was partway down to nudge it past an obstruction behind his Adam's apple. He also had to watch out for the breast bone; he says striking it with the sword was like a blow to the solar plexus, only from the inside.

Cecil strongly advises against trying this at home but feels a few pointers are in order just in case. As you might guess, the sides of the sword must be dull so they won't slice up your throat on the way down. But the point can be sharp, the better to impress the rubes, provided the sword isn't long enough to puncture the bottom of your stomach. (If it does anyway, you're in trouble; you could get peritonitis.) The sword should be wiped before and after swallowing: before to wipe off any dust, which might cause you to retch, and after to remove stomach acid that could corrode the metal.

Mannix eventually became dissatisfied with swords, partly because many smartarse spectators were convinced the blade somehow folded up into the handle. He began swallowing neon tubes, then all the rage among the more daring carnies. The tube was specially fabricated of thin glass and doubled over into a tight U so that all the electrical connections were on one end. The lighted tube could be seen glowing through your skin, proving you had swallowed it. "A lovely act," Mannix quotes a fellow performer as saying. "I was very nearly taken sick myself." The drawback was that the tubes occasionally shattered in the throat, bringing the swallower's act, career, and sometimes life to an abrupt end.

There were many other equally perverse variations. Mannix took to swallowing a giant corkscrew, "which made my Adam's apple leap around like a flea on a hot griddle as it went down and this gave a particularly horrible effect that went over big." He once got into a swallowing contest with another performer who downed a red-hot blade. The secret? The guy first swallowed an asbestos scabbard offstage. This same character later swallowed a sword plus scabbard on stage, removed the sword, then plucked a handful of paper flowers and a large American flag from the scabbard (still in his throat, natch), whereupon the orchestra launched into "The Star-Spangled Banner." OK, it's not everybody's idea of a great job, but it sure sounds like more fun than the steno pool.

I found an obscure reference to a place called the Grand Guignol in Paris. It said some pretty twisted stuff happened there for the amusement of others. Do you know anything about it? Was it theatrics or the real McCoy (or should I say McCabre)? How do you pronounce Grand Guignol?—Mike McGary, Dallas

Well, we can't have you prowling around Paris looking for the Grand Goog-nole, Mike: you say it Gron Geen-yole. Not that you're going to find it no matter how you say it; the place closed in 1962. Too bad. I bet it would have been a trip.

The Theatre du Grand Guignol, for years one of the leading tourist attractions of the French capital, was the classic shock theater, special-

izing in productions designed to horrify and sicken. No show was considered a success unless at least a couple audience members fainted or upchucked on their shoes. In its latter years, what with competition from Hollywood horror films and real-life nightmares like Auschwitz, the Grand Guignol became pretty campy. But in its day it produced some truly terrifying theater that explored, admittedly for low commercial purposes, the dark limits of what could be accomplished on the stage.

In some ways the subject matter of the Grand Guignol wasn't all that different from what you can see today in any number of *Friday the 13th*-type slasher movies. But there were a couple key differences: this was live, in-your-face, and sometimes all-over-your-clothes theater conducted in a disconcertingly intimate space: the place seated only about 285, and the stage measured just 20 by 20 feet. Equally important, the plays, which were short and usually ran three or more to a bill, partook of the queasily amoral outlook that we are pleased to think of as peculiarly French. The characters typically were brutal louts, hapless victims, or both. The guilty often went unpunished. Lovers and friends routinely betrayed one another. For comic relief the producers might throw in a sex farce featuring the lineup of seedy characters and illicit affairs you'd pretty much expect in the land of the feelthy postcard—a harmless enough business in itself, but in context adding to the air of Parisian sleaze.

The Grand Guignol's main stock in trade was gory special effects (and they were only that; we're not talking snuff theater here). In description today the effects seem pretty tame, but remember that they were carried off at close range, with no retakes, using stuff that was scrounged mainly from the drugstore and the butcher shop. Eyeball gougings were perennially popular, animal eyes being especially useful for this purpose because they could be relied upon to bounce when hitting the floor. Then you had your disembowelings, your self-mutilations, your throat slashings, your rapes, your acid thrown in the face, your flesh ripped from the bone . . . predictable stuff, I suppose. But in the most effective Grand Guignol plays the effects were coupled with a shrewd grasp of the psychology of horror plus an over-the-top gallic love of the nutso that can weird you out even today. Historian Mel Gordon, in *The Grand Guignol: Theatre of Fear and Terror* (1988), recounts some of the plots:

- The innocent Louise is unjustly locked in an asylum with several insane women. A nurse assigned to protect her blithely leaves for a staff party as soon as Louise falls asleep. The insane women decide that a cuckoo bird is imprisoned in Louise's head and one gouges out her eye with a knitting needle. The other crazy women are freaked and burn the gouger's face off on a hot plate.
- Two brothers have an orgy with two prostitutes at a lighthouse. The lighthouse beacon goes out and one of the brothers realizes a boat containing their mother is heading toward the rocks. But the drunken lighthouse keeper has locked the beacon door. The brother goes nuts, blames everything on an earlier blasphemy by one of the hookers, slits her throat, and throws her out the window. "The boat with the men's mother crashes against the rocks," Gordon says. "In a religious frenzy, the [brothers] decide to burn [the other prostitute] to death. After pouring gasoline on her, they incinerate her and pray." The end. And you thought *The Texas Chain Saw Massacre* was sick.

Where did the Grateful Dead get their name? What does it mean? I've heard a lot of tales, but I'll believe only you.—S. Seidman, Stevenson, Maryland

I *am* a rock of comfort, ain't I? The official story on the Grateful Dead, as related by Jerry Garcia in the book *Playing in the Band*, is as follows: "We were standing around in utter desperation at Phil [Lesh]'s house in Palo Alto [trying to think up a name for the band]. There was a huge dictionary, big monolithic thing, and I just opened it up. There in huge black letters was 'The Grateful Dead.' It . . . just canceled my mind out."

I'll say—how often does the phrase "grateful dead" pop up in the average dictionary? But it turns out Garcia may not have hallucinated the whole thing after all. In the *Funk & Wagnalls Standard Dictionary of Folklore, Mythology and Legend*, we find a page headed "GRATE-FUL DEAD" in big type. Beneath this is an entry to the effect that the "grateful dead" is a motif figuring in many folktales.

Further investigation has turned up a rare volume of folklore entitled *The Grateful Dead* by G.H. Gerould (1908), lent to me by Straight Dope reader Charles Kroon. In it we find a typical grateful-dead story:

"Graf Willekin von Montabour . . . learned that a beautiful and rich maiden had promised her hand to [whichever] knight should win a tourney she had established. Thereupon he set forth and came to the place announced for the combats. There he found lodging in the house of a man who would only receive him if he paid the debts of a dead man, whose body lay unburied in the dung of a horse-stall. Willekin was moved by this story and paid seventy marks, almost all his money, to ransom the corpse and give it suitable burial. He then

had to borrow money from his host in order to indulge in his customary generosity. On the morning of the jousting he obtained from a stranger knight a fine horse on condition of dividing everything he won. He succeeded in [beating] all the other contestants, and so wedded the maiden. On the second night after the marriage the stranger entered his room and demanded a share in the marital rights. After offering instead to give all his possessions, the hero started from the room in tears, when the stranger called him back and explained that he was the ghost of the [presumably grateful] dead, then disappeared." Definitely puts a different spin on "Sugar Magnolia," I'm sure even hardened Deadheads would agree.

In other Dead news, I learn that John Epler, a leading bug authority and loyal Straight Dope reader, has named a newly discovered species of chironomid midge after the Dead, namely *Dicrotendipes thanatogratus*. (*Thanatos* is Greek for death, *gratus* Latin for grateful.) Abrim with boyish enthusiasm, he sent the band a note, but can you believe it, the ingrates (oh, rich irony!) never bothered to reply! Maybe they were turned off by the gauche commingling of Latin and Greek. Or maybe they're just too jaded. Whatever, when John names his second new bug, you can be sure *I* won't forget the thank-you note.

Grateful Dead: Not Ungrateful After All

As John Epler may already know, the Dead are no more efficient than they have to be. The mail answerers are rummaging through the backlog in search of the Dicrotendipes thanatogratus *note. Your column was the first anyone had heard about it, and it's a nice flash.*

For the record, naming the Dead took place at the house on High Street in Palo Alto on a November afternoon in 1965. The name was found in a regular Funk and Wagnalls dictionary, probably the 1956 edition.

Gerould's book on the "grateful dead" legends is lovely. Stith Thompson also discusses them. [Typically the hero pays a dead man's debts so his corpse can be buried. Later a stranger, who turns out to be the grateful dead man, joins the hero and offers his help, on condition that all winnings be equally divided.]

Is the grateful dead man tempting you? Are you making a moral de-

cision? The flat hit you get from the words "grateful dead" can be en-
hanced by pondering what life situations the g.d. tales represent.
When you listen to such tales you're living on that level of symbolic
transaction.—Bill Legate, San Rafael, California

You're living on a level of symbolic transaction? Jeez, what happened to sex, drugs, and rock 'n' roll?

Wil Wheaton, in Stand by Me, *posed a very interesting question.*
Mickey's a mouse, Donald's a duck, Pluto's a dog . . . what the hell was
Goofy? Enclosed is a bribe—the largest I could afford.—Britt R., Seattle

A year-old Seattle Mariners ticket is your idea of a *bribe*? Not to cast aspersions, but a *current* Mariners ticket isn't exactly a siren's call to my ears. Equally depressing is your failure to grasp cartoon conventions. For starters, Pluto isn't a dog, he's a *dawg*. So is Goofy. The difference is that Goofy is a human dawg, whereas Pluto is a dawg dawg (or dawg,[2] if you're into the new math). You can tell a dawg dawg from a human dawg because the dwag gets naked and walks on all fours and the human doesn't, though admittedly this isn't the acid test it used to be.

Educated people—leastways, educated people who've just chatted with the Disney archivists—know Goofy first appeared anonymously in *Mickey's Revue* (1932), looking essentially as he does today except older. In the wonderful way of cartoons, he then got younger, meanwhile adopting various aliases, including Dippy Dawg, Dippy the

Goof, and Mr. Geef before settling on Goofy in *Orphans' Benefit* (1934). So if the guy has an identity crisis, it goes back a long way.

A friend and I were discussing the fate of the "singing nun," popular for a time in the '60s when we were kids. We agreed she left the convent, entered into a lesbian affair and, in a state of despondency over money matters, committed suicide. But neither of us can remember exactly why. Could you possibly help?—Hethryn Haryse (?), Los Angeles

Let's not make this any more lurid than it already is, Hethryn (or whatever your name is—I swear, what this country really needs is a good course in handwriting). It's true that the "singing nun," also known as Janine (spellings vary) Deckers, committed suicide in Belgium in 1985 along with her companion of 10 years, Annie Pecher. However, popular belief on this score notwithstanding, Cecil does not know whether the two were lovers, and frankly does not feel it is any of his business. Or, if you don't mind my saying so, of yours.

The two women were in despair because the center for autistic children they had founded had gone under for lack of funds. The Belgian government was also dunning Deckers for back taxes of between $47,000 and $63,000, although she said she had given all her music earnings to her convent. Deckers, who had become a Dominican nun in 1959, recorded "Dominique" as a tribute to the founder of her order. In 1963 it made number one in the United States, selling 1.5 million copies. Deckers left the convent in 1967 before taking final vows, partly to pursue a recording career, but never repeated her earlier success. After her death at 51 or 52 (the two women washed down massive doses of barbiturates with alcohol), she did receive the highest honor our society can bestow: a full-page obit in *People* magazine.

Chapter 5

Critters

This may seem like a stupid question, but hey, I have no pride. Our psychotic dwarf rabbit, Slick, has an unusual urge to chew on things. He does it pretty indiscriminately and I have some chewed up T-shirts to prove it. Annoying as this is, my sister claims if he didn't do it, he would die. She showed me a gruesome picture of a woodchuck with incredibly long and deformed chompers, and says that's what would happen to Slick if he didn't chew. Is this true? How can I remedy this?—Josh Ingle, Salem, Oregon

You may think this question is stupid, Josh, but it's Kierkegaard compared to some of the stuff I get. Like the three dweebs who mailed me a dirtball from under the bed so I could tell them what was in it. (Answer: dirt.) Lotta days when I open the mail I feel like I should wear rubber gloves.

Rabbits and a few other critters have teeth that grow continuously throughout their lives—in the middle-size breeds, about five inches per year for the upper incisors (front teeth) and about eight inches for the lower ones. The teeth abrade away against one another, giving the rabbit a constantly sharp edge.

Once in a while you get a rabbit with a *malocclusion*, which generally turns out to be the world's worst case of underbite. Since the top and bottom teeth don't meet, they don't wear away against one another and grow to truly horrifying lengths. This prevents the rabbit from eating, threatening it with starvation.

The only treatment, according to my rabbit handbook, is to "cut [the teeth] back to normal length with sharp side-cutting pliers every three or four weeks," an operation that on Cecil's Scale of Grossness is maybe one notch below sheep gelding. Luckily, normal rabbit teeth are self-adjusting, given an adequate supply of chewing material. T-shirts, however, aren't an essential part of the mix. You ever think of trying, say, a carrot?

On a recent afternoon around the lunch counter, my colleagues and I were discussing the attributes of the chicken egg when someone asked, "Which end of the egg comes out first, the round end or the pointed end?" Of course we all took a position, and while wagering of serious money did not take place, our reputations are on the line. I naturally thought of you to answer this question.—Mark Olson, Las Vegas, Nevada

Cecil's initial thought was: these guys have been spending too much time playing the nickel slots. The more I thought about it, however, the more this question began to nag. At last I turned to Cornell University professor Kavous Keshavarz, poultry czar on the Straight Dope Science Advisory Board. According to Professor K., the egg initially moves through the chicken's oviduct small end first. When it reaches the uterus, however, it hardens (that is, the shell calcifies), rotates 180 degrees, and makes the rest of the trip big end first. This may sound

like doing it the hard way, but actually it's the most efficient way to push the egg. When the muscles of the chicken's uterine and vaginal walls squeeze the egg's small (i.e., back) end, it squirts forward and out into the cold cruel world.

How did the myth that cats sometimes steal people's breath when they sleep get started?—Rick Weaver, North Bay, California

Well, not to be Mr. Paranoid or anything, but I'm not totally sure it's a myth, and neither are some cat writers, as we shall see. No question, people have been getting freaked about cats for a long time. One cat book notes that to many people, "cats may still presage evil, particularly if they are black; they may still, as has been widely held throughout the world, cause the death of a child by creeping upon it and sucking its breath." Furthermore, we read, "Lilith, the dark goddess of Hebrew mythology, changed herself into a vampire cat, El-Broosha, and in that form sucked the blood of her favorite prey, the newborn infant." The authors described such beliefs as "without factual substantiation."

Maybe, maybe not. Some cat-care experts—folks who presumably would laugh off unfounded legends about cats—warn against allowing a cat into a room with a newborn baby. "Cats like warm spots to sleep," one writer says. "Attracted by body heat, they may curl up alongside a baby, but this habit must be discouraged as there is a danger that the cat might unwittingly suffocate the child."

Cecil is willing to concede this fear may be exaggerated. It may be

that cats over the years have been unjustly blamed for cases of crib death, whose cause is not well understood. Still, if you've got a little one on the premises, no sense taking any chances.

Facts About Cats, Part 1

It's hard to believe a person in the 1990s could still believe that cats can "suck the breath out of babies." No reputable cat-care book has ever suggested that a cat will "suffocate" a baby! I have over 50 cat books in my possession, and have lived with cats for 34 of my 39 years. My cats sleep next to me at night, and the only thing that concerns me is that I might roll over and crush them! You are an irresponsible reporter. If you had half the brains and personality of a cat you could accomplish much more than writing for a cheap throwaway paper.—Donna Kentnor, West Covina, California

Listen, honey, at least I've got something to sleep with besides a cat. One cat book that warned about the danger of suffocating a baby was *You and Your Cat* by David Taylor (1986); it seemed plenty reputable to me. Is the danger exaggerated? Maybe, but read on.

Facts About Cats, Part 2

As a passed-out drunk freshman in a Michigan State dorm room about 32 years ago, I can attest to cat breath thievery—or at least to cat-assisted attempted suffocation. Unconscious in my bunk bed, I was unaware that one of my academic neighbors had let a small stray cat into my room during the night. The next morning I awoke with really fuzzy vision and undeniably hairy tongue. Naturally I thought I had achieved a truly remarkable hangover. I raised my hands to give my eyes a serious rubbing (I was lying flat on my back), when much to my surprise I discovered a large furry growth protruding at least three inches above my face.

Disorientation is not the appropriate word, but it'll have to do. I pulled my arms back to my sides and froze while I tried to make sense of the situation. About that time the furry growth began to purr, as kitties will do when touched. EUREKA! I had a cat on my face. Totally disregarding the cat's ability to extend its claws, I grabbed it and flung it across the room. I developed a cat fur allergy that stuck with me for 25 years, but at least it didn't steal my breath.

Cats like to cuddle up to things warm and rhythmic—I've seen them asleep atop operating electric motors, so it's probably best to keep them out of nurseries. Baby's face would be too much to resist.—Kirby Metcalfe, Dallas

Where do pigeons go to die? I've only seen maybe two dead pigeons in my life. Considering how many there are, the streets should be littered with them. Is there a pigeon graveyard?—Ken Ellyson, Dallas; similarly from Bobbie Warshau, Evanston, Illinois and Betty Pryde, Novato, California

What is this? Just a few years ago everybody wanted to know where the baby pigeons were. Now all I get is letters asking what's become of the dead ones. I blame it on the cults.

You don't see many dead city pigeons for a couple of reasons. The first is that scavengers make pretty quick work of them. Insects alone can reduce a deceased pigeon to a heap of feathers and bones in a week or two. Rats, dogs, or other animals may drag the carcass off into some secret corner for a late snack. City sanitation crews occasionally stir themselves to scoop up a couple.

The other reason you don't see dead pigeons is that old and feeble ones usually hole up in some out-of-the-way place so they won't be seen by predators. Nooks and crannies in and around buildings are always popular, but I'd say the pigeons' favorite spots are the ironwork underneath viaducts. I recently inspected one near the office of the newspaper that publishes my column. I found the surrounding area littered with decaying remains—mostly former editors sleeping it off, but a bunch of dead pigeons, too. Naturally, I paused for a moment of respectful silence. For the pigeons. I mean, pigeons and editors both do the icky on the stuff you cherish most. But at least the pigeons don't think, "Wow, now it *sings*."

Reports From The Field

I thought you might want to know that there is indeed a pigeon graveyard in Dallas. I have had the opportunity, if not the pleasure, of touring the old American Beauty flour mill on South Ervay Street. After having been abandoned for 15 years, the building now houses the remains of several hundred pigeons, in every stage of decay from recently deceased to crumbling skeletons.

As an interesting aside, the vast majority died flat on their backs with their wings spread and their little feet in the air.—Janice-Mary Cunningham, Dallas

Hmm, just like the cockroaches we reported on in *The Straight Dope*, pages 24–25. As soon as I get that big NSF grant, we'll get to the bottom of this once and for all.

My girlfriend's mother claims that when she was a child many years ago in Virginia, a "hoop snake" once chased her by forming itself into a circle, gimbaling its rotational axis to horizontal, and, balancing perfectly, rolling down a hill at her. I intimated that I wasn't quite convinced (I fell out of my chair laughing). My girlfriend, however, did not share my sentiments. She respects your opinion highly and asked me to ask you if it was possible. Well?—John Sandow, Chicago

I love country folk, John, but let's face it, they're the product of generations of inbreeding. Folklore about hoop snakes is well-known to herpetologists but universally dismissed. I quote from *Snakes of Virginia* (Linzey and Clifford, 1981): "The 'hoop snake' tale is usually applied to the mud snake [*Farancia abacura*] and to the rainbow snake [*Farancia erytrogramma*]. Supposedly, the snake takes its tail into its mouth, forms a hoop, and rolls after the nearest human. It then tries to 'sting' the person with its tail. Should the snake jab a tree instead, the poor plant immediately wilts and dies. The whole story is, of course, nonsense."

To be fair, there's a germ of truth to the legend. While a hoop/mud snake cannot sting with its tail, it does have a hard spine back there that can draw blood when thrashed vigorously. What's more, the snake tends to form itself into a flat, hooplike circle when relaxed. If you were an impressionable six-year-old prowling through the swamps and you came across such an apparition, you might easily imagine it was about to hoist itself to the vertical and roll after you. The only problem is, the former six-year-old who became your girlfriend's mother still believes it.

Our cat seems to be left-handed. Is that possible? Are animals right- or left-handed, as humans are? If so, how come, and what can be inferred from that about the meaning of life?—Pierre and Daniella, Montreal, Quebec, Canada

Life is pretty much meaningless. However, if you play your cards right, it can still be a million laughs. Proof: the carefree existence led by your humble columnist, who gets paid big money to answer questions like this.

Not that I'm the only one. I have before me a research paper entitled "Paw Preference in Cats Related to Hand Preference in Animals and Man," by J. Cole, University Laboratory of Physiology, Oxford, England. Professor Cole sounds like a person (we will hereinafter assume a male person) after my own heart. If he represents the cream of the British intelligentsia, no wonder they lost the Empire.

To test feline handedness, or pawedness as you prefer, Professor Cole had 60 randomly selected cats reach into a glass tube for some rabbit meat. Of the 60, 35 showed a noticeable preference for one paw over the other (i.e., same paw used in at least 75 out of 100 tries). Of the 35, two-thirds were left-pawed. Cecil finds this interesting because

he himself is a lefty, a much-oppressed minority. Previously I have not had much use for cats, but when I see one now I will think: "Hey, bro!"

Paw/claw/whatever preference is actually pretty common in the animal world, having turned up in most species tested, including parrots (mostly lefties) as well as rats, monkeys, and chimpanzees (50–50 right versus left). Why should there be a preference? One plausible guess is that it helps the animals learn faster. Professor Cole noticed that cats with a dominant paw figured out how to get the rabbit meat out of the tube faster than the ambidextrous cats. Presumably if you practice constantly with one paw, you become more skillful than if you squander your playing time on two.

My uncle told me that once when he was cutting chickens' heads off on his farm, one chicken didn't die, but rather lived headless for two weeks. He told me he put it on display and charged admission to see it. He fed it through the rectum and gave it water from an eyedropper. Evidently he made a great deal of money from this chicken. Is this possible?—Jack Saltzberg, Montreal, Quebec

Your uncle may well be putting you on, Jack—I certainly maximize the baloney when talking to *my* nephews—but sure, it's possible. In fact, a story along these lines appeared in the October 22, 1945, issue of *Life* magazine.

L.A. Olsen, a farmer in Fruita, Colorado, had attempted to decapitate a Wyandotte rooster named Mike for purposes of supper. Perhaps

moved by last-minute remorse, or possibly just because he was uncoordinated, L.A. didn't aim too well and chopped off just the top two-thirds of Mike's head. This sheared off the frontal lobes, rendering the bird totally incapable of thinking about Immanuel Kant but leaving enough of the brain stem to take care of breathing, blood circulation, and the like.

Mike's owners, knowing an opportunity when they saw one, put him on exhibit at 25 cents a throw in Salt Lake City, then as now a center of sophisticated entertainment. They fed him with an eyedropper by way of his unclosed esophagus. *Life,* ever the paragon of good taste, published a close-up photo of this for the benefit of skeptics. Another shot shows Mike in the barnyard being eyed by his anatomically complete brethren. "Chickens do not avoid Mike who, however, has shown no tendency to mate," the caption notes helpfully.

This sort of thing evidently occurs fairly often. When Dear Abby ran a column on it a while back she got clippings and eyewitness reports about headless-but-living chickens from all over the country. The phenomenon has even found its way into literature, namely Garrison Keillor's *Leaving Home*. If you don't think it happens in humans, too, you've never had a close look at the contestants on *Let's Make a Deal*.

How did some medieval Europeans come to display lions on their coats of arms? Few if any would have been able to see a real lion during their lifetimes.—Zach Church, Washington, D.C.

You never heard of Daniel in the lion's den? So much you have to explain to these postreligious Generation Xers. Lions once ranged more widely than any other land mammal. While there were none in Europe during the Middle Ages (they had become extinct in Greece, their last European outpost, by A.D. 100), they survived in considerable numbers in the Middle East and North Africa. Medieval Europeans had regular contact with these areas, and presumably with lions, via trade and (in the Middle East) via pilgrimages and the Crusades. The last Middle Eastern and North African lions weren't wiped out until this century.

But even if medieval Europeans had had no contact with the big cats at all, they'd probably still have had a thing about lions. Lions show up in the art of China, after all, even though none has ever roamed there. Lions early on attained mythic stature and became embedded in the culture, after which point it didn't much matter whether the real thing was around or not. No animal has been given more attention in art and literature. C.A.W. Guggisberg, in his classic book *Simba*, says the lion is referred to 130 times in the Bible. The lion can be found in Stone Age cave drawings and no doubt has been considered king of beasts since the dawn of man.

The high regard in which lions traditionally have been held accounts, to a large extent, for their greatly reduced numbers today. They have always been considered the premier game beast and men have slaughtered them in vast numbers to prove their manliness. But it seems certain lions would survive in human recollection as a symbol of nobility and courage even if, as may well happen, all living specimens were destroyed.

When I look at dinosaur skeletons in museums the thing that always impresses me is their incredible size. It has occurred to me that perhaps these animals could grow to such enormous size because effective gravity was lighter then. If earth spun faster at the time of the dinosaurs, then centrifugal force might have counteracted gravity enough to make a substantial difference in the weight of massive animals. What are the scientific merits of this idea? I read somewhere that the earth's day is getting shorter by a fraction of a second every year. Extrapolating backward, how much faster [etc.]—Andrew Murphy, Philadelphia

We have two questions here, Andrew—the one you asked, and the one you would have asked if the drugs hadn't kicked in first. The best that can be said for question #1 is that if you mention it to a stranger on the bus you're guaranteed to get the seat to yourself. Question #2 is more interesting: why were dinosaurs so big? Some theories:

- *Dinosaurs had to be big to reach the leaves on the tops of the trees.* This is the answer favored by fourth graders. It probably was a factor in the size of some dinosaurs, notably brachiosaurus, a plant-eater described as basically a crane on legs. But dinosaurs were huge whether they ate plants or not. One estimate puts their median weight at two tons.
- *Dinosaurs had to be big because they were a) cold-blooded, or b) warm-blooded.* Paleontologists have been debating whether dinosaurs were warm-blooded or cold-blooded for 25 years, and the great size of the animals has been enlisted as an argument on either side. Cold-blooded advocates say dinosaurs were big because their sheer thermal mass protected them against the sudden temperature swings to which small cold-blooded creatures were vulnerable. Objection: "bulk homeothermy," as it's called, only works in animals weighing more than a ton; some dinosaurs were smaller.

Warm-blooded advocates say dinosaurs had to be big because their uninsulated skin made them easily chilled. Great size gave

them a lower ratio of skin surface to volume and thus reduced heat loss. Objection: come on, they couldn't wear sweaters? There have to be easier ways to stop heat loss than putting on twenty thousand pounds. Equally to the point, how did they survive long enough to get big?

• *Dinosaurs had to be big because the early mammals had taken all the small slots, ecologically speaking.* It's thought mammals were more agile than the relatively stiff-limbed dinosaurs and thus better equipped to survive. Objection: OK, but why couldn't mammals have become huge, too, and beaten out dinosaurs at both ends of the size continuum?

The question may never be resolved because so much about dinosaurs is unknown and, given the limitations of the fossil record, may be . . . well, I don't know that it's completely unknowable. But Cecil can appreciate that it's a lot easier holding forth on your latest grand theory in the faculty room than excavating in some former swamp with a spoon.

Why is it that some dogs walk by moving both legs on one side of the body at the same time, while others (most?) walk by moving the front leg on one side at the same time as the rear leg on the other side?—Tim Silva, Washington, D.C.

You won't believe this—I didn't believe it, until I checked the files—but there is actually an answer to this question. Moving both legs on one side of the body forward at the same time is called "pacing." It's generally considered an easier, slower method of locomotion. Moving diagonal pairs of legs forward at the same time is called "trotting." It's more efficient since the body doesn't roll as much and is usually regarded as a step up from pacing speed- and coordination-wise. There are many exceptions to the foregoing; some dogs can move pretty fast while pacing. Personally I'm content to locomote on two legs rather than four, except when I've had a very, very bad night.

From The Straight Dope Message Board

Subj: chewing gum anesthesia
From: Mostrim
   Anyone familiar with the theory that your senses and faculties are numbed or less cognitive while chewing gum . . . or is it just me???

From: TUBADIVA
   It's just you.

Subj: Meaning of life
From: MVonren
   Why were we all born only to suffer and die?

From: TicklinLad
   Because some of us, in between being born and suffering and dying, can make great contributions to the general welfare of mankind. Others of us make smaller contributions to a lesser portion of mankind, and still others only send answers to questions on the Straight Dope Message Board.

From: Nnymmph
   I guess that this is a corollary to the question: Why does God allow pain and suffering? I think the answer fits for both questions:
   SO WE CAN HAVE LYRICS TO COUNTRY-WESTERN SONGS!

From: Diannecar
   You know what happens when you play a country and/or western song backward, don't you?
   You get your wife back, you get your dawg back . . .

C h a p t e r **6**

To Your Health

As a child I was told that the best way to treat a minor burn was to hold a piece of ice against it, and to this day I'm convinced it works. Uniced burns redden and swell, while iced ones often leave no mark at all. But judging from the reactions I get when I explain this medical miracle to others, you'd think I was using garlic to ward off vampires. Please, Cecil, tell me this isn't just some silly superstition and that putting ice on burns really works. Also, what's the word on using aloe for burns and scrapes? I think it helps but am not about to say so with-

*out authoritative support—if people think ice is weird, imagine what
they'll make of mysterious plant ointments.—Beth, Chicago*

Yeah, witchcraft trials can be such a hassle. But you're safe with me.
Clinical studies have shown that cold (although not ice per se, for fear
of frostbite) can speed burn healing significantly. It's not unreasonable
to suppose that in minor cases it may prevent reddening and swelling
altogether.

One of the more striking demonstrations of the usefulness of "water cooling," as it's called in trauma circles, was provided by a doctor
in (appropriately) Iceland named O.J. Ofeigsson, who wrote several
articles touting the benefits of cooling in the 1960s. He reported the
case of a 40-year-old woman whose right arm at age two had been
badly burned from hand to armpit by boiling milk. Someone had had
the presence of mind to put the little girl's arm into a bucket of cold
water immediately—but only up to the elbow. Thirty-eight years later
the woman's arm from the elbow down was fine but her upper arm
was disfigured by deep scars. I've got the photo right here.

You might be thinking: come on, doc, you didn't see her until 38
years later, how do you know what really happened when she was two?
Well, OK. But animal studies—studies in which animals were intentionally burned, I feel obliged to note—suggest the woman's story
could be legit. Animals whose burns were immersed in ice water
within 30 minutes after occurrence and kept there for a half hour
healed much more quickly and thoroughly than those where soaking
had been delayed for an hour or put off altogether.

Why does cooling burns work? Doctors aren't sure, but studies suggest cooling prevents the tiny blood vessels in the skin from clogging,
inhibits dehydration, and slows the formation of certain harmful
chemicals. The point is, it works.

Dabbing aloe vera juice on a burn, scrape, or other minor skin injury also seems to speed up healing. Nobody's sure why aloe works, either, but like cooling it seems to prevent formation of harmful
chemicals and kills bacteria besides.

Not every folk remedy is so salubrious. Ever been told to dab a burn
with butter? Don't. Butter isn't sterile and you'll just increase the
chances of infection.

In days of old, doctors wore metal disks with a hole in the middle on their heads, which made them look like a coal miner or a shaman. What was the disk and where did it go?—Evan and Yishai, Oakland, California

Cecil has heard various terms for this, but the simplest, most descriptive, and therefore most unmedical is "head mirror." It was used in examinations of the ear, throat, and other, ah, body cavities. To use, you swung the head mirror down so that you could look through the hole in the middle with one eye. Then you positioned a light source so that it shone on the mirror's parabolic surface. By moving your head just so, you could reflect the light rays down the patient's throat or whatever, the better to illuminate items of interest without obstructing the view.

Just about all doctors used head mirrors at one time and they became, along with the stethoscope, one of the symbols of the profession. But they could be a bit of a hassle to use and they did make you look like a space alien, so today many doctors prefer a penlight or other examining device. Some ENT (ear-nose-throat) specialists still use head mirrors, though, so look one up if you get nostalgic.

Is there really such a thing as a pathological liar? If so, why does one become one?—Scott Riedel

Why not? Looking at Washington on the one hand and the O.J. trial on the other, you've got to figure it gives you a lot of career options. The term is, however, somewhat imprecise. The best definition was put forth 50 years ago by L.S. Selling: "a person having a constellation of symptoms . . . characterized psychopathologically by a very definite tendency to tell untruths about matters which perhaps could be easily verified and which untruths may serve no obvious purpose." This enables us to distinguish a pathological liar from, say, a lawyer, whose distortions of the truth are easily detected by anybody not serving on the jury but which do serve the obvious purpose of getting his murdering slime of a client off. More generally, we may say that John, the adulterous husband played by Peter Gallagher in the movie *sex, lies, and videotape*, is not a pathological liar because his deceptions serve the obvious purpose of enabling him to get laid. Thus we see that habitual

liars are of two kinds: on the one hand, pathological liars, who are pathetic losers, and on the other hand, skilled liars, who constitute the national ruling class.

What makes pathological liars lie is not well understood although it seems pretty clear there isn't any single cause. Some people exhibit what's known as "pseudologia fantastica," in which they present wild yarns as fact. Again, skill is a factor—your journeyman fantasts can maybe swing a gig with the *Weekly World News*, while those who really have the gift can try the *Washington Post*. On the other hand, if your lying is so inept that you don't qualify even for journalism . . . well, there's always broadcasting. I have a report, for example, of a "35-year-old right-handed Caucasian male"—that's enough to put you on your guard right there—who suffered from "pathological lying associated with thalamic dysfunction." Due apparently to a brain impairment he had a 10-year history of repeated lying about everything from his personal finances to where he'd put the Kleenex. Years ago he'd have wound up in the gutter but today, thank God, he can be a guest on Jerry Springer.

Not all cases of pathological lying are associated with a neurological disorder. Psychologists also blame such conditions as "superego lacunae" or "a need for the patient to produce narcissistic gratification." I love the word "lacunae," and because I love it I can say for a fact that anyone using it has no concept whatsoever. Seems clear enough to me that some people lie because they profit from it, some fib because they're sick, and some do it because they're lying sacks of sh*t.

I'm 48 years old. A few months ago, a small growth appeared on the upper side of my left forearm. It looked like a wart, but I went to a doctor recently and had it excised and biopsied. It was a squamous cell carcinoma. The doctor told me there was almost nothing to worry about since squamous cell is one of the least dangerous forms of cancer. Still, it's hard not to stress about this. I trust your always excellent feedback. What is a squamous cell carcinoma? Do they metastasize at predictable rates? How much do I really have to worry about? If it makes any difference, I smoked cigarettes off and on for 30 years, but quit for good 14 months ago.—Neil Flowers, Santa Cruz

Nothing like cancer to make an aging baby boomer realize he's not a kid anymore. Not to argue with your doctor, but "least dangerous" is not a term I would apply to squamous cell carcinoma. It is much less dangerous than some cancers, but it can spread and it can kill you. What's more, if you've had it once, there is significantly increased risk that you will get it again. See a doctor immediately about any new growths. Also, while the damage has probably already been done, I'd skip any future sunbathing—squamous cell carcinoma appears to be directly related to solar exposure.

Skin cancer in general is extremely common, accounting for a quarter to a third of all cancers. New cases appear to be increasing rapidly, perhaps because of the thinning ozone layer; some call it an epidemic. There are three main types: basal cell carcinoma, squamous cell carcinoma, and melanoma. Basal cell is the most common by far, with more

than 500,000 new cases a year. It's also the least dangerous. Basal cell carcinomas grow slowly and seldom spread; deaths are rare. Squamous cell carcinoma also occurs fairly frequently, with about 100,000 new cases per year, but the prognosis isn't as bright; this type of cancer kills about 2,000 people a year. Still, it's a lot less serious than melanoma, the most dangerous of all skin cancers. About 32,000 new melanomas are reported each year; 6,500 of this number will die of it.

Diagnosing skin cancer is something you want to leave to the pros, but in general basal cell carcinomas are smooth while the squamous cell kind have a sandpapery feel ("squamous" means "scaly"). Melanomas typically affect pigmented areas such as moles and birthmarks. Squamous cancers usually show up in areas most exposed to the sun such as the head, neck, and the back of the hands and forearms, often on sun-damaged skin (roughened, wrinkled, discolored, etc.). Light-skinned people are more vulnerable than dark; men get them twice as often as women.

The cure rate for S-C carcinomas is on the order of 90 percent—not an entirely comforting figure. The thinner and smaller the tumor, the better the odds it won't recur. One study reported a 99.5 percent cure rate for growths less than one centimeter in diameter but only 59 percent for those larger than three centimeters, a compelling argument for not procrastinating if you've got some suspicious bumps.

Your smoking probably had little to do with your carcinoma. The real culprit was baking on the beach when you were a kid. One study concluded that using an SPF 15 sunscreen till age 18 could reduce the number of nonmelanoma skin cancers 78 percent. Never-tan, always-burn types would be smart to use SPF 25 to 30, and what the hell, a big umbrella and a muumuu might not be such a bad idea, either. Better a little dorkiness now than a biopsy later.

The 50th anniversary of D-Day leads me to ask a timely question. Many American men began smoking while serving in the armed forces in WWII. The Red Cross even distributed free cigarettes to the troops. Most of these men became addicted to cigarettes, smoked throughout their lives, and now many have died of smoking-related illnesses. I wonder—have more men died from smoking connected with their WWII service than died as battle casualties in that war?—Bill Phillips, Seattle, Washington

Great question, I thought when I first read this, and easy to answer. Shows you what I know. I called the National Cancer Institute; the American Lung Association; the National Heart, Lung, and Blood Institute; the Veterans Administration; the American Cancer Society; the Center for Addiction and Substance Abuse at Columbia University; the National Center for Health Statistics; the Metropolitan Life Insurance Company; and the federal Office of Smoking and Health.

Result: nothing, although if I were younger and lived in the 404 area code I might have asked the woman at the OSH for a date. One researcher I spoke to did venture that smoking-related deaths among WWII vets could probably be computed, but it would take six months. Plenty fast if you're funded by the government, I thought, but I'm on deadline.

I retired to the library to see what I could scare up with a little common sense and the *World Almanac*, supplemented as necessary by the medical journals. I learned that 14.9 million people served in the U.S. armed services during WWII. I then made some simplifying assumptions: a) all 14.9 million were male (actually around 2 percent were female), and b) they were statistically reflective of U.S. men as a whole, meaning that 51 percent smoked (as of 1965, anyway), 19 percent were former smokers, and the typical smoker had 20 or fewer cigarettes a

day. I then applied an estimate from an article entitled "What Are the Odds That Smoking Will Kill You?" (Mattson et al, *American Journal of Public Health*, April 1987): at age 35, the chances of a moderate smoker (fewer than 25 cigarettes a day) dying of a smoking-related disease by age 65 are 8.7 percent; for a former smoker, 4.2 percent. The youngest WWII vets today are past retirement age, so if Mattson and friends are right, smoking to date has killed at least 780,000. Total U.S. battle deaths during WWII: 292,131.

You realize that from the standpoint of statistical reliability, the preceding is about one jump ahead of a Ouija board and in all likelihood greatly understates the actual smoking-related death toll. (Cecil offers this caveat after having consulted further with the National Cancer Institute.) Individual daily smoking consumption is probably higher than reported in surveys; what's more, smoking-related deaths climb sharply after age 65. One study (Peto et al, *Lancet,* May 1992) suggests that a staggering 20 percent of all deaths in developed countries are attributable to tobacco. Applying this to WWII vets, we come up with nearly three million smoking deaths, 10 times the number of combat deaths. But that number is still low, since men smoke more than the population as a whole. So take a stab—four million smoking deaths? Five million?

Sure, your skeptics will say cancer victims are older, and die when they've only got a few good years left under the best of circumstances, whereas soldiers are cut down in the first blush of youth. But we're talking a difference of an order of magnitude. I say we definitely should have heavied up on the Doublemint and nixed the Lucky Strike.

One of the presents my wife and I got at our wedding was an original 14-inch Fiestaware cut plate, given to us by my grandfather. The plate is our favorite color: red. (Well, Fiesta calls it red, but actually it's more of a red-orange.) While we were admiring the plate my mother had to throw in her customary wet blanket. "You be careful!" she said. "Don't eat off that plate or let food sit on it! I read in an article that red-colored Fiestaware is highly radioactive."

My wife didn't buy this for a second, but I scare easily. Cecil, is red Fiestaware really radioactive? Is there a serious danger or is it one of those deals where we'd have to eat 600 meals a day off the thing for

3,000 years before we'd be in real danger? And why red?—Max
Shenk, Alexandria, Virginia

You'd better sit down for this. The pigment in red Fiestaware contains, among other things, uranium oxide. The Homer Laughlin China
Company, which began making Fiestaware in 1936, was forced to dis-
continue the red version in 1943 so the uranium could be diverted to
make atom bombs.

Gives you pause, no? Well, don't get too alarmed. The actual
amount of radioactivity is extremely low—less than the normal background radiation you get from rocks and stuff. Homer Laughlin says
they've kept tabs on the workers who used to make Fiestaware—who
obviously were at greater risk than the end users—and they've never
detected any unusual health problems.

The real problem, if in fact it's a problem, is that uranium is a heavy
metal, as is lead, another red Fiestaware ingredient. In 1981 the New
York State Department of Health warned that both could leach into
food, particularly if it's acidic. Eat enough tomato sauce or whatever
off red Fiestaware, they argued, and you could wind up with stomach
disorders, kidney dysfunction, and God knows what else.

Homer Laughlin disputes this. One company official told me he and
his family eat off red Fiestaware all the time, and says you'd only run
into trouble if you ate acidic foods off the stuff for years and never
washed the dishes. If so, I have an old college roommate whose days
are numbered, but normal humans are probably in the clear. If you're
still concerned, hang the dish on the wall instead of eating off it.

Fiestaware, incidentally, is being made again after a 14-year hiatus.
There's no lead in it now and no red either, unfortunately. Instead, we
get trendy colors like black—a regrettable surrender to fashion that
has also afflicted such noble products as the lava lamp. But I guess it's
better than no Fiestaware at all.

Why is it that Native Americans died from European diseases
brought by the Europeans but Europeans didn't die in great numbers
from Native American diseases?—Bob Kelso

There may have been at least one Native American bug that wiped
out a few boatloads of Europeans; see below. But in general you're

right: percentage-wise, and probably absolute numbers-wise, a lot more Native Americans died of European diseases than did Europeans of American diseases. The natives had no resistance to smallpox, influenza, or plague, or even to mild (to us) diseases like measles. Entire populations were virtually wiped out, with some Atlantic Coast tribes losing 90 percent of their adult members. Some historians go so far as to say European diseases reduced the precontact population of the New World as a whole by 90 percent or more. One says the population of central Mexico was reduced from 25 million in 1519 to 3 million by 1568 and to only 750,000 by the early 1600s—3 percent of the preconquest total.

Granted, some of these horrifying numbers may be arrived at by exaggerating the size of the original population. One researcher says there were 18 million people living north of Mexico before Columbus, but a more conservative estimate puts it at four million and some say only one million. Maybe there were only 12.5 million pre-Columbian Mexicans, not 25 million. Even so, we're talking 94 percent mortality for central Mexico, maybe 87 percent for the Americas overall— thereby reducing the population from 80 million in 1500 to 10 million 50 years later. One can make a good case that it was European germs rather than European military prowess that conquered the New World. One can also argue that disease led to the African slave trade. The conquistadors would have been happy to enslave local labor except that it was dead.

Why were the natives so vulnerable? The best guess is that Europe had been a crossroads for war and commerce for millennia and so had encountered an extraordinary number of pestilences, while the Americas were isolated and had not. Europeans had also spent a long time around domestic animals, which were the source of many of the most virulent diseases to afflict humans in the Old World. In contrast, Native Americans had few domestic animals. As a consequence, Europeans had developed some resistance to disease but Native Americans hadn't.

That's not to say Europeans were immune. While millions of Native Americans died of European diseases, millions of Europeans died of European diseases, too. In some years 25 percent of European immigrants died at sea, often of diseases such as typhus that they had picked up in the ports they had just left. Epidemics were common in Europe; it was not uncommon for a town to lose a third of its population to some new outbreak. Armies invariably lost more soldiers to disease than to combat. (Judging from U.S. figures, this remained true up until World War II.)

By comparison to Europeans, historian Thomas Berger says, Native Americans were remarkably healthy. Most lived not in unsanitary cities but "in small, isolated bands and were therefore less likely to spread diseases over large geographical areas." Berger even claims the few germs they carried with them during the original migration across the Bering land bridge didn't survive the Arctic "cold screen"—a little hard to believe, since the humans made it through OK.

However Edenic the New World may have been, it may have harbored one bug that did kill a lot of Europeans: syphilis. The first-known cases of syphilis showed up in Italy in 1494, and we know what happened in 1492. Many believe the Spanish contracted syphilis in Hispaniola (Haiti and the Dominican Republic) and gave it to the Italians and French at the siege of Naples. Bone damage characteristic of syphilis found at pre-Columbian New World archaeological sites supports this view. But others say syphilis was merely an old European disease that prior to 1500 had been improperly diagnosed. Even if it did originate in the Americas, syphilis was little enough payback for the disaster visited on the original inhabitants of the Americas by the subsequent ones.

I've heard off and on for years that talcum powder is asbestos. Recently I was reading Coroner *by Dr. Thomas Noguchi, and in the section on Janis Joplin where he talks about cutting agents used in heroin, he comes right out and says talcum powder is asbestos. If this is true, Bhopal, India, just took second place in the egregious industrial negligence contest—I'm selling my Johnson & Johnson stock before the nasties hit the fan. Is talcum powder asbestos? If it is, why is it sold for use on babies when it's being removed from brakes, schools, and workplaces at a cost of millions?—Michael G. Kramer, Los Angeles*

Tom Noguchi is a sweet guy, but on the subject of talc, at least, he's about as reliable as a two-dollar alarm clock. Talcum powder, also known as talc, is not asbestos, although the two are mineralogically related. (They're both silicates.) Sometimes talc is *contaminated* with asbestos, though, and that's the source of all the problems.

What problems, you ask? Try ovarian cancer. For a while it was thought talc itself caused it. A 1982 epidemiological study found that women who dusted talc on the skin near the vagina or on sanitary napkins had one and a half times the normal risk of ovarian cancer. If they dusted it on both places, they had three times the risk. The researchers surmised that the talc worked its way up the reproductive tract to the ovaries and there went about its dirty business. (Baby girls were thought to be less at risk than adults because they were exposed

to talc for only a few years and their reproductive tracts were too immature to transport the talc particles.)

A subsequent lab study, however, failed to find any sign that talc was actually transported to the ovaries in this way. In 1987 the cancer research arm of the World Health Organization officially absolved talc of suspicion.

The consensus today is that asbestos contaminants in talc are the real culprit. Asbestos, of course, can cause both cancer and lung disease and is dangerous even in minute amounts. In 1976 the cosmetic makers' association called upon its members to keep their talc products asbestos-free. Johnson & Johnson says its baby powder never had it, never will, and blames the whole thing on low-class "industrial" (i.e., noncosmetic) talc. If you'd just as soon not take any chances, you'll have to be careful; talc can be found in a variety of consumer products, including dusting powders, deodorants, chalk, textiles, pills, and soap.

What is it with sickness and cold temperatures? Countless times I have heard it said that winter is "cold and flu season." Mom always said to put my hat and galoshes on or I would catch pneumonia or my death of a cold. But I'm no dope. I know disease is caused by germs, not cold. From what I can remember of high school biology (not much), germs don't like cold any more than we do—in fact, it kills them. So how come people get sick more often in the winter? Or do they?—Ryan Joseph, Chicago

Seems like a reasonable question, doesn't it? Too bad there isn't a reasonable answer. All the research of the past three decades has succeeded in doing is undermining the old wives' tales about wet feet causing colds and such without putting anything in their place. Here's what we know so far, and it ain't much:

- The cold, wet feet, etc., don't make you more susceptible to the common cold. Several researchers, obviously graduates of the Joseph Mengele School of Medicine, had people sit in cold tubs and whatnot for extended periods to see if they'd catch more colds. By and large they didn't.
- If anything, long stretches of cold temps mean you'll catch *fewer*

colds, presumably because the germs die off. People who "winter over" at Antarctic research stations seldom get colds except when they host germ-laden visitors from warmer climes.

• We don't have indisputable evidence that winter is "cold season." Most cold sufferers don't see a doctor, and no central record is kept of the colds that doctors do hear about.

• Winter *is* flu season, but not always. The influenza pandemic of 1918–19, which killed at least 20 million people worldwide, reached peak virulence throughout most of the world during the late spring and summer and topped out in the United States in October.

Still, most flu outbreaks peak in January or February. Why? Figure that out and you may be hearing from the Nobel committee. Cecil's mother's theory is that cold "lowers your resistance" to disease. Sounds plausible, but during major flu outbreaks the winter months typically bring an equally sharp upward spike in flu in all parts of the country. Sure, Chicago gets a little brisk in the winter. But L.A.?

Something besides the cold obviously is at work. Maybe it's that even in southern California during winter folks keep the windows closed and stay indoors more, giving them a chance to exchange more germs. If we want to get really creative, we may note that if you want to catch the latest bug there's nothing like going to church, and the one time people are sure to go to church is

Christmas. Hence (maybe) the January outbreaks. OK, so I'm reaching. But nobody knows for sure.

• Respiratory infections, setting aside colds and flu, seem to be more common in winter. But some think that's because of misdiagnosis. For example, what may appear to be sinusitis—runny nose, congestion, and so on—in fact may be simply a result of "cold stress." Cold stress is a direct bodily response to cold (like shivering, say), not something caused by germs.

Cold stress symptoms can last several days but eventually go away by themselves; so do most respiratory infections. Since most doctors don't send out for tests, there's no telling what the real problem was. Cold stress is most pronounced when the weather changes suddenly, which is when many folks seem to get colds. Maybe they haven't got a cold, they just *are* cold, if you follow me.

Psychological (as opposed to physical) stress may also play a role. A study published in the *New England Journal of Medicine* reported that the more psychological stress people were under, the more likely they were to get colds. Cecil can personally attest that cold weather and sunless days can be tough on the psyche. So maybe in the interest of stress mitigation you should pop for a week in Puerto Vallarta—and while you're at it, tell that in-your-face boss of yours to take a running jump.

I have heard many times that smoking commercially available filtered clove cigarettes is "ten times worse for your lungs than normal cigarettes." I suspect this is just an urban legend, but if it is true maybe I should quit smoking cloves. Are cloves worse than other cigarettes?—Summers Henderson

The "ten times worse" figure is probably an exaggeration, but this is no urban legend. At least two teenagers died after smoking clove cigarettes during the clove craze of the mid-1980s. Five others were hospitalized and 250 others reported breathing difficulties, including coughing up blood.

Called "kreteks," clove cigarettes are imported from Indonesia and were first brought to California by Australian surfers. Typically they're a 40–60 mix of shredded clove buds and tobacco. Sales rose from 15 million in 1980 to 150 million in 1984 but plummeted thereafter following reports about health problems, including a warning from the American Lung Association. Clove cigarette importers claimed that the media were whipping up antikretek hysteria, pointing out that 80 billion had been sold worldwide in 1984 and that Indonesians had been smoking them for a century without massive loss of life (due to smoking kreteks, anyway).

But we're not talking candy cigarettes here. Kreteks produce more tar, nicotine, and carbon monoxide than ordinary cigarettes. The active ingredient in clove cigarettes is something called eugenol, on which little research has been done. But there is reason to believe it promotes lung infections or allergic reactions in vulnerable individuals. One of the two clove fatalities involved somebody with a cold; the other victim had a history of severe allergies. Part of the original appeal of clove cigarettes was that they were healthier than the all-tobacco variety; that's clearly not the case.

Enclosed are two of the many articles on the death of Gloria Ramirez, who became known as "the toxic lady" because she downed several medical attendants with her fumes. Pesticides, nerve gas, cervical cancer, kidney failure, cardiac arrest, crystals in blood, and other obscure causes were cited in these and many TV reports. Did they ever find out what killed Ms. Ramirez and made the workers sick?—J. Pilla, Tucson, Arizona

What killed the 31-year-old Ramirez was no big mystery. She died of kidney failure due to advanced cancer of the cervix. What stumped people was what caused all those emergency room staffers to keel over. Nearly two dozen vomited or passed out, six wound up being hospitalized, and at least one suffered complications that persisted for months. Nobody's sure exactly what happened, but investigators have come up with a promising theory, as we shall see.

It all began when the terminally ill Ramirez began having heartbeat and breathing problems at her home in Riverside, California, on the evening of February 19, 1994. Paramedics rushed her to Riverside General Hospital, administering oxygen en route. Shortly after arriving at the ER she passed out.

Dr. Julie Gorchynski tried to fix Ramirez's fluttering heartbeat by

shocking her with defibrillation paddles. A short time later a nurse took a blood sample with a syringe. Dr. Gorchynski smelled ammonia and felt dizzy. The nurse keeled over. Dr. Gorchynski took the syringe and sniffed it. She smelled ammonia again and noticed the blood had funny straw-colored crystals in it. Seconds later she blacked out and went into convulsions.

Soon medical staff all over the place were retching and fainting. The ER was ordered evacuated. Further attempts to revive Ramirez failed, and she was pronounced dead. The body having been sealed in an airtight casket, the experts arrived to clean up and figure out what had gone wrong.

They didn't get very far. An autopsy conducted by doctors wearing space suits revealed that Ramirez was suffering from a urinary blockage, among other things. But no known toxic chemicals were found. An inspection of the ER's plumbing and ventilation systems and whatnot also turned up nothing.

Baffled officials came up with one inane explanation after another. The coroner's office said the ER staff were sickened by the "smell of death." The California Department of Health Services blamed the whole thing on mass hysteria. This POd the victims no end, particularly Dr. Gorchynski, who was in the worst shape. She was in the hospital for two weeks, stopped breathing repeatedly, came down with hepatitis and pancreatitis, and later developed bone rot in her knees.

Finally some folks with IQs in the triple digits got into the act. Scientists at the Forensic Science Center at Livermore National Laboratory found a chemical called dimethyl sulfone ($DMSO_2$) in Ramirez's blood. Dimethyl sulfone is a reaction product of dimethyl sulfoxide (DMSO), a solvent sometimes used by cancer patients as a home pain remedy.

Neither DMSO nor $DMSO_2$ is especially dangerous. But while reading up on the subject a Livermore scientist came across a related chemical, dimethyl sulfate ($DMSO_4$). $DMSO_4$ is a powerful poison gas, and it can cause nearly every symptom suffered by the Riverside ER staff.

The Livermore scientists hatched the following hypothesis: 1) Ramirez doses herself with DMSO. Due to urinary blockage, the stuff builds up in her bloodstream. 2) Oxygen administered by the paramedics converts the DMSO in her blood to a high concentration of $DMSO_2$. 3) When the $DMSO_2$-laden blood is drawn out in the syringe and cools to room temperature, crystals form (this was confirmed by experiment). 4) $DMSO_2$ is converted to $DMSO_4$ by some unknown mechanism (the defibrillation shock?) and clobbers the medical staff. 5) The volatile $DMSO_4$ evaporates without a trace.

Step four is obviously the weak link. The Livermore scientists have proposed some possible chemical scenarios. While skeptics have raised objections, Livermore's Pat Grant tells me, "There weren't any showstoppers." Those people got zapped by something, and right now this is the best explanation we've got.

Another Theory

The Los Angeles weekly *New Times* has come up with a possible alternative explanation for the toxic lady episode: the hospital where the incident occurred may have been the site of a secret lab used to illegally manufacture the drug methamphetamine. In stories appearing in the May 15–21 and September 11–17, 1997, issues, staff writer Susan Goldsmith reports that "meth chemicals" may have been smuggled out of the hospital in IV bags, one of which was inadvertently hooked up to the dying Ramirez. This triggered the round of nausea, headache, and other symptoms that put six ER workers in the hospital.

"Those smells and symptoms are classic to meth-fume exposure," a forensic chemist who analyzes drug-lab materials is quoted as saying.

Meth manufacturing is said to be big business in Riverside county, where the hospital was located—authorities have shut down more than 1,000 meth labs since 1988, and many more remain undetected.

Still, you gotta think: a secret meth lab in a major hospital? A meth lab, moreover, that's run by people so stupid they somehow allow an IV bag full of meth chemicals to wind up in the emergency room? Hard to believe. On the other hand, Goldsmith points out, the authorities never took the elementary precaution of testing the IV bags to see what was in them. Cover-up or just incompetence? Right now it's anybody's guess.

From The Straight Dope Message Board

Subj: Sea Monkeys
From: MtRyder
    What are Sea Monkeys and where can I find info about them?

From: EntropyNut
    Sea Monkeys are just brine shrimp. Brine shrimp live in brackish water and deposit eggs that are highly tolerant of dessication (drying out). When you buy sea monkeys, they send you a bunch of dried brine shrimp eggs, you put them in water, and they hatch. Bingo.
    I live next to about a trillion (give or take 10^{12}) brine shrimp. If you want info on them, come to Utah, stick your head in the Great Salt Lake, and take a look. Impressive! Just don't drink the water.

From: JKFabian
    If you look really hard—and I mean, really, really, really hard—you can see the happy sea monkey family just as they're pictured on the package!

From: Misanthr
    You can buy Sea Monkeys at Toys "R" Us (at least you can in Raleigh, NC). It's pretty cool because even if you forget about them and never feed them or let the water evaporate—just let the container dry out completely—you'll find the gunk at the bottom contains more

eggs—some that never hatched the first time around and some that were produced when the Sea Monkeys mated (very interesting to watch, by the way, as well as seeing pregnant female SMs). Then buy more of the stuff that makes the eggs hatch and add water. More Sea Monkeys!

From: SuesZ
Check out the Sea Monkey message board for plenty of info. Yes, really! Look under Interests and Hobbies.
Is this the Information Superhighway or what?

Subj: My FBI File
From: ChwYunFat
How can I find out if there is an FBI file on me? And, if there is one, how can I get a copy?

From: Magik4U2
Your rights in this regard are codified in the Freedom of Information Act and the Privacy Act. The FBI, being a law enforcement agency, may have information that they cannot be compelled to release—information regarding an ongoing investigation, for example. That's the stuff you get during discovery.

From: Bookwrm847
You could join the FBI and get a position as a file clerk.

From: Toy Drone
If the FBI won't hire you, you could always start something like "Joe's Bureau of Investigation," and make secret files on FBI personnel. Then, perhaps a deal could be struck.

From: TMcT
<<How can I find out if there is an FBI file on me? And, if there is one, how can I get a copy?>>
You can probably assure that you get one by hanging out outside of a federal building or embassy and staring at it day after day. You'd sure get a file then.

From: Captain677

My grandmother got a copy of her FBI file but all the documents were completely blacked out.

From: PinkyDVM

Your *grandmother*? Man! I thought my grandmother was tough when she killed a snake with her walking stick!

Games

In baseball, why do batters always pound the plate with the bat when they step up to hit?—D.H., Chicago

If I put my mind to it, I imagine I could cook up some pop-anthropological explanation about how it's an aggressiveness display, like bulls pawing the earth before charging. However, there's a simpler explanation: you hit the plate with the bat to gauge the distance, the better to get yourself positioned properly.

Every race I've ever seen on an oval or round track, be it between humans, animals, or autos, is run in a counterclockwise direction. What explains this?—I. Cohen, Dallas, Texas

How do these things get started? I've gotten several letters asking why races are "always" counterclockwise, and I notice my fellow toiler, *Omni* magazine game czar Scot Morris, has written a lengthy treatise on the subject. Scot came up with the following list of counter-clockwise phenomena: the Indianapolis 500 and other auto races, track and field events, Roller Derby, indoor bicycle races, horse races, speed skating, merry-go-rounds and other carnival rides, revolving doors, the chariot race in *Ben-Hur*, the customary flow of people around an ice-skating rink, the usual direction in which people spin Hula Hoops, the base runners in baseball, cable-operated model air-planes, and tornadoes and hurricanes in the Northern Hemisphere.

To be sure, Morris concedes, there are a lot of clockwise phenomena as well: the direction of the pieces on a Monopoly board; the "on," "higher," or "tighten" direction on knobs, dials, faucets, lightbulbs, screws, and bottle caps; dialing on a rotary telephone; record turntables; and turning a manual can opener, eggbeater, or pencil sharpener. But most of these—at least the ones that involve exertion—are easy to explain: most people are right-handed, and righties have more strength turning clockwise than the other way.

The counterclockwise phenomena are a different story. On the theory that there might be some dark link to our primeval past, Morris asked several distinguished anthropologists, but no luck. He morosely concludes, "the bias toward moving our whole bodies in counterclockwise cycles undoubtedly can be traced back to the right-handedness of our species and of every human society yet discovered, but how the one led to the other is unclear."

Before we despair, however, we would do well to inquire a bit further. Some of these supposedly counterclockwise phenomena in fact aren't always counterclockwise. Horse races, for example, are commonly run in a counterclockwise direction in this country, but European tracks are less standardized and "the horses run clockwise on most of them," one writer notes.

Similarly with auto racing. Oval tracks for stock-car racing are common in the United States; they're counterclockwise because in stock cars the driver is on the left and if he loses control and crashes into a wall the right side will absorb most of the impact. (Presumably it's also easier for a driver on the left to cut a tight left turn.) In Europe, serpentine grand-prix-type courses are more common, and judging from the photos a good number of them are run in a clockwise direction.

It's true track events (i.e., foot races) are always run counterclockwise, but that's because track geometry, direction of travel, etc., are set by international agreement to ensure comparability of times. I could go on, but frankly Roller Derby isn't my cup of tea, and anyway I'm sure you see my point: counterclockwise travel isn't the implacable law of nature some make it out to be.

She Goes Both Ways

Your answer to the question on counterclockwise races was a tad off, at least on human races. In 24-hour, 48-hour, 72-hour, and 6-day (human) races on tracks, every so many hours (typically four to six) the direction is reversed to spare the runners' knees. Going in the same direction constantly puts a lot of torque on the knees and reversing evens things up.

The longer the race, the more crippled we become anyway, so I hate to imagine how we'd look if this weren't done. To put it mildly, we walk funny after these events. And I'm not making this up. I've done my share (well, not yet) of 24-hour, 48-hour, and 6-day races, setting a few American and world records winding and unwinding around the track. I plan to resume racing when I move to Albuquerque in a matter of months. Cheers.—Myra J. Linden, Key Biscayne, Florida

I was talking about traditional track events, Myra, not endurance contests. But your letter does support my main point, which is that such events aren't always run in a counterclockwise direction.

A baseball-playing friend stymied me with this question. Seven batters step up to the plate in one inning, all from the same team. The inning ends and no one has scored. How? We came up with bases loaded, two pop-outs, a grand slam, and one more pop-out, when the other team claims the grand slam hitter didn't tag third and the four runs are nullified. But we regard this answer as a copout, and the guy won't tell us the solution. Help!—Rene C., Chicago

Another one of those days when I not only have to give the answers, I have to clean up the questions, too. An essential condition you left out is that no substitutions can be made in the lineup. If you *do* allow substitutions, the number of players who can step up to the plate is limited only by the number of players you've got suited up. Even a casual baseball fan like me knows you can substitute batters freely during an inning.

As for your appealed grand slam strategem, I wouldn't call it a copout. I'm obliged to call it wrong. Still, you're on the right track, as we shall see. Failing to tag a base is what we call an appeal play. The runs are nullified only if the opposing team appeals to the umpire before the next pitch. Since you throw in an intervening out, the runs stand. I learn this from rule 7.10 of my *Official Baseball Rules*, the holy writ of the sport.

Here's the correct solution, helpfully supplied by loyal Straight Dope reader Kirk Miller of Richardson, Texas:

"Bases are loaded (three batters). Two outs (two more batters). The sixth batter hits a grand slam home run, but fails to touch first base. The umpire throws a new ball to the pitcher, and the seventh batter steps up to the plate. The pitcher successfully appeals that the home run hitter failed to touch first base. The umpire signals the third out, and no runs count. (Had the batter failed to touch second, third, or home, one or more runs would have counted.)

"Note: The defensive team cannot appeal the missed first base until the ball is put into play, which is done by the pitcher stepping up on the pitching rubber while holding the ball (when the seventh batter steps up to the plate). So they couldn't appeal until the seventh batter got up; hence, the number of batters in the conundrum (seven instead of six)."

Nice, eh? Follow up with this next stumper and you'll have 'em convinced you're a baseball god. Nine players have been named most valuable player in two consecutive years. Coincidentally they constitute a complete lineup (all positions covered). Name the nine.

SURPRISE ANSWER: Hal Newhouser, pitcher, 1944–45; Yogi Berra, catcher, 1954–55; Jimmie Foxx, first base, 1932–33; Joe Morgan, second, 1975–76; Ernie Banks, shortstop, 1958–59 (he played short in the '50s, so no snotty letters please); Mike Schmidt, third base, 1980–81; Mickey Mantle, outfield, 1956–57; Roger Maris, outfield, 1960–61; Dale Murphy, outfield, 1982–83. Hope you can turn this to profitable use on your next trip to the corner saloon.

The Amateurs Get Into The Act

Here's another good trivia question. In one year, the MVPs in the National League, the American League, the National Football League, and the American Football League (before they merged) all wore the same number. Name the players. HINT: the number was 32. ANSWER: in 1963, Sandy Koufax of the Dodgers, Elston Howard of the Yankees, Jim Brown of the Browns, and Cookie Gilchrist of the Buffalo Bills were MVPs. I can't tell you how much money this has netted me over the years.—Dave O., Chicago

Hope you didn't spend it, Dave, because you're going to have to give it back. Only three of the four MVPs in 1963 wore number 32—Koufax, Howard, and Brown. The fourth MVP wasn't Cookie Gilchrist of the Bills, but Clem Daniels of the Raiders. He was number 36.

Two questions that bug me: 1) Why can't pitchers hit? 2) Why do catchers tell the pitchers how to throw?—Earl Adkins, San Rafael, California

Finally, a question that makes you *think*. Easy stuff first: Catchers tell the pitchers what to throw because the two have to agree on the pitch, lest the pitchers heave it where the catcher ain't. If the pitcher did the signaling, everybody in the ballpark would see it; ergo, it's up to the guy with the big mitt. The pitcher can shake off the catcher's signals if he wants to, although occasionally he does so at some peril to his ERA, as demonstrated in the movie *Bull Durham*.

As for pitchers, they can't hit for basically two reasons: 1) they don't bat often enough to get good at it, and 2) natural selection. The latter being more cosmic, we'll start with that.

Pitchers are essentially defensive players, and are selected for their defensive skills. No pitcher ever got called up to the majors because

he was a great hitter. Ditto for shortstops and catchers, also not noted for their prowess at the plate.

Outfielders aren't in on every play, so they can survive in the big leagues with mediocre defensive skills as long as they can crank out the hits or homers. Pitchers don't have that luxury. So you get guys who can pitch it through a brick wall but can't hit in triple digits.

Making things worse is reason #1: pitchers don't get much practice. A National League starting pitcher would be lucky to get 100 at bats a year, whereas a regular position player might chalk up 500 or more. The fact that starters are being yanked earlier in the game today makes things worse. With only so much coaching time to spread around, most NL clubs don't even have their pitchers take batting practice except on the days they're pitching. (AL pitchers, of course, don't routinely bat at all because of the designated hitter rule.)

But there's nothing about pitchers that makes them physically unable to hit. The classic case is Babe Ruth, who began his major league career as a pitcher and had a lifetime record of 94–46 (a ratio so lopsided some say Ruth would have gone into the Hall of Fame if he'd never hit a home run). During his pitching years Ruth averaged around .300, frequently playing outfield or first base on his off days. More recently there was Don Newcombe, who in 1955 hit .359 in 117 at bats with the Dodgers.

Why don't we see guys like that anymore? Mainly because pitchers have become victims of their own success. What with split-fingered fastballs and all, pitching has become a sophisticated art. Batting averages have dropped even for the best hitters. For a part-time slugger like a pitcher, the situation is hopeless. These days you can hope to become good at hitting *or* pitching, but not both.

The perception that some number combinations appear more frequently than others in the various state lotteries leads me to wonder: do all number combinations have equal probability, or is there some mathematical quirk that would allow certain number combinations to appear more often than others?—Douglas J. Stark, Houston

What you want, Doug, is what is known as a system. I know of only one system that's a sure thing: 1) dream up some cockamamie lottery-beating scheme of your own, preferably involving a personal computer (hey, it's the '90s), and 2) sell it to 50,000 guppies at $29.95 a pop. Dozens of entrepreneurs have already done just that, and it's a safe bet they're better off financially than the people who buy their dubious wares.

In some games of chance, of course, systems do work. Card counting in blackjack, for instance. That's because every card played in blackjack is a card that can't be played again. If you keep track of which cards are left, your ability to bet shrewdly improves. In the typical card-counting system you count the 10-point cards (10, jack,

queen, king) and bet more heavily when an unusually large number of them remain in a dwindling deck, since they mean trouble for the dealer.

Not so in lotteries, where the game begins afresh with every drawing. If the numbers are drawn at random—a big *if*, as we shall see— all the number combinations are equally probable. Occasionally you may notice what seem to be suspicious patterns among the winning numbers, but these mean nothing. One of the hallmarks of random numbers is that pseudopatterns occasionally arise—the million-monkeys-with-a-million-typewriters syndrome in action.

Still, gamblers looking for an edge will grasp at anything. There are two main "scientific" approaches to picking lottery numbers: hot numbers, and due numbers. Hot numbers are ones that have been coming up a lot lately, while due numbers *haven't* come up and supposedly are overdue.

Statisticians say the due number system is strictly for the birds. Number-generating systems are either biased or they're not. If they're biased, obviously you want to go with whatever numbers the bias favors. If they're not biased, all the numbers have equal probability and there's no point using a system.

Hot number systems are a little more interesting. Generating truly random numbers is tougher than you might think. It's quite possible for the machines used in lottery drawings to have some minor mechanical peculiarity that causes certain numbers to come up slightly more often than others. Purveyors of hot number systems say their programs will detect those subtle biases and use them to your advantage.

Trouble is, lottery officials are as hip to bias as the wiseguys who write computer programs. They know if their drawings do show bias, the betting public will eventually discover it and start betting heavily on the hot numbers. That means more winners dividing up every pot, lower average payouts, and less interest (and fewer bets) on the part of gamblers. So the people in charge do everything in their power to ensure that the winning numbers are as random as human ingenuity can make them.

One common type of state lottery uses a machine that blows numbered balls around in a glass bowl until eventually the winning numbers drop into a chute. Normally there are several machines and several sets of balls. Before each day's drawing, a preliminary lottery is held to determine which machine and which ball set to use. The public is not told which machine/ball set combo is used on any given day and in any case the ball sets are replaced periodically. So it's impossible to develop the kind of track record a bias-detecting program requires.

The one feature a number-picking program can offer that might actually do you some good is a feature that selects numbers at random—or, equally usefully, avoids numbers that are picked often—e.g., 31 and below, heavily bet by those who insist on picking their birthdays. The idea is that if you do win, you'll have to share the loot with fewer cowinners. A reasonable notion, perhaps. But divvying the boodle is not a major problem for most people who play.

Why is a football called a pigskin?—Ben Schwalb, Laurel, Maryland

Because calling it a pig's *bladder*, which is what it actually is (or was), is a bit too real even for football players. In the days before vulcanized rubber, animal bladders were easily obtained, more or less round, readily sealed and inflated, and reasonably durable—just the thing if you wanted to play the medieval equivalent of soccer. In later years the bladder might be covered with leather (not necessarily pigskin) for added protection.

The main drawback of a pig's bladder was that inflating it by way of the obvious nozzle was too grotty for words. Still, it was an improvement over what the English traditionally regard as the original football, namely the noggin of an unsuccessful Danish invader. If you were offended by the bladder's aesthetics you could always stuff a leather casing with hay or cork shavings or the like, but such balls lacked zip.

Happily for the sensibilities of modern youth, pigs' bladders faded from the scene not long after intercollegiate football began in 1869. One account indicates rubber bladders were being used in 1871, and probably they were around long before that, Charles Goodyear having patented vulcanization in 1844. Couldn't have been too soon for me.

The *real* question here, if you don't mind my saying so, is how footballs got to be prolate spheroids ("round but pointy," for you rustics) rather than perfectly spherical. As usual with these pivotal episodes in history, it was an accident. Henry Duffield, who witnessed the second Princeton-Rutgers game in 1869, tells why:

"The ball was not an oval but was supposed to be completely round.

It never was, though—it was too hard to blow up right. The game was stopped several times that day while the teams called for a little key from the sidelines. They used it to unlock the small nozzle which was tucked into the ball, and then took turns blowing it up. The last man generally got tired and they put it back in play somewhat lopsided."

The odd shape of the ball, eventually enshrined in the rules, was turned to advantage with the introduction of the forward pass in 1906, which was made possible by the fact that you could grip the ball (barely) around the narrow part. Passing got a lot easier in the 1930s when the rules committee ordered the watermelon of previous decades slimmed down by an inch and a half, opening the door for the modern aerial game. How fortunate for the future shape of the game that the Ivy Leaguers of yesteryear didn't have any more lung power than today's.

Questions We're Still Thinking About

A while back there was a lot of news about some nut in Scotland who went to a school and killed 16 or 17 kids. I noticed repeated references in the early stories concerning the killer's habit of writing letters to the editor. My questions are: 1) Have a lot of mass murderers been found to have written letters to the editor prior to their killing sprees? And 2) Is writing to your column a sign of violent mental instability?—J.T. Colfax, San Francisco

Oh, I don't think so. If one judges from the return addresses, less than 1 percent of my correspondents write from prison. Of course there is that fellow David English, who sent me a letter a while back exhibiting an unhealthy interest in a book entitled *If We Can Keep a Severed Head Alive*. But he probably writes to Ann Landers, too. Besides, give me some credit. I'm keeping Slug Signorino off the streets.

8

Body Language

I've heard all the jokes; now I want some facts. I'm in my mid-sixties and partially bald. Yet I can barely keep ahead of trimming the hair growing in my nose and ears. What gives?—Ernest Hobbs, Columbus, Ohio

This problem, which is common among men as they age, is a manifestation of the law of conservation of hair. When you were young the

manly fluid filled your whole being, but as you got older a lot of it boiled off. By now it doesn't even reach the bottom of the old brainpan. The sad result is that hair grows in your nose and ears rather than on top of your head. The plus side is that you can now watch *Pocahontas* with the grandkids without thinking, "Whoa, nice rack."

Unfortunately, that's about it for definitive statements on this subject. I note that my friend David Feldman frittered away parts of two of his *Imponderables* books before concluding that not much was known about this. His findings:

1. Excessive hair is called hypertrichosis.
2. Hairy ears are an inherited trait that some geneticists believed was passed along on the Y (male) chromosomes.
3. They don't believe this anymore.
4. In 1984 two doctors in Mineola, New York, announced that hair in the ear canal plus a crease in the earlobe were signs that you were susceptible to heart attack (strictly speaking, that you had coronary-artery disease, i.e., narrowing of the coronary arteries).
5. In 1985, having been accused of misconstruing the data big time, the doctors conceded that hairy, creased ears were pretty useless as a predictor of heart attack.

Actually, Dave touched only lightly on item five, but I figured I'd better clarify the lack of clarity on this point.

Having further reviewed the medical literature, I can add the following to the above:

1. Even less is known about hairy noses than hairy ears.
2. In men hairy ears are probably pretty common. In the Mineola study 74 percent of the men had them. Unfortunately you can't tell how old they were because the only average age provided applied to a group of men and women mixed together. Obviously a little more time needs to be spent on statistics in the medical schools serving Mineola.
3. It sure is hard to figure out what medical authors are talking about when they use words like "tragus" and "pinna" without telling you what they mean.
4. The tragus is the pointy projection on the front side of your ear opening. Interestingly, tragus can also mean any of the hairs

growing at the entrance to the ear. So I guess what you've got there, Ernest, is a bad case of tragus on the tragus.

5. The pinna, according to the dictionary, is the "external part of the ear," but some medical authors figure it really means the external part of the ear except the tragus.

6. I bet hair on the tragus is what's really important, but maybe that's just because I have it.

7. Some people think men in certain ethnic groups, such as those found in parts of India and Sri Lanka, have hairier ears than usual. However, you couldn't prove it by me, inasmuch as the admittedly sparse literature on the subject suggests that hairy ears are pretty common all over. In any case, the Indian researchers think if you've got them you might have diabetes, too.

8. You can get hairy ears as a result of using minoxidil and, boy, does it look gross.

9. While not having hairy, creased ears doesn't necessarily mean you *aren't* prone to heart attacks, if you do have them—and if in other respects you seem like the heart-attack-prone type—you're in trouble. Ninety percent of the guys with hairy, creased ears in the Mineola study had coronary-artery disease.

10. I sure wish the people who published the relatively small number of ear-hair papers had had their acts a little more together, because it's just about impossible to determine from their work whether ear hair becomes more common in men as they age and if so, where on the ear and with what indications for your health. But it's not like counting ear hairs is a job that's going to attract the great minds of our times.

11. Some great mind is going to have to do a lot of this work over if we're going to come to any firm conclusions about ear and nose hair.

12. But it's not going to be me.

When eating ice cream and sno-cones too fast I often get a "cold headache." What causes this? What would happen if you kept chowing down on those frozen treats?—Chuck Nevitt, Dallas

The standard medical term for this phenomenon is "ice cream headache"—an expression so clear and comprehensible it obviously

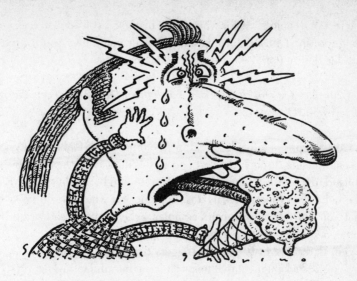

was settled on by mistake. Probably that accounts for the scarcity of research on this universal (well, pretty darn common) human condition. One recalls the attention given some years back to a complaint someone had been shrewd enough to name "hypoglycemia." Can you see getting big money to study Folks Feeling Vaguely Punk?

Ice cream headache occurs most frequently after you've worked up a sweat or during very hot weather. Typically it starts when you cram too much cold stuff into the roof of your mouth. It reaches a peak in 25 to 30 seconds that can last from several seconds to a couple minutes. Most people feel it deep in the front of the head, although if the ice cream gets stuck in the vicinity of the tonsils you may feel the pain behind your ears. Cold farther down the throat produces no headache.

The cause of ice cream headache is far from clear. One plausible explanation is that the cold causes constriction of blood vessels near the point of contact, which in turn causes the blood to back up painfully inside the head.

Ice cream headache occurs in maybe a third of the general population but in over 90 percent of migraine sufferers, who feel it in the same place they get migraines. (Many migraine victims take precautions with frozen desserts for just that reason.) Researchers believe migraine and ice cream headache are physiologically similar, the difference being that migraine sufferers are abnormally sensitive to stimuli the rest of us ignore. As for what would happen if you applied the cold continuously, I imagine a migraine sufferer could give you a pretty graphic description. I don't expect it'd be fun.

Why does the sun darken skin but lighten hair?—Listener, Garry Meier show, Chicago

Cecil's representative little Ed, well-intended but feeble as always, was able to get through the first part of this answer on the air but was obliged to have the second part explained to him by another caller. Explained to him incorrectly, as it turned out, but when all you know is that you don't know you can't complain when you get shown up by someone who doesn't even know that.

Sun darkens skin because it triggers the production of melanin, a brownish-black pigment that helps filter out harmful ultraviolet rays. It lightens hair because the UV light triggers the breakdown of these selfsame melanin molecules into simpler and evidently less colorful compounds. The exact mechanism by which this is accomplished is not as clear as it might be. "The ionic pathway probably begins by nucleophilic attack of the peroxide anion on the o-quinone grouping," says one medical text, clearly written by the kind of guy you wouldn't want to have season tickets next to at the ball game. The melanin in both skin and hair is meant to protect the other tissue, but in skin it's renewed (and thus the skin gets darker) whereas in hair it's not, hair being dead. An answer little Ed will spit out quicker next time it's asked.

In novels of yesteryear you could barely get through a chapter without some female character fainting. But women rarely faint today. Was all that swooning just literary license? If not, why don't women faint as much now?—Felix Krull, Dallas

It's all the fault of the media. In the 1800s, writers helped to create "the cult of female invalidism," which held that women were such delicate creatures that they'd faint at the slightest provocation. Women were as much at fault as men for perpetuating this idea—they loved to make a scene by fainting at a dramatic moment.

Fainting wasn't just an act, though. Partly it was the result of incredibly constrictive Victorian clothing. A fashionably dressed woman wore

37 pounds of clothing in winter, of which 19 pounds were suspended from the waist. She also had herself shoehorned into a corset that compressed her waist to an average of 20 inches. Corsets distorted the rib cage and made it difficult to move or even breathe. In a crowded room you'd have women keeling over right and left. Add in poor diet, lack of exercise (too masculine), and quack medical practices such as leeching, and it's a wonder a woman could remain upright at all.

Corsets and the cult of invalidism helped create fashionable female diseases such as chlorosis (vaguely akin to anemia) and neurasthenia (chronic nervous exhaustion). These largely disappeared after World War I. But that's no reason to feel smug. What with anorexia and bulimia, we've just substituted one set of disorders for another.

I have some leg problems and one of the workmen in my building told me to give my creaking joints a squirt of WD-40. He said they all swore by it and that it had been written up in a medical journal but he was unable to be more specific. Is there any basis to this?—Jeanne B., Chicago

What do these guys figure you are, the Tin Woodsman? WD-40, a petroleum distillate, is for mechanical joints, not human ones. The WD-40 folks say that while they've heard of this folk remedy (it was on the cover of a supermarket tabloid a couple years ago, next to a story about the Human Bigfoot from Outer Space), they've done no studies on it and "we do not recommend it." An arthritis specialist was equally unencouraging.

When we broached this subject on a radio talk show recently (hey, anything for a laugh), we did turn up one guy who'd tried it and said it helped. But he freely admitted he might have been imagining things.

Got an earful about some other home remedies, too:

- *Putting cayenne (hot) pepper in your boots will keep your feet warm.* There may actually be something to this, because a mild local irritant such as pepper (or liniment, for that matter) will bring warmth to the skin surface. Interestingly, there's a cream on the market called Zostrix containing capsaicin, the active ingredient of pepper, which in addition to being an irritant apparently inhibits a neurotransmitter that conveys pain. Zostrix is used for shingles and arthritis, so perhaps you should heave the WD-40 and sprinkle hot pepper on your extremities instead. Maybe a little A.1 sauce, too. It might not cure what ails you but you'll leave a good-tasting corpse.

- *Touching your earlobe with a burned finger will ease the pain and prevent blisters.* I got this from a woman named Bonnie, who says a heating repair guy she told about it laughed at first but now swears by it. Bonnie also reported that a friend burned her palm on a hot plate. Figuring this was too much dermal acreage for the earlobe trick, the friend applied said palm to her stomach. Some miraculous results. Hey, if people believe in psychoanalysis, why not this?

From The Straight Dope Message Board

Subj: ice in urinals
From: Jerryvan01

Why do many of the bars that I happen to find myself in put ice in the urinals in the bathroom? Is it just the kinds of places that I go (House of Beer, Brat Stop, etc.) or is it something that they do at the high-class joints also?

From: VCRogers

They put ice in the urinals of at least one high-class joint—the Pointe Hilton at Tapatio Cliffs in Phoenix, AZ. The ice is put in the urinals in the morning; it melts in a few hours and is not, to my knowledge, replenished until the next day.

This is the only place, high-class or low-, that I've ever encountered this custom, and I have no idea what it's for.

From: JILLGAT

Is it kinda °fun° to melt it? Many people like to pee in the snow for this reason.

From: Toy Drone

<<Why do many of the bars that I happen to find myself in put ice in the urinals in the bathroom?>>

Oh my God, those are urinals?!

From: Larasaurus

Toy—you can bet I won't be frequenting your lemonade stand.

From: OpenMind12

We used to dump ice in the urinals at the bar I worked at for two reasons:

1. Dumping ice on the floor made a mess.
2. Dumping ice in the sink made it too cold to wash glasses.

OK, we know the beer drinkers love to watch it melt, too.

Simply, it's a convenient place to dump ice you don't want anymore.

From: CKDextHavn

I've been at a private club that not only puts ice in the urinals, but replenishes it on a regular basis during the course of an evening. (Don't ask.) They claim it keeps the smell down.

From: CecilAdams

Ahem. Cecil has made his own inquiries, and as often happens, people agree there's a reason for the practice, but disagree on what the reason is. Some possibilities: 1) The melting ice acts as a sort of slow, continuous flush. We call this the trickle-down theory. 2) Ice cools the air around the urinal. Cool air sinks, which serves to contain the smell. 3) Cold discourages the presence of drain flies (family Psychodidae), so called because drains and urinals and such are where they like to lay their eggs. 4) Fun to melt, helps users aim better, compensates for poor male sanitary habits.

Personally I think this is one of those things that works on a lot of levels.

From: ITURI

I've never seen ice in a urinal (well, I've only been in a men's john once), but what I did see were those little pink deodorizer things in the bottom of them. Scribbled on the wall above the urinal was, "Don't eat the mints."

Getting Religion

When people want to express total pointlessness, they sometimes say a thing is as silly as "arguing over how many angels could dance on the head of a pin." This argument is supposed to have taken place between Byzantine theologians or medieval scholars, or somebody. But I'm beginning to think the fathers (and mothers) of the church are getting a bad rap. Try as I might, I can't find any source that identifies when this argument took place, who discussed it, and what they said. Did this arcane debate really occur, or is this a case of ecclesiastical leg-pulling?—David F., Belle Fourche, South Dakota

I see from your letterhead that you're a minister, Dave. What's the matter, you couldn't ask the Big Guy yourself?

Let's get a couple things straight. First, you're misquoting the saying in question. According to unimpeachable sources, it's not how many angels can dance on the head of a pin, it's how many can do it on the *point* of a *needle*—which, of course, makes more sense. Second, the earliest citation I can find is from a book by Ralph Cudworth in the seventeenth century, which is suspiciously late in the day.

Valuable insight on this question is provided by Isaac D'Israeli (1766–1848), the father of British prime minister Benjamin Disraeli. Isaac was an amateur scholar who published several books of historical and literacy "curiosities," which were quite popular in their day. D'Israeli lampooned the Scholastic philosophers of the late Middle Ages, notably Thomas Aquinas, who were famous for debating metaphysical fine points.

Aquinas wrote several ponderous philosophical tomes, the most famous of which went by the awe-inspiring title *Summa Theologica*, "summary of theology." It contained, among other things, several dozen propositions on the nature of angels, which Thomas attempted to work out by process of pure reason. The results were pretty tortured, and to the hipper-than-thou know-it-alls of the Enlightenment (i.e., D'Israeli's day), they seemed a classic example of good brainpower put to nonsensical ends.

For example, D'Israeli wrote, "Aquinas could gravely debate, Whether Christ was not an hermaphrodite [and] whether there are excrements in Paradise." He might also have mentioned such Thomistic puzzlers as whether the hair and nails will grow following the Resurrection, and whether or not said Resurrection will take place at night.

D'Israeli goes on to say, "The reader desirous of being merry with Aquinas's angels may find them in Martinus Scriblerus, in Ch. VII who inquires if angels pass from one extreme to another without going through the middle? And if angels know things more clearly in a morning? How many angels can dance on the point of a very fine needle, without jostling one another?"

I have not been able to turn up the text D'Israeli refers to (my seventeenth-century files are just a mess), but it sounds like the work of some would-be comedian. Martinus Scriblerus (dimestore Latin for "Martin the Scribbler") is a pseudonym of a sort in common use among Enlightenment satirists, and the quoted items are burlesques of actual treatises in Aquinas's *Summa*.

Fact is, Aquinas did debate whether an angel moving from A to B passes through the points in between, and whether one could distinguish "morning" and "evening" knowledge in angels. (He was referring to an abstruse concept having to do with the dawn and twilight of creation.) Finally, he inquired whether several angels could be in the same place at once, which of course is the dancing-on-a-pin question less comically stated. (Tom's answer: no.) So the answer to your question is yes, medieval theologians *did* get into some pretty weird arguments, if not quite as weird as later wise guys painted them.

What's the poop on this Dianetics stuff? Is it a religion, a life-view, or another P.T. Barnum scam? L. Ron Hubbard's ads make it sound like the best thing for humanity since cable TV. However, all these years of reading your column have made us skeptical. Is it worth wasting our time and money on this stuff, or is it just more garbage from money-grubbing con artists?—Rob and Junior, Los Angeles

Well, Cecil wouldn't waste *his* time and money. But you know, some people pay to get beaten with canes. Maybe you'd get a kick out of Dianetics, more commonly known in its religious incarnation as Scientology. The teachings of the late L. Ron Hubbard (he died in 1986) have been described as "the poor man's psychoanalysis." There are those who believe this means that if you're not poor when you start, you will be by the time you're done. It takes thousands of dollars' worth of training sessions to achieve "clear"—the Scientological equivalent of enlightenment—and there have been repeated claims that the whole thing is just a hugely profitable scam. Scam or not, it's definitely huge. At its peak the cult was reportedly taking in $100 million a year, and in 1986 was said to have assets of $280 million.

The evidence suggests Hubbard was sincere in his beliefs, at least at the outset. Originally a writer of hack science fiction, he published *Dianetics: The Modern Science of Mental Health* in 1950. The book argued that the brain was analogous to a computer with two independent memory banks, the Analytical (conscious) Mind and the Reactive (subconscious) Mind. The latter is full of "engrams" (traumatic memories), which interfere with the operation of the Analytical Mind and cause personality problems and ailments such as asthma and arthritis.

During "auditing" (therapy), the "pre-clear" (patient) can "run" (relive) and thus conquer the traumatic experiences. Once "clear," the patient would have super powers: total recall, high IQ, perfect health, and for all I know X-ray vision. Except for the inflated payoff, the parallels to Freudian analysis are obvious, including 1) the high hourly fees you pay to learn this stuff from the experts, and 2) the great likelihood that the whole thing's BS.

Dianetics inspired a brief vogue for kitchen-table auditing. But the medical establishment condemned it and many early enthusiasts became disillusioned when they didn't get results. Undiscouraged, Hubbard repackaged Dianetics a few years later as a religion called Scientology, throwing in some new elements of Eastern mysticism. He now argued that we are all "thetans," or immortal spirits. Through auditing we can explore previous lives (74 trillion years' worth), free our inner being, and gain control over the material world. A key element in this is the "E-meter," a biofeedback device consisting of a galvanometer, some wires, and two soup cans.

By establishing a religion Hubbard was able to set himself up as a font of revelation rather than a scientist and thus control the movement. He also hoped to deflect outside criticism and, indeed, might have succeeded in doing so had it not been for his own implacable paranoia. He established thought police, conducted purges, and declared his critics "fair game," who "may be deprived of property or injured [or] tricked, sued or lied to or destroyed."

As a result of such threats, Scientology has been frequently investigated and sometimes banned in different countries. The FDA even tried (in vain) to ban the E-meter, claiming it was a quack medical device. Ron's attempts to fight back only made things worse. In 1979, for example, his wife and ten other Scientologists were convicted of burglarizing and wiretapping government offices.

Even Cecil has been the target of the Scientologists' wrath. Not long after my column on Scientology was published in the newspapers, I got a call from a radio show producer asking me to answer questions from listeners on the air. This happens fairly often and I didn't give the timing much thought. When the first caller lambasted me for dissing L. Ron, I started to get a little suspicious, and when every caller for the next half hour did the same I knew I'd been set up. Not that they laid a finger on me argument-wise. But swatting mosquitoes for 30 minutes isn't my idea of fun.

In 1984 several former Scientology officials claimed Hubbard told them to divert $100 million of church funds into foreign bank accounts. The church denied any wrongdoing, but you see the pattern. Whatever may be said for Scientology as a philosophy (and there are those who say it has helped them), its reputation as an organization is one of unmitigated sleaze. Get mixed up with these people at your own risk.

Thanks for the scoop on Dianetics. Now how about Transcendental Meditation? Relaxation I can see. Cleansed thought processes, sure. But levitation?—Anonymous, Greensboro, North Carolina

Little do you know. Awhile back somebody sent me a flier with the startling news that the Fourth Annual Continental Yogic Flying Competition was about to be held in Washington, D.C. The featured performers were the "top Yogic Flyers in the continent" competing in four events: the "50 meter dash, 25 meter hurdles, high jump, and long jump—all performed in the traditional cross-legged yogic sitting position." It is one of the regrets of my life that I didn't get a chance to go, but I did read the story about it in the *Washington Post*. Said story

was written by my old college roommate Steve. I'm not saying I arranged this. But my operatives are well placed.

The concept of competitive levitation didn't catch me entirely by surprise. I first heard about it in a general way from another old college roommate (Cecil had a lot of roommates) named Thom, who's been doing TM since the late '60s. Thom, who remains pretty rational despite 20 years of communing with the Maharishi, said he'd done some levitating himself, though I've never actually seen him in action.

None of this, however, prepared me for the 50-meter aerial dash. When I called Thom to ask about it—he was one of the 1,200 who attended the event in D.C.—he freely conceded it was "a sight to behold." The contestants weren't continuously airborne; rather, they proceeded by a series of hops—all this, mind you, in full lotus, the familiar yogic sitting position.

A skeptic might say it's ridiculous to call hopping levitation, but Thom says it's merely the first stage of a three-stage process. Stage two, which apparently no one has achieved yet, is hovering, and stage three is full-scale flying. I would pay serious money to see a demonstration of the latter in full daylight, but I gather that, at the moment, it's pretty far down the road.

TMers see levitation not merely as a novel method of transportation but as a mighty blow in the struggle for cosmic consciousness and world peace. According to David Orme-Johnson, a researcher at Maharishi International University, "Thirty-one sociological studies conducted throughout the world document that the quality of life in society significantly improves when as little as the square root of one percent of a population practices TM-Sidhi Yogic Flying together in one place." Orme-Johnson was one of the authors of a recent scientific paper purporting to show that levitation and related techniques had reduced the violence in Lebanon.

Wait a sec, you say. Reducing the violence in *Lebanon*?

My reaction exactly. Nonetheless I've been quite the little trouper in trying to get both sides of the story. I've had long talks with TM spokespeople to find out what scientific basis they have for thinking levitation works. While I don't doubt these people are sincere, all they can give me is a lot of half-baked mumbo jumbo about "quantum field theory" and the like.

I'm not claiming I went through all the math. But the notion that one could prove yogic flying had reduced the violence in Lebanon, as Orme-Johnson claims to do, is preposterous on its face and suggests that either 1) the exotic statistical techniques used in the social sciences are far less reliable than previously believed, 2) the techniques were improperly employed, or 3) these guys are lying through their teeth. I'll be charitable and say #2 seems like the obvious choice. Reviewers of the paper in question (*Journal of Conflict Resolution*, 32(4): 776–812) said as much. The fact that the researchers were true believers does nothing to increase one's confidence in the results. As the cold-fusion fiasco some years ago makes clear, scientists are as prone to self-delusion as anybody else.

That's not to say meditation per se, TM-style or otherwise, is a bad thing. The claimed health benefits probably are a placebo effect (i.e., if you think something is going to help you, chances are it will). But a lot of people seem to enjoy chanting mantras and at a few hundred bucks a pop the basic TM course isn't all that expensive. Learning yogic flying, on the other hand, could set you back a stiff three grand. My feeling is, if you gotta hop, go buy a trampoline.

What can you tell me about the Masons, i.e., politics, bylaws, who belongs, etc.? I have always assumed they were one of those semisilly men's associations like the Elks or the Odd Fellows, but occasionally you hear rumors of something more sinister.—Kathy P., Chicago

Masonry is probably harmless, but I feel it is my duty to stir up doubt. Besides, it's not like you're the first one to hear rumors. The Catholic Church and other major denominations have repeatedly condemned Freemasonry for its allegedly pagan tendencies. For a long time Catholics who became Masons were automatically excommunicated. In 1987 the Anglican Church reaffirmed that Christianity and Masonry were "incompatible."

The origins of Freemasonry are obscure. The best guess is that it's an outgrowth of medieval stonemasons' guilds that began after the mid-1500s. As construction of Gothic cathedrals ceased and the number of real (or "operative") masons began to dwindle, some of the guilds began to accept nonmasons, often members of the upper classes.

These men, called "accepted" masons, enjoyed the ritual and secrecy that, in the Middle Ages, had been necessary to transmit the skills of the craft and prevent outsiders from horning in. Eventually there were no operative masons at all and Masonry became a kind of fraternity, retaining such trappings of stonemasonry as the apron worn at formal functions and the familiar compass-and-square symbol.

Over the years a long-winded Masonic ritual has grown up, full of cornball references to Knights of the Brazen Serpent and the like. There are also "secret" signs and handgrips, which initiates are never supposed to reveal lest they suffer a fate worse than death. (In reality, books on Masonic rituals can be found in many public libraries.) In shaking hands, for example, a Master Mason will press his thumb between the other guy's second and third knuckles, thereby identifying himself to initiates while leaving others clueless.

Clerical objections to Freemasonry are based in part on its quasi-religious overtones. In the ceremonies open to members of lower degree (there are 33 degrees, or ranks, in all), reference is made to the Great Architect of the Universe, whom initiates are encouraged to think of as the God of their own religion.

If and when they climb a little farther up the ladder, however, they learn that the real name of the Great Architect is Jahbulon. According to British journalist Stephen Knight, Jahbulon is a combination of the names Jahweh; Baal, the god of the Canaanites, whom the Jews regarded as false; and Osiris, the god of the Egyptians. Ergo, Freemasons are pagans.

This accusation shocks most Masons, few of whom take the rituals literally, at least in English-speaking countries. (French lodges reportedly are more openly atheistic.) Masonic apologists argue that Jahbulon represents a sort of primitive ecumenism. But leaders of established churches recoil at the suggestion that their conception of the godhead is no more valid than that of the golden idol crowd.

Another (and to the nonreligious, more serious) charge made against Freemasonry is that it is a conspiratorial self-help society whose members look out for one another to the detriment of non-Masons. In some areas so many big shots belong that Masonry has become a kind of parallel Establishment, and it is widely assumed that members get first crack at jobs, preferential legal treatment (many cops and judges are "on the square," as the Masonic saying goes), and so on. The extreme example of this is Italy's infamous P-2 lodge, whose members included hundreds of prominent officials, some of whom traded confidential information, influenced government decisions, and pulled strings for one another.

American Masons have included such prominent figures as Gerald Ford and Robert Dole, meaning we had an all-Masonic presidential ticket in 1976. Nonetheless, there has been little concern recently about excessive Masonic influence in this country. This is not the case in countries such as England, where Masons constitute a much larger percentage of the population. Knight's exposé, *The Brotherhood*, created a sensation in 1983 and no doubt was partly responsible for the Anglican crackdown.

Personally I think it's all paranoia. But next time you're in London you might want to press between the knuckles when shaking hands and periodically intone "so mote it be." Maybe it won't help. But who knows?

Of the 27,000-plus so-called Christian religions, about 99½ percent worship on Sunday. However, all biblical indications are that the Sabbath or Lord's Day is the last day of the week—that is, Saturday. Isn't every priest, minister, and TV preacher helping us break a commandment by holding worship services on Sunday instead of Saturday? They use the excuse that the Resurrection occurred on the first day of the week, Sunday. Still, nowhere in the Bible does the Lord say, "thou shalt change the Lord's Day from the last to the first day of the week."—Saint Michael of San Antonio, Texas

One of the great things about founding a new religion, bro, is you get to do things any way you want. The Sabbath, which marks the last day of Genesis, on which God rested, is mainly a Jewish tradition. The Lord's Day, on the other hand, is strictly a Christian one.

Christians often call the Lord's Day the Sabbath, but don't get the wrong idea. Though Christians obviously borrowed a great deal from Judaism, they felt no obligation to worship on the same schedule that the Jews did. Admittedly at times it was expedient to do so. In the early days, when Christianity was considered a kind of postgraduate Judaism and most converts were Jews, it was customary to observe the Sabbath and the Lord's Day (Sunday) back to back. Not only was this convenient, it had a certain metaphorical significance: the Sabbath commemorated the seventh day, the completion of material creation, while the Lord's Day, sometimes called "the eighth day," signified the start of the creation of God's kingdom on earth, the Church.

Dual Sat.-Sun. worship was uncommon outside Palestine and most Christians celebrated Sunday alone, Sunday having been the day of the Resurrection. As it happened, the Roman name "Sunday" (Latin *dies solis*) meshed with the Christian idea that Jesus was the new sun, the light of the world. The Lord's Day and Sunday have been linked ever since.

I am currently reading a book entitled The Lost Books of the Bible. *Being interested in Bible history, I thought it might be an interesting diversion, but I was not prepared for what I found. It claims that when Jesus was young, he killed a couple of boys and a schoolmaster because they displeased him. Jesus comes off as an arrogant bad seed in these supposedly ancient texts.*

My question is: were these books truly a part of the original Bible, and if they were suppressed for obvious reasons, does the Catholic Church, or any church for that matter, acknowledge their existence? How do they explain Jesus' bad temper? Is this why there is very little about Jesus' youth in the current Bible?—Dan Olmos, West Hollywood, California

You can see why the book in question wouldn't be the ideal text for a Sunday sermon. After recounting three murders in two pages, one passage concludes, "Then said Joseph to St. Mary, henceforth we will not allow him [Jesus] to go out of the house; for everyone who displeases him is killed." This is the Prince of Peace?

The "lost books" are part of the apocrypha, quasibiblical works not included in the official Bible. There are several dozen of these, dating from both Old and New Testament eras and exhibiting considerable variety in length, completeness, and credibility. In some corners of the early church a few of these were considered inspired, but they were ultimately excluded from the formal canon for one reason or another. The remaining books, which account for the bulk of the material, have always been regarded as spurious by the mainstream church and include works condemned as heretical or fraudulent.

In 1820 a number of the apocryphal books were compiled into a sort of alternative Bible called *The Apocryphal New Testament*. This was republished in 1926 as *The Lost Books of the Bible* and reprinted in 1979; the last version is what you saw. The 1820 book was itself an aggregation of two English translations published in 1736 and 1737. The original works were a serious attempt to advance Bible study, but the subsequent publications, arguably in 1820 and certainly from 1926 onward, were an attempt to play the scandalous aspects for all they were worth.

The homicidal-Jesus stories come from something known as the Infancy Gospel of Thomas. (This is to be distinguished from the better-known but equally apocryphal Gospel According to Thomas, about

which more below.) Several versions of the Infancy Gospel dating back to about the sixth century A.D. have come to light; all are copies of earlier texts.

As near as scholars can make out, the Thomas story originated in the mid-second century A.D., subsequent to the four canonical gospels (that is, Matthew, Mark, Luke, and John). Some say it was based in part on Luke; the two books share the story of Jesus scourging the moneylenders at the Temple. It is one of the few portrayals, spurious or not, of Jesus' early life, which no doubt accounts for its continued circulation after eighteen hundred years.

The Infancy Gospel has never been proposed for inclusion in the official Bible. Many of the early Christian writers who were influential in deciding what books belonged in the canon regarded it as heretical. In it the young Jesus is fully aware that he is a god and performs miracles for sport, which is at odds with the usual Christian emphasis on Jesus' humanity.

The book is not a literal account of Jesus' early life. All of the Gospels, including the canonical ones, were based on oral traditions collected after Jesus' death and to a greater or lesser extent were intended to support a doctrinal point of view. In antiquity the Infancy Gospel was linked to sects that held that Jesus was God disguised as a man, rather than God become a man. Many of the stories have parallels in tales of the Buddha and other religious figures.

I mentioned there is another Gospel According to Thomas, a collection of 114 sayings attributed to Jesus that was discovered in Egypt in 1945. It is taken more seriously than the Infancy Gospel and, while not as outrageous, is equally troubling in its way. It ends, "Simon Peter said to them, 'Let Mary leave us, for women are not worthy of life.' Jesus said, 'I myself shall lead her in order to make her male, so that she too may become a living spirit resembling you males. For every woman who will make herself male will enter the kingdom of heaven.'" The best one can say is that it may represent the view of the compiler rather than the maker of heaven and earth.

Is there any major religion that believes there is no life after death or any continuation or reincarnation whatsoever?—Azbug, Berkeley, California

Are you kidding? Absolutely everybody, including atheists, believes in life after death. Eleanor Roosevelt died and you're still alive, yes? I rest my case. The question is not whether there is "any continuation or reincarnation [of life] whatsoever" but whether 1) you continue to enjoy some sort of *personal* existence after death, and 2) whether there is a spiritual or immaterial realm that transcends death. On the latter point every religion I have ever heard of argues for the affirmative— else why have a religion?—but there is disagreement on point #1.

Buddhists, strictly speaking, do not believe in an immortal individual soul and in fact much of Buddhist teaching is aimed at the extinction of personal desire. Other eastern religions don't take it that far but do say the proper aim of individual souls is to merge anonymously with the Great Font of Existence. Old Testament Jews did not have a fully worked-out idea of the afterlife until late in the game and even today one may argue that personal salvation in Judaism is secondary to the deliverance of the Jewish people as a whole.

Apparently it was the Egyptians who first popularized the idea of a personal postmortem paradise, an idea since adopted by Christians and Muslims. But it's not true, as your question seems to suggest, that the chief appeal of all religions is the chance to cheat Mr. Death.

A Question

You claim that "it's not true ... that the chief appeal of all religions is the chance to cheat Mr. Death." What, then, is their major selling point?—A. Buddy Tobias, Austin, Texas

Why, the promise of obtaining some clue to what it's all about, Alfie. Isn't that enough?

Who is this St. Jude dude? Why are people always thanking him in the classified section of the newspaper?—Lisa K., Madison, Wisconsin

I am continually shocked at how little the coming generation knows about the realm of the spirit. Saint Jude is the patron saint of hopeless causes. Also known as Jude Thaddeus, he was one of the 12 apostles, but other than that virtually nothing is known about him. According to

the *Oxford Dictionary of Saints*, his job as lost-cause czar "is said to have originated because nobody invoked him for anything since his name so closely resembled that of Judas, who betrayed the Lord." In other words, he was so hard up for work he'd jump at the chance to intercede for you.

Devotion to Jude first began in the late 1700s in France and Germany. If he comes through for you today, one gathers, you're supposed to manifest your gratitude publicly. Who originated this practice? I dunno. But I'll bet he moonlighted selling classified ads.

From The Straight Dope Message Board

Subj: Karaoke
From: Inkcon
    Where did karaoke get started and where did the name come from?

From: DC3454
    Karaoke started in Japan. The exact definition is "empty orchestra," meaning that all words, music, and background voices are supplied while you supply the lead vocals. Karaoke will live forever because, as a "karaokaholic," there is nothing you will ever hold in your hand as addictive as a microphone. The instant gratification of applause will outdo your wildest imagination. I once had a standing ovation of

over 500 people and I can tell you that there is NO other feeling like it.

I am so addicted to this incredible and harmless form of entertainment that I now make my living as a K.J. (karaoke jockey). I always say, "If you only sound like a buck I can make you sound like a million." I'm also verrrry gentle with karaoke "virgins."

From: LilethSC
Was the ovation when you finally STOPPED singing?

Chapter 10

Consuming Passion

Why does the label on a bottle of Pine Sol say, "It is a violation of federal law to use this product in a manner inconsistent with its labeling"? Exactly what uses are unlawful? We'd hate to be sent up the river on a Pine Sol rap.—Hank Keedy and James Nielock, Chicago

What, you think this is *funny*? OK, it's funny. But as you know if you've ever tried a few gosh-Myrtle-did-you-remember-the-bomb jokes at the airport, you don't want to try kidding the feds. Disinfectants are legally classified as pesticides, which are regulated by the Environmental Protection Agency. A warning is required on the labels of all such products, regardless of their potential threat to the biota. Strictly speaking, the EPA could nab you if you used too high a concentration of Pine Sol (or Lysol or what have you) or, for that matter, too low. This may seem like a classic case of bureaucratic overkill—you can just imagine EPA SWAT teams swooping down on Grandma to see if she's mixing the Pine Sol right—but actually it does make some sense. Insecticides kill insects, and nobody doubts they ought to be regulated; disinfectants kill microorganisms, so it stands to reason they should be regulated, too.

Lest you be overcome with paranoia, be assured that much of the EPA's enforcement effort is directed at disinfectant manufacturers, to see that their products are registered and labeled with the proper directions and so forth. On the consumer side, they usually just keep tabs on larger users—hospitals and day-care centers, say. They'll only check up on an individual when there's an injury or a citizen complaint. Ergo, if you're into serious Pine Sol abuse, make sure you do it out of sight of the neighbors. Sanctions, should it come to that, range from a warning letter for a first offense to fines and even criminal prosecution. For what it's worth, most EPA citations of individuals involve weed killers and pesticides; nobody I spoke to could recall a disinfectant bust. Always a first time, though. Not that I want to encourage eco-crime, boys, but you could be Pine Sol's answer to the Exxon Valdez.

I've bought many cigarettes in my years but all of them have been class A cigarettes. I've seen third-class mail, grade B beef, and C average math, but why no class B cigarettes?—JShaft666, via AOL

We're not big on smoking around here, Shaft, but we figure whatsoever concerns humanity should concern us. So we called up Cliff at the federal Bureau of Alcohol, Tobacco, and Firearms (and don't those sound like the ingredients for a great camping trip?). Cliff revealed the following facts:

1. Federal revenooers recognize two kinds of cigarettes—small cigarettes (class A), which weigh up to three pounds per thousand and
   are taxed at $12 per thou; and large cigarettes (class B), which weigh
   more than three pounds per thousand and have a tax rate of $25.20.
2. Total class A cigarettes produced in fiscal 1996: 755 billion.
3. Total class B cigarettes produced in fiscal 1996: zero.

We thought: boy, this sounds like an extremely useful classification system. What OTHER kinds of nonexistent cigarettes can we dream up
categories for? Concrete cigarettes! Electrical cigarettes! Cigarettes
with stainless-steel linings!

This just shows what a bad attitude we have. Cliff patiently explained that in fiscal 1995, there were 83,000 class B cigarettes produced, and 105 million taxed.

We thought about this. Then we asked the obvious question:
"Huh?"

"They must have been cleaning out the inventory," Cliff replied.
Cigarettes aren't taxed until they're put into sales channels. The class
B cigarette market was rapidly declining.

This doesn't sound like a market that is declining, we thought. This
sounds like a market that has dropped dead. We asked Cliff: Had he
ever *seen* any class B cigarettes?

Sure, Cliff said. We then heard the sounds of someone rummaging
around in what we took to be the ATF's Big Drawer of Cool Stuff.
"There's a hookah in here!" Cliff exclaimed at one point. But at last he
found what he wanted. A brand called Cigarettellos. He was cagey
about who the manufacturer was, no doubt having a certain paranoia
about spilling the beans on the tobacco industry to weasels from the
press. But we found out. Cigarettellos were manufactured by Nat
Sherman International, a purveyor of fine tobacco products in New
York City and for many years one of the few makers of class Bs.

On the horn with Joel Sherman, president of Nat Sherman International, we ascertained the following truths:

1. Cigarettellos were ordinary cigarettes except that they were 6½
   inches long. This gives you a clue as to the long-term marketing
   problem faced by this brand. You're conspicuous enough smoking
   one of those 100-millimeter jobs. Who wants to be seen waving a
   cigarette the size of a welding electrode?

2. Nat Sherman also made several other brands of large cigarettes, including Fantasia (which were rolled in multicolored paper), and MCD Double. As near as Joel could recall, they had been introduced as novelty items in the 1960s. But they sold in minuscule quantities, mostly through specialty tobacco shops, and they were a pain to make. After losing money on them for 30 years, Joel figured the market was telling him something, and what it was telling him was, "Don't make these cigarettes." So around 1995 he threw in the towel.

3. The brands are still made in four-inch class A versions, however. Just in case you wanted to re-create the class B experience with scissors and Elmer's glue.

But Joel, we said. You pulled the plug on a product that was moving 105 million in its last year. This number is minuscule? Wasn't all us, said Joel. He recalled something about one of the majors test-marketing a class B cigarette that had extra circumference rather than length. We are not seeing the sexiness of this, and apparently neither was anyone else. The product was withdrawn.

So now you're thinking: damn, no more class B cigarettes! There is a hole in my life that shall never be filled. I suppose you could bum one of Cliff's 'tellos, but if not, never fear: you can still get class B *clove* cigarettes. We know this because our assistant Jane found some in a smoke shop. They're not big, they're more lethal than all-tobacco smokes, and why they don't show up in the ATF statistics even Cliff can't explain. But class B is class B.

I'm not sure when I first began noticing the arcane titles at the tops of paper bags (samples enclosed), but, seeing them once, I began to note others in great variety. Since they don't seem to indicate paper weight or bag size, what are they? And why the Boy Scout names?—Mary Shen Barnidge, Chicago

I've had it on my list to look into this, Mary. Had it on my list for four years, to be precise, since that's how long ago your letter arrived. However, I feel that from the standpoint of improving with age, a good question is like a fine wine.

No argument, the marks on paper bags can be pretty strange. Your

samples include one that consists of a flag on which is inscribed AD-VANCE 4, and beneath that the enigmatic word WA-HA. This must be the Boy Scout name you refer to, although the influence of the Shriners cannot be entirely discounted. Another set of marks consists of the word TRINITY above an inverted triangle, with, in one version, the word TOREADOR below, while another has TOREADOR SQUAT. I am familiar with the concept of doodly-squat, of course, but must confess that toreador squat is, to me at least, a notion that is entirely new.

We at the Straight Dope are nothing if not resourceful, however. I called up the folks at Stone Container Corporation, the leading maker of paper bags, and learned that Wa-Ha, Toreador Squat, etc., are all trade names applied to various styles and sizes of paper bags by manufacturers. Wa-Ha is an "SO grocer" bag made of brown kraft paper by the Great Plains Bag Company. Great Plains had a thing for Indian names; its line of bags included Dakota, Mohican, Wampum, Teepee, and Super Chief. SO stands for self-opening—if you hold the bag by the half-moon cutout at the top and give it a sharp flip, it'll open by itself.

Toreador and Toreador Squat are natural kraft bags made by Trinity Bag & Paper Company—the Squat variety, as we might have predicted, being squatter in shape than the regular kind. You also enclosed samples of Wolf and Tornado bags; both are white SO grocer bags, the former made by Union Camp Corporation, the latter by Trinity.

You've also got your Terrier, your Titanic, your Sweepstakes Chunky, and scores of other names ranging from the charming to the prosaic. Why so many? We can but guess, but I would venture to say that in the paper bag business you need all the creative outlets you can get. Sadly, the whimsical names of yore are slowly fading away. Great Plains and the bag-making operations of Trinity B&P, for example, were bought by Stone Container, which has phased out Toreador Squat in favor of the more informative but unpoetic Natural Shorty.

The number on the bag, in case you wondered, indicates its capacity. Your smaller units, called bags or grocers, have numbers from ½ to 25, signifying the approximate weight in pounds of sugar or flour the bag can hold. Your bigger varieties, known as sacks, are sized in fractions of a barrel, e.g., ⅙, the size most commonly found in supermarkets.

On the bottom of most plastic containers I've noticed a triangle-shaped symbol indicating that the container is recyclable. In the middle of this symbol is a number ranging from 1 to 6 or higher. I know these numbers have something to do with the classification of plastic products, but what is the difference between a 1 and 2 or 6 in terms of recycling? Finally, why do most recycling centers take type 1 or 2 containers but not 3 through 6? Where are we supposed to take these other products so they can be recycled? I want to recycle but it is hard to do with all this confusion.—J. R. Richards, Sterling, Virginia

Things are more confused than you realize. The main problem is that the triangle symbol, more commonly known as the "chasing arrows" symbol, doesn't indicate recyclability, contrary to wide belief. The number just indicates the type of plastic. The numbers range from 1 to 7, 1 through 6 being the most commonly used plastic resins while 7 is miscellaneous. It's important to keep the types separate when recycling because they have different melting points and other characteristics and if you throw them all into the pot together you wind up with unusable glop.

Although it's technically possible to recycle most plastics, recycling types 3 through 7 is rare because using virgin material is cheaper. Things are better with type 1 (polyethylene terephthalate or PET, used for pop bottles) and type 2 (high-density polyethylene or HDPE, used

for milk and detergent bottles). Twenty-seven percent of type 1 is recycled, including 41 percent of plastic pop bottles, because type 1 containers usually are easy to sort and clean, the stuff can be used to make a lot of products, and virgin-type 1 feedstock is relatively expensive. Type 2 is less attractive (for one thing, it's hard to get rid of the smell from old milk bottles); still, the bottles are big and easy to sort out of the waste stream. About 7 percent of type 2 plastic is recycled.

Types 3 through 7 you might as well throw away. Recycling rates for these materials range around 1 percent or less. Some recycling operations won't even take types 1 and 2, arguing that plastic items of whatever type are so bulky in proportion to their value that it's a waste of fuel to send out a truck to haul them away. The recycling rate for all plastics is a dismal 4.5 percent, compared with 53 percent for aluminum.

Some environmentalists think it's deceptive to use the chasing-arrows recycling symbol on plastic packaging since it fools people like you into thinking the product is likely to be recycled when the overwhelming probability is it won't. In 1993 and '94 representatives of the National Recycling Coalition and the Society of the Plastics Industry attempted to work out an improved symbol that would address this objection. The effort went aground on—get this—the new symbol's shape. The final proposal called for replacing the chasing arrows with an ordinary triangle and adding a letter to the numbers (e.g., 2B) to indicate various grades within each type of plastic as a sorting aid. SPI's board approved the plan but NRC's refused, saying the triangle and the recycling symbol looked too much alike and suggesting a square or rectangle instead. SPI claimed a rectangle would increase industry retooling costs 400 percent—a triangle would let plastics companies modify existing molds, hammering the chasing arrows into a triangle with the equivalent of a chisel, whereas a rectangle would mean making new molds at great expense. In the absence of an agreement, the old system will remain in place indefinitely, since 39 states now require it and only a united front on the part of recyclers and plastics companies would persuade state legislatures to enact a change.

So what are you supposed to do? Given the difficulty of recycling plastic, a lot of environmentalists say it's best to avoid disposable plastic when possible. Of the plastic you do buy, recycle types 1 and 2, rinsing all items out carefully first. Above all, don't mix in types 3 through 7 (unless your local recycler specifically says they're OK), plastic without a code, or random garbage. Some poor stiff will have to muck through the junk sorting it out later if you do.

Old Plastic In New Bottles

In response to your recent opus on plastics recycling, I thought you might want to update the Teeming Millions regarding the enclosed.—Rob Grierson, Evanston, Illinois

The enclosed article, which is misleadingly headlined, MIXING PLASTICS IS NOW OK, describes a new plastics recycling process developed by Northwestern University's Basic Industry Research Laboratory. (Actually, the basic process was developed in Germany to recycle tires; NU's contribution was to adapt it to plastics.) The process, known as "solid-state shear extrusion," uses a "twin-screw extruder" to pulverize a random collection of old plastic under high pressure. Unlike conventional grinding methods, this causes the plastic not simply to mush together but to recombine in ways not yet fully understood. The result to some extent is new plastic that I'm told can be used to make "high-value products." The high-value product shown at a demonstration a while back was a souvenir key chain, but I guess everything's relative. The new process promises to be everything current plastic recycling methods aren't: cheap and hassle-free, since any mixture of old plastic can be used as feedstock.

The key word above is "promises." The new process was only recently introduced and has not yet proven itself in the marketplace. Several companies have expressed interest but commercial application is still a ways off. Until your local recycler specifically tells you otherwise, do not, repeat do not, mix different types of plastic. Not that I have any doubts whatsoever about the viability of this thing, but in 1959 the magazines said we'd soon all be living in underwater cities and I'm still waiting for those, too.

What's the Straight Dope on speed reading? Evelyn Wood commercials in the late '70s showed people casually zipping through impressive-looking tomes, apparently having benefited from one of Evy's speed-reading courses. The concept, as I recall it, was that one learned to read not word-by-word but line-by-line and eventually paragraph-by-paragraph. It was claimed that in spite of the breakneck speeds you would "achieve a higher level of comprehension." It all seemed a bit implausible at the time. Anyway, speed reading seemed to disappear until recently, when it was reintroduced on those late-night mail-order "infomercials." What's the scoop?—John Ashborne, Chicago

I'm not saying it's a scam. People used to think mustard plasters did something, too. But the benefits have been exaggerated. Speed reading is what you might call the Ronald Reagan approach to reading—you get the text's general drift while remaining largely innocent of the details, sometimes embarrassingly so. Several trained speed readers were once asked to read a doctored text in which the even-numbered lines came from one source and the odd-numbered lines from another. The speed readers read the material three times (average speed: 1,700 words per minute). Did they understand it? You bet, the speed readers said. Did they notice it was two separate passages mixed together? Uh, no.

Claims that speed readers comprehend just as well as ordinary

readers are probably spurious. In one early comprehension test speed readers scored a seemingly respectable 68 percent. But it turned out the test was so easy that people who had never read the material at all scored 57 percent.

To find out the truth about speed reading we turn to researchers Marcel Just, Patricia Carpenter, and Michael Masson, all spiritual graduates of the Cecil Adams Cut-the-Comedy School of Scientific Investigation. Just and Company tested three groups: speed readers, normal readers, and "skimmers"—that is, people who were told to read rapidly but had no special training.

The researchers found that the speed readers read a little faster than the skimmers (700 wpm versus 600 wpm) and much faster than the normal readers (240 wpm). But the speed readers' comprehension was invariably worse, often a lot worse, than that of the normal readers. What's more, the speed readers out-comprehended the skimmers only when asked general questions about easy material. When asked about details, or when reading difficult material, the skimmers and speed readers tested equally poorly.

Conclusion: speed reading might help you read TV cue cards faster, but for technical stuff, the kind speed-reading boosters want us to read faster so we can whomp the Japanese, it's pretty useless. Reading seems to be like losing weight—there's just no fast and easy way to do it. For more, see *The Psychology of Reading and Language Comprehension*, Just et al., 1987.

There's a question that's been burning in the unscrubbed corners of my mind for a long time. We are told that Ivory Soap is "99 and $^{44}/_{100}$% pure." What's in the other $^{56}/_{100}$% (or if 0.56% if you prefer)?—Peter Holland, Chicago

I don't know that our primary concern ought to be the $^{56}/_{100}$ths, Peter. As a legendary economics professor once put it, the real question is, "99 and $^{44}/_{100}$% pure what?" Since you asked, however, the remainder consists of "foreign and unnecessary substances." Bear with me a second and I'll give you the results from the lab.

It all started in 1881 when Harley Procter, son of Procter & Gamble cofounder William Procter and a legendary soap salesman in his own right, decided he needed a new angle to hawk Ivory Soap. Then as now people were impressed by scientific testimonials, and Harley decided if he could come up with a lab test showing Ivory was "purer" than other soaps, he'd win sales.

Trouble was, there wasn't a standard for purity in soap, so Harley hired an independent scientific consultant in New York to concoct one. The consultant concluded that a 100% pure soap would consist of nothing but fatty acids and alkali. You see now why the Ivory slogan is so cryptic. If you announce to the world that what you're selling is "99 and $^{44}/_{100}$ths fatty acids and alkali," you're not going to sell a lot of soap.

A definition of purity having been arrived at, Harley sent out some Ivory Soap for analysis and compared it with earlier analyses he'd had done of castile soap, regarded at the time as the best soap available.

He was gratified to discover that by his consultant's definition, Ivory Soap was purer than the castile soaps. The impurities consisted of uncombined alkali, 0.11%; carbonates, 0.28%; and mineral matter, 0.17%. Total: 0.56%. Thinking that "99 and $^{44}/_{100}$% pure" had just the right touch of technical authenticity to appeal to the great unwashed, so to speak, Harley began sticking the phrase in Ivory advertisements, and another classic marketing slogan was born.

Did the Swiss army really use the Swiss army knife?—Matthew Steiner, via the Internet

But of course. I know this because I heard it from one Tanya, a Swiss citizen living in the United States whose father served in the Swiss army. Tanya confirms that her dad was issued a regulation Swiss army knife not unlike the ones we civilians are familiar with. I was going to ask Tanya for more details, but unfortunately I lost her phone number, one of the hazards you face in this business when you start doing research via talk radio rather than the library. But I'm confident Tanya would have told me that the main difference between her father's knife and the ones you're familiar with was that the handle was anodized aluminum rather than red plastic. (Red is supposed to make the knife easier to find when dropped in the snow, a mishap to which military personnel are apparently immune.) I am also certain she would have told me the knife was furnished with the standard soldierly assortment of tools, consisting of a thick stainless-steel blade, two screwdrivers, a can opener, and an awl. That is, unless her father was an officer, in which case his knife might have included a corkscrew. The privileges of rank.

Two Swiss manufacturers, Victorinox and Wenger, each supply 25,000 knives annually to the Swiss army, which amounts to a little more than one day's production. The rest of the two companies' vast output—together they produce about seven million knives a year—is mostly exported, the United States being by far the largest customer. (Non-Swiss knockoffs are also available; the real thing will have Victorinox or Wenger stamped on one of the blades.) Hundreds of models are available, ranging from a basic two-blade version to a 31-tool octopus that will let you do everything from rebuilding an Edsel to picking your teeth. You can get tools ranging from corkscrews and magnifying glasses to aspirin-bottle-cotton pullers. There's even a model with a blade that will let you perform—I am not making this up—an emergency tracheotomy, no doubt inspired by an actual emergency tracheotomy performed with a SAK aboard an airliner in flight. The in-store demonstrations must be quite a sight.

The modern Swiss army knife dates back to 1891, when Victorinox founder Karl Elsener began supplying the Swiss army with knives made in Switzerland, previous army blades having been manufactured in Germany. The original wooden-handled knife featured a blade, a screwdriver, a can opener, and a punch, but Elsener didn't really hit his stride until 1897, when he invented an officer's version that used a special spring mechanism to enable more utensils to be added without increasing the size of the handle. In 1908 the Swiss army decided to split the contract, with half the order going to Victorinox, in the German-speaking part of Switzerland, and the other half to a firm run by rival cutlery maker Theodore Wenger, headquartered in a canton where everybody spoke French. They claim they did this in the interest of national harmony, but they may have also figured a little competition would keep the price down. If so, they were right. Today you can get a Swiss army knife for as little as nine bucks.

American GIs discovered the Swiss army knife during the World War II era, but it's only in the last 20 years or so that it has become a mass-market item in North America. Today the knife has become emblematic of almost comical versatility. Some feel the knife is overrated, and Cecil must say his personal panacea for life's little crises is duct tape and drywall screws. But neither would be much help in an emergency tracheotomy. All things considered, a Swiss army knife is probably still your best bet.

Why are magazines dated anywhere from a week to a month later than the time they actually appear? Newspapers don't presume to print August 1 on a paper that hits the streets July 31.—W.J. O'Neill, Los Angeles

It's all a ploy. These days, what ain't? What you see on news-magazine covers, at least, is not the publication date but what is sometimes called the "off-sales" date—that is, the date on which dealers are supposed to pull the magazine from the stands. It's the equivalent of the "fresh-until" date on milk. The feeling is that if people see a cover date a few days in the future, they'll figure they're getting the latest poop, even though the magazine may actually have been sitting on the rack for quite a while.

For the most part it's a harmless illusion, but some magazines look a little silly in retrospect. A prime example is the December 12, 1941, issue of *United States News*, predecessor of *U.S. News & World Report*. You'd think word of that little hoo-ha at Pearl Harbor on December 7 might have filtered in to *USN* by December 12, but no. One cover headline begins noncommittally, "If War Comes in the Pacific . . ."

Newspaper types such as myself might have you believe we are somehow above all this. Bah. We're lying scum just like everybody else. The evening edition of many dailies bears the next day's date, and of course you can get Sunday papers Saturday morning. Newspapers simply benefit from the fact that they're lining birdcage bottoms within hours of publication, so nobody notices if their headlines (and datelines) are occasionally overtaken by events.

Around the time of the 1996 summer Olympics I heard a radio commercial for a camera. At the end of the spot the announcer mentioned that it was the official camera of the U.S. Olympics. It occurred to me that not only is there an official camera for the Olympics, but probably an official paper towel, laundry detergent, and frozen yogurt. How far do they take this "official" business? And exactly how is

it determined what the official camera is anyway? Is there some rigorous Olympics Testing Committee for cameras, or does it all come down to payola?—Brett Bayne, Los Angeles

Payola is such an ugly word, Brett. Let's say it's free enterprise in action.

As you suspect, there's no product Olympics in which hard-working businesses (hmm, should they be amateurs? would you want them if they were?) compete for the honor of providing the athletes with cameras, beer steins, and other necessities of life.

The actual selection process is simple: you pay the money, you get to be an official sponsor. It's not cheap. Top-of-the-line sponsors of the Atlanta summer games reportedly had to shell out more than $50 million each in the form of cash, goods, and services. All told, close to $1 billion was raised in this way during the four-year Olympic cycle.

Most people have no illusions about what it means to be a sponsor, be it of a TV show or a sports event: you cough up some cash in hopes of gaining commercial advantage. What confuses the issue is the "official" business. Olympic sponsors are not required to contribute an official Olympic anything to the games. However, the big companies interested in becoming Olympic sponsors often sell things that the Olympic organizers need.

So the two sides strike a deal. Nissan, say, agrees to provide the Olympics with the thousands of vans, light trucks, and utility vehicles it needs for the duration of the games. In return the company is allowed to advertise the Nissan Quest as the Official Import Minivan, the Nissan Pathfinder as the Official Import Sport Utility Vehicle, and so on.

Similarly, Texaco is the Official Petroleum Provider, Visa is the Official [credit] Card, and Coca-Cola provides the official soft drinks.

It's an exclusive arrangement. You can bet if you grabbed a can of soda pop in the Atlanta Olympic Village it wasn't a Diet Pepsi.

Is there an official Olympic everything? Just the opposite. The trend over the past several olympiads has been toward fewer sponsors paying more money. There are still plenty of official Olympic souvenirs, but it's not like the old days, when you couldn't walk down a grocery aisle without a half-dozen official Olympic products falling into your cart.

The organizers of the Atlanta games did offer promotion rights to suppliers who weren't sponsors in return for a deal. But don't expect to see ads for the official Olympic forklift or toilet paper. Promotion by suppliers is restricted to the trade press.

Which brings us to that camera commercial you heard. It's for the Cameo Motor EX Olympic edition from Eastman Kodak, one of ten worldwide Olympic sponsors. The Cameo is one of two official Olympic cameras, the other being Kodak's Fun Saver Pocket 35, the Official One-Time-Use Camera. They were the only cameras on sale at Olympic shops during the games. The Fun Saver was also given to athletes and attendees at the closing ceremonies.

Bestowing the "official" label on these cameras was strictly Kodak's decision. Why the Cameo Motor EX? Since first writing, you have informed me that you called Kodak's 800 number and were told "with rather surprising honesty that sales of the camera were waning, and this was probably a mere marketing ploy."

Horrified Kodak spokespeople were quick to deny this, pointing out that the Cameo is Kodak's best-selling nonthrowaway camera. But still, is it a marketing ploy? Of course. Is the whole "official" products business a bit silly? You bet. Is it a monstrous scam? Look at it this way. The Olympics are a good show, they separate corporate America from a billion dollars that would otherwise be spent on who knows what foolishness, and they help Kodak sell a few more cameras. How upset can I get?

Why is there an expiration date on sour cream?—Al Malmberg, Colorado Springs, Colorado

Al, you nut! I mean, just spelling it out for the benefit of the slow, it's already sour, right? Unfortunately, as commonly happens, I'm obliged to spoil your little joke with the facts. Probably you have the idea that they make sour cream by taking ordinary cream and letting it sit out on the windowsill for a couple hours. By and by somebody gets a whiff, goes, "Yo, that's sour! Ship it!" and two days later you're spreading it on a blintz.

But that's not how it works. It's true they start with light cream or the equivalent. Having pasteurized it, which kills most of the microorganisms that make raw milk go sour, they then dump in a special bacterial culture that produces lactic acid. If I know my bacteria—and I did stand in line once to get tickets for a Kiss concert—they produce

the lactic acid by excreting it, which you then pay to eat. Chilling the sour cream after the bacteria have had 12–16 hours to do their thing halts the "ripening" (i.e., souring) process, resulting in a product that is merely tangy rather than completely rank. But bacterial action doesn't totally stop, and if the sour cream sits around long enough it will eventually become so sour (or moldy) that it's inedible. The same will happen to virtually any dairy product, since some sour-inducing microorganisms invariably survive pasteurization. Thus the expiration dates. We may think of sour cream, therefore, as occupying the bracingly tart but brief interval separating the hopelessly bland from the unspeakably vile. A perfect analogy to the locations on the cultural continuum occupied by Barney the Dinosaur, myself, and Howard Stern.

Betty: In The Bottle At Last

Now we know. They were just saving her [Betty Rubble] for a special occasion.—Jim Siterlet, Urbana, Illinois

My faith in humanity is restored, sort of. Jim, who obviously shares Cecil's sympathy for the oppressed, remembered the column I wrote years ago lamenting the absence of Betty Rubble from bottles of Flintstones chewable vitamins. Manufacturer's excuse #1: she looked too much like Wilma. Manufacturer's excuse #2: "The vitamin die had

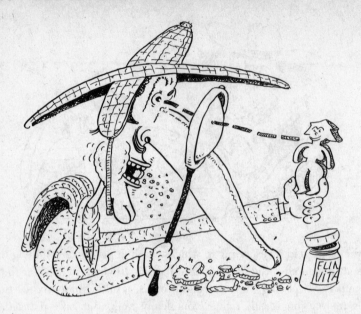

limited room and in a toss-up between Betty and Wilma, Betty lost out because her slim waist kept breaking." In other words, she lost out because she watched her weight! Is this the message we want to send to impressionable young consumers?

But let's get serious. We all know what really happened.

First male marketing genius: OK, we got the main stud in there, we got his buddy, we got his wife, the kids, the pet dinosaur, the car . . . what are we leaving out?

Second male marketing genius: Uh, Betty.

First MMG: So what's more important—your car, your pooch, or your best friend's wife?

(They look at each other.)

First MMG: This is a family product.

Second MMG: Pitch the babe.

When I first wrote about Betty I was as a voice crying in the wilderness. However, a sense of the injustice of it all gradually seeped into the awareness of the American public. The movement got a boost when the movie *The Flintstones* came out. Actress Rosie O'Donnell, whose portrayal of Betty was unjustly overlooked at Oscar time, was asked about Betty's whereabouts during an interview on *Eye to Eye with Connie Chung*. Her consciousness instantly raised, Rosie cried,

"Something has to be done! Hand me the phone. I'm going to call my agent."

The thing snowballed from there. One hundred and fifty women named Betty formed the Betty Club and circulated a petition. Radio DJs, long known for their social concern, circulated their own petitions. An Atlanta rock band decided to call itself Betty's Not a Vitamin. Sensing that popular sentiment was turning against them, the makers of Flintstones vitamins, now known as Bayer Corporation, resolved to put things right, provided they could make a couple bucks in the process. They launched a "Find Betty" promotional campaign, offering big prizes if you could find "icons" of Betty (although apparently not an actual vitaminic representation) in specially marked packages of Flintstones chewables. They also asked the American public to vote on whether Betty should get into the bottle on a permanent basis. "Vote?" Americans asked. "We're supposed to vote on fundamental questions of justice? Hey, why not?" Bayer set up "prehistoric voting booths" (I didn't ask) at malls in major markets and also launched an 800 number.

Final results: 15,281 in favor, 1,492 against. Betty was in. Since something else had to go to make room, a Bayer spokesman said, "we decided to bag the car." Unanswered question: who are these 1,492 jerks who voted no?

One last thing. The Bayer PR folks traced the genesis of the "Where's Betty?" movement and say it all began with a 1994 mention in *Spy* magazine. Nothing against *Spy*, but this is a crock. My column about Betty was reprinted in *More of the Straight Dope* in 1988. But what can you expect? Sometimes I'm so far ahead of the curve I get there before they even open the ballpark.

Is it true that, as my father says, companies that produced maps (Rand McNally, etc.) make up some little bitty towns and dot them around their map design so they can tell if anyone copies it? Has anyone ever gotten lost trying to find one of those made-up towns?—Susan Owen, College Station, Texas

You are talking about "copyright traps." They are devious. They exist. In a world of high-level conspiracies that are completely imaginary, it's a relief to discover one that's not.

For the record, the folks at Rand McNally swear on a stack of road atlases that they would never use copyright traps. However, they admit a small regional map company called Champion they acquired a while back did put a trap into a map on at least one occasion. The trap consisted of a nonexistent street stuck into a map of a medium-size city in New York state—a fact that was gleefully revealed on a network news show.

On investigating, Rand McNally found some smart-aleck cartographer (and you know what a wacky bunch they are) had gone ahead and done the wicked deed entirely on his own. Whether the guy committed other cartographic sabotage I do not know. But the possibility of additional fakery does exist—and may for a while, since checking every detail of a map is a huge job. Not that I'd get into a panic about it, but on your next road trip you might want to bring a flashlight just in case.

Nowheresville

I thought you'd like to know a little more about the often-discussed but never officially acknowledged practice of putting copyright traps on commercial maps. The closest I've ever come to finding such a trap is the fictional town of Westdale, which appears on the 1982 Rand McNally Road Atlas map of metro Chicago. By 1986 it had disappeared.

I also enclose some illustrations from Mark Monmonier's book How to Lie with Maps, *which show some phony towns added to a map of Ohio as a prank.—Dennis McClendon, Chicago*

It happened to Brigadoon, why not Westdale? Although I have to say the industrial suburbs west of Chicago seem like an unpromising locale for an enchanted vanishing village. The folks at Rand McNally claim it was all an honest mistake. They say a real estate developer submitted a plan for a community called Westdale that was approved but never built. Somehow this found its way into the Rand McNally Road Atlas and years went by before anybody noticed.

This story is slightly fishy; the area in question, though unincorporated, was built up decades ago. But a Rand McNally spokesman reasonably inquires, "Why would we put in copyright traps and then not tell anybody they were there?" If one assumes the main value of traps is deterrence, good question.

Errors of this sort apparently happen fairly often. In his book Mark Monmonier shows several "paper streets"—planned but not built—on an official map of Syracuse, New York.

Of course, when it comes to map errors, you can't overlook the possibility of a little good-natured sabotage. Monmonier mentions two prank towns appearing in an official map of Michigan, the edge of which showed portions of the neighboring state of Ohio. Some diehard Wolverine fan in the mapmaking department decided that would be a good place to put the nonexistent towns of "Goblu" (Go Blue, get it?) and "Beatosu," referring to the University of Michigan's traditional rival Ohio State. If you had to spend all day staring at squiggly lines and benday dots, you'd need some way to let off steam, too.

Map Traps: The Smoking Gun At Last

Perhaps the enclosed clipping will put an end to any agnosticism about map companies inventing fictitious geographic detail for copyright purposes.—Robert Carlson, Los Angeles

Reader Carlson encloses a clipping from the March 22, 1981, *Los Angeles Times* about the Thomas Brothers map company, which publishes maps of southern California. The article says:

"[Thomas Brothers vice president Barry Elias admits] that the company sprinkles fictitious names throughout its guides. . . . 'We put them in for copyright reasons,' he said. 'If someone is reproducing one of our maps (as with a photocopier) and selling them, we can prove an infringement.'

"Of course, the make-believe streets are little ones. The mythical avenues normally run no longer than a block, dead end, and are shown with broken lines (as though they are under construction).

"Elias revealed that the guides for San Bernadino and Riverside counties have the heaviest concentration of fictitious streets— 'between 100 and 200. . . . We try to come up with names that would fit in with the area [such as La Taza Drive and Loma Drive]. . . . Spanish-sounding names are very big now.' "

So that accounts for all those lost-looking folks you see around L.A. The grim effects of drugs? Nah. Thomas maps.

Come To Think Of It, They Look Pretty Lost In Wisconsin, Too

Looking at a recent map of Madison I noticed that it showed a friend's house was located in a city park, and didn't show another park at all. So I called the map company [Badger Map, Wonder Lake, Illinois], and they were quite straightforward in pointing out that errors are intentionally introduced to protect the copyright on their maps. —Dennis W. Gordon, Madison, Wisconsin

So there we have it. And now I may as well come clean. Every time I publish a book a few subverters of public order write in to point out what they claim are mistakes. Mistakes, my arse. Copyright traps.

From The Straight Dope Message Board

Subj: Jamie Lee Curtis
From: DisRob
Is Jamie Lee Curtis a hermaphrodite? Please explain. It seems half the U.S. population has heard this. The other half says, "No way!"

From: Magik4U2
Jamie Lee Curtis is not a hermaphrodite although she is unusual genetically. My wife's obstetrician told us about it and explained it in detail because I was interested. I got the impression that this was common knowledge in the obstetric community.

From: JILLGAT
WHAT is common knowledge, for godsakes?

From: LAKendall
What I have heard is that she isn't a she, genetically, at all. All embryos start out looking female—that's the basic stock—but those with

a Y chromosome develop male characteristics. Some males (XY chromosome carriers) don't develop the external sex organs, staying apparently female. The problem is only noticed at puberty, when the girl doesn't start getting periods. Though these people are sterile, they're often terrifically attractive—they become tall, slim-hipped, and a fascinating blend of masculine and feminine.

From: KTchai

What's the clinical term for it?

From: BMaffitt

Testicular feminization is the term for at least one possible condition she could be suffering from. Don't know if that's what she has (if she, in fact, has anything).

From: Wdpat

I have a feeling most females would like to look as asexual as Jamie Lee Curtis.

From: Guenever1

Did he just say that Jamie Lee is or isn't a hermaphrodite???

Hermaphrodites have both copulatory organs (I thought), but not always breasts. Now, does she have a . . . a . . . well . . . you know . . . a . . . that thing . . . oh God, I can't believe I'm saying this:

Does she have a peeny or a woo-woo or both?

From: JKFabian

Woo-woo? Guen, thanks so much for increasing my vocabulary today. "Down there" just wasn't cutting it.

From: Guenever1

You're quite welcome. Always happy to help.

From: WilsonSA

I remember reading an article about Jamie Curtis that mentioned that arriving guests to a party were surprised to see her strip naked and change in public. Presumably, they didn't notice anything out of the ordinary or we would have seen the headline in the *Enquirer*.

From: Shebu44

That's assuming all the other guests at the party were "normal," which is always a subjective term.

From: WilsonSA

It was Hollywood.

From: Ezotti

There you go.

From: ChiGirl676

An interesting side note to all this is when she was on David Letterman the other night she mentioned that both of her children are adopted. Granted there are many reasons for adopting children, but it would fit in with her possible genetic oddities.

From: PaulWalto

I would still consider JLC an extraordinarily beautiful and sexy °woman° even if it were proved that she was genetically a kangaroo.

From: Songbird61

Let's put this to rest, kids . . .

I went to the same college as Jamie Lee (University of the Pacific in Stockton, CA) . . . and through the normal kinds of things that go on in dormitories, I can assure you she has all the normal female attributes and that's all. Most of us wished we had her attributes . . .

From: Wheatley

Jamie Lee Curtis has testicular feminization, or androgen insensitivity syndrome. She has XY sex chromosomes, and is therefore °genetically° male. Patients such as this have testicles, though they generally remain undescended, or in the abdominal cavity. In this position, they pose a great risk of malignant transformation, and are therefore removed at the time of diagnosis. Other than that, there is no "male organ" (as a previous response termed it) to remove. The reason is that females develop their external sexual characteristics as a result of absence of the testosterone levels seen in men (women, obviously, have a much lower level). In androgen insensitivity, the target cells for testosterone (an androgen) are insensitive to the hormone. Hence the name. So the testicles pump out the testosterone just like any good boy's should, but the cells that are supposed to get the signal don't recognize it. The patient therefore develops female sex characteristics—breasts, vulva, and the external two-thirds of the vagina, which ends in a blind pouch. There is no cervix, uterus, or fallopian tubes present (these require an XX genotype). Therefore, as stated in a previous post, these patients are recognized generally when they fail to menstruate.

You may have heard something about this during the recent Olympic games. Testing for athletes' genetic sex is now commonplace, and sometimes the results surprise everyone. It's not uncommon for young women athletes to have amenorrhea (not menstruate) as a result of their physical and dietary habits, so the condition might go undiagnosed longer in this set of people. It is also said that women with testicular feminization are taller and more athletic in build, and therefore perhaps there are disproportionate numbers of them among young women athletes. And they are women; girls; female. They are raised that way, they function that way, and there is no reason to call them otherwise (just take a look at JLC). To do so would just unnecessarily stigmatize them. For the same reason, the term androgen insensitivity is preferred to testicular feminization, and, when discussing the condition with a patient, the term "gonad" is used instead of "testicle." I'm sure it is traumatic enough to learn you're not every bit as female as you thought you were.

From: PMuste

So, Wheatley, you're saying she really is a kangaroo?

From: CecilAdams

Fun's fun, kids, but let's get serious. The sole evidence for the belief that Jamie Lee Curtis suffers from hermaphroditism, testicular feminization, or what have you is that:

1. She has slim hips.
2. Her kids are adopted.

Not to cast aspersions on any of the contributors above, but they had better evidence at the Salem witchcraft trials. I'm not about to call up Ms. Curtis and ask because, first, I would have every expectation of being told to buzz off; second, if she did answer and denied the story, no one would believe her; and third, it is no damn business of mine or yours anyway.

Then again, maybe I'm just being old-fashioned. Maybe NOBODY should have secrets. Tell you what, Wheatley, pull down your pants and let Dr. Tyson take a look.

A Scientific Bent

Everyone is familiar with Teflon, that nonstick surface no self-respecting housewife can do without. If'n it works so well slippin' and slidin' yer flapjacks, how do they get it to stick to the pan in the first place?—Richard Lavine, via the Internet

Smart-aleck radio hosts think this one is sooo funny. Obviously they don't remember the first Teflon pans in the 1960s, which required special nonscratchy cooking utensils, lest you scrape the Teflon off.

Fact is, the reaction when Teflon was invented pretty much consisted of, "Whoa, Teflon, the nonstick miracle! So tell us, genius, how do we make it stick to the pan?"

Teflon, known to science as polytetrafluoroethylene, is a pain to work with because it's nonsticky in all directions, the pan side (the bottom) as well as the food side (the top). Teflon is a fluorinated polymer, a polymer being a passel of identical building-block molecules linked together to make a long chain—the stuff of most plastics. Fluorine, due to certain electrochemical properties you'll thank me for not explaining now, bonds so tightly with the carbon in Teflon that it's virtually impossible for other substances, e.g., scrambled egg crud, to get a chemical-type grip or, for that matter, for Teflon to get a grip on anything else. In addition, the finished Teflon surface is extremely smooth, giving said egg crud little chance to get a mechanical-type grip.

So how do they get Teflon to stick to the pan? First they sandblast the pan to create a lot of microscratches on its surface. Then they spray on a coat of Teflon primer. This primer, like most primers, is thin, enabling it to flow into the the microscratches. The primed surface is then baked at high heat, causing the Teflon to solidify and get a reasonably secure mechanical grip. Next you spray on a finish coat and bake that. (The Teflon finish coat will stick to the Teflon primer coat just fine.) Works a lot better than the early Teflon pans, but you can still ruin Teflon cookware by subjecting it to extremely high heat. This causes the bonds between some of the carbon atoms to break, giving other undesirable stuff a chance to bond thereto and making the Teflon look like Jeff Goldblum in the last reel of *The Fly*.

Scientists continue to search for something better, and recent reports suggest they may have succeeded. Dow Chemical researcher Donald Schmidt has come up with another fluorinated polymer that can be used like paint and cured with moderate (as opposed to high) heat. Even better, you wind up with a coating that's nonsticky on only one side, presumably the outside. The only drawback: Schmidt's coating won't withstand heat. That doesn't matter if you're trying to make, say, graffiti-proof wall tile, but don't look for Schmidtlon-coated frying pans anytime soon.

I'm enclosing an article that poses a question that had never occurred to me before: Why is the night sky dark? According to the author of the article, Robert Cowen, "the traditional answer holds that the universe is expanding so fast that light from the distant stars is degraded and thinly spread." Another theory suggests, "the darkness is better explained by the simple fact that the universe is of finite age. Galaxies have not had time to flood the sky with starlight." Excuse me, but aren't we overlooking the obvious here?—Bill, Nanaimo, British Columbia

This is one of those questions so bizarre that only serious drugs or an astronomer could be behind it. But it's not as nutty as it might seem. We can rule out one obvious answer right off the bat: the night sky isn't dark merely because the sun goes down. The stars alone ought to be enough to make the night sky intensely bright.

Think about it this way. If we assume the universe contains an infinity of stars scattered in endless space, we should see a star in any direction we look. It's like being in the middle of a forest—all you can see in any direction is tree trunks. The sky should be so completely filled with pinpoints of light that they should all merge into a uniform white glow.

Clearly it doesn't work that way, a puzzle astronomers call "Olbers's paradox." Why not? We can nix a few possibilities:

- *The light emitted by the most distant stars is so faint it's below the threshold of vision.* Forget it. You can't see an individual glowing atom, but you can see zillions of them massed together in a candle flame. The same ought to hold true of a horde of distant stars.
- *The most distant stars are obscured by interstellar dust.* Won't work either. The dust would absorb so much light it'd eventually start glowing itself.

So what does explain the paradox? After 400 years of debate on the question, there is now fairly wide agreement among astronomers: there just aren't enough stars in the observable universe to fill up the night sky.

Your reaction to this may be: It took scientists 400 years to come up with *that*? No wonder we still haven't found a cure for the common cold. But I'm making the answer seem simpler than it is. We don't really know how many stars there are. What we do know is that however many there are, we can see only a finite number of them.

The oldest stars are about 10 billion years old, meaning that the greatest distance starlight can have traveled is 10 billion light-years. So the only stars we could possibly see are those within a 10 billion light-year radius of us—the light from stars farther away has yet to reach us. The few jillion stars in our corner of the cosmos (aka the "observable universe") don't have the collective candlepower to illuminate the night sky. (True, as time goes on, light from more distant stars does reach us, but meanwhile some close-in stars are dying out.)

So that's why the night sky is dark. All right, it's a complicated way of telling you what you might have guessed anyway. But sometimes the obvious ain't.

Is it true that cow, sheep, and termite flatulence does more damage to the ozone layer than fluorocarbons? How much damage do human farts do?—Mojo, Washington, D.C.

I'm glad you wrote, Moe, because it gives me another chance to point out the sad decline in reporting skills in the daily press. You were no doubt moved to write by a story in the *Washington Post* headlined FEED, ANIMAL FLATULENCE AND ATMOSPHERE. It described the work of one Donald Johnson, an animal-nutrition specialist at Colorado State University, who supposedly has been studying cow flatulence. According to the story, animal flatulence "contributes in a large way to the potentially catastrophic warming of the globe, the 'green-

house effect.' " Each cow emits 200 to 400 quarts of methane gas per day, or 50 million metric tons per year.

Only trouble is, cows *don't* emit 400 quarts of flatulence a day. According to Professor Johnson, they emit 400 quarts' worth of *burps*, known in polite circles as eructation. The *Post*, in other words, doesn't know one end of a cow from the other! And this is the paper that broke Watergate—although, to be fair, I don't suppose they assign their top reportorial resources to the cow burp beat.

Details aside, animal methane does present a definite threat to the biota. It's believed 18 percent of the greenhouse effect is caused by methane, putting it second on the list of offending gases behind carbon dioxide. Methane breaks down in the atmosphere to form carbon dioxide, ozone, and water, all of which absorb heat. The temperature of the atmosphere rises, the ice caps melt, and next thing you know you're pumping the Atlantic Ocean out of your basement.

There are several major sources of methane: rice paddies (methane-producing bacteria thrive in the underwater environment), swamps and wetlands (ditto), mining and oil drilling, landfills, termites (although there's still some controversy on this one), "biomass burning" (notably in the Amazon rain forest), and animals. Ninety percent of animal methane is produced by ruminants (i.e., cud-chewers). These include sheep, goats, camels, water buffalo, and so on, but most of all cattle, of which the world has an estimated 1.2 billion.

Ruminants eat hay and grass and stuff containing cellulose, which can be digested only by special microbes that live in the ruminants' guts. Unfortunately, the microbes are sloppy eaters, and about 6 or 7 percent of what they consume winds up as methane. Thus the problem.

Now, you're probably saying, what the hey, cows have been around forever, how come all of a sudden they're a threat? All we know is this: atmospheric methane has been increasing at the alarming rate of 1 percent a year, and something's got to be causing it. The world cattle population is thought to have increased in the last decade, and Lord knows the Brazilians don't feel like taking any more heat for torching the Amazon. So hey, let's blame the cows.

Is there hope? Professor Johnson thinks a timely application of antibiotics in cattle feed could retard the microbes' methane production. But by and large antibiotics are already in use in the United

States, while in many third-world countries cattle forage out in the fields, making antibiotics difficult to administer.

In other words, we've got still another largely insoluble problem that threatens to end life as we know it. Sometimes I just wish one of these looming disasters would go ahead and happen, just to end the suspense.

Two questions. 1) Why do you blow on hot coffee to cool it, but you blow on your hands in winter to warm them up? 2) How come vegetables have no fat, but vegetable oil is 100 percent fat?—Dick Wolfsie, WIBC, Indianapolis

You broadcast guys are such a pain. But when you're a person such as myself who is single-handedly keeping the book industry afloat, you do what you gotta to promote the product.

1. I suppose we could get into the physics of heat transfer. Then again, try this: your breath (98 degrees F or thereabouts) is cooler than the coffee, so the coffee cools. It's warmer than your near-frostbitten hands (perilously close to 32 degrees F), so your hands get warm. Any other questions?
2. Vegetables are low fat, but they're not *no* fat. Any living cell has fat in its cell membranes and elsewhere. In vegetables the fat content typically is less than 1 percent, but it's higher in the seeds, from which most vegetable oils are made. Some vegetables are pretty fatty even if we ignore the seeds—olives and avocados, for example. Olive oil is one of the few types of vegetable oil that is made from the flesh of the plant, as opposed to the seed. They'd probably make avocado oil from the flesh, too, if there were any market for avocado oil, which there isn't. Be that as it may, the fat storage bodies in avocado flesh are what makes it smooth and creamy.

Complaints

In reference to your column about blowing on coffee to cool it: You blow on coffee to cool it not because your breath is cooler than the coffee but rather to induce convection cooling. Your blowing on it removes

the hot air from directly above the coffee and replaces it with cooler air from the environment, thus speeding up the cooling process in the same way a convection oven speeds up the heating process.—Samuel Pullara, Chicago

Your explanation of the blow hot/blow cold question is, dare I say it, full of hot air. It's all in how you blow. Here's why. When you warm your hands, you blow steadily with your mouth open. This allows a greater volume of warm air to reach your cold hands. But to cool a hot cup of coffee, you first pucker. This causes the air to do interesting things before it reaches your cup: 1) The narrower opening reduces the volume of gas that escapes. 2) The increased pressure compresses the air. 3) The velocity of the escaping air increases. According to Boyle's law . . . at a constant temperature the volume of a definite mass of gas is inversely proportional to the pressure [blah, blah]. When a gas is allowed to expand adiabatically through a porous plug the temperature of the gas changes. This rate of change is known as the Joule-Thompson differential [blah, blah]. As the rapidly expanding air leaves your mouth, it sweeps along neighboring molecules by adhesion (Van der Waals force) [blah, blah]. Thus we . . . see that air that normally blows hot ceases to do so whenever it is compressed and allowed to expand. Isn't science fun? [Two single-spaced pages, two equations, one poem deleted.]—*Michael Godfrey, Cupertino, California*

Science *is* fun, Mike, and whatever it is you're doing, that's fun, too. I know this because when I showed your comments to the Straight Dope Science Advisory Board they laughed. Suffice it to say no one believes you can pressurize air significantly by puckering your lips.

Pullara's objection is more serious. I've gotten several similar notes. Here's another: "You are forgetting that the latent heat of vaporization of water is very high. When you blow on your coffee, you replace the vapor-laden air above the coffee with dry air, allowing evaporation to proceed at the maximum possible rate. The temperature of your breath is not important. The coffee is not cooling by conduction of heat directly to the air but by shedding heat in the steam that comes off the coffee."

Cecil was skeptical that the temperature of your breath was unimportant, as indeed he was obliged to be, since it was the heart and soul of his answer. So, having consulted on the net, I retired to the Straight Dope Laboratory and Kitchen of Tomorrow and performed an experiment. I heated a cup of water to boiling, stuck in a candy thermometer, started the timer, and noted the temperature every 60 seconds. It took 25 minutes for the water to cool down to 100 degrees F. (I noted the whole thing on graph paper. I can be very professional when I want to be.) Then I did the same thing again, only this time I set up Mrs. Adams's hair dryer so that it directed a stream of air over the water. With the dryer on the "cool" setting (85 degrees F), low speed, the boiled water dropped to 100 degrees F in under seven minutes. Then I repeated the process with the dryer at the "hot" setting (180 degrees F). The water dropped to 100 degrees F in under eight minutes. Conclusion: the temperature of the airstream (e.g., your breath) isn't irrelevant, but it's pretty damn close. To confirm, I did the experiment yet again, only this time I directed the airstream directly at the water, as opposed to over it. Contrary to what my theory compelled me to predict, the water cooled off even faster, reaching 100 degrees F in less than four minutes with the dryer on the "cool" setting and under five minutes on "hot."

In sum, your breath does *not* cool the coffee because it's cooler than the coffee; it cools it because it increases the coffee's rate of evaporation. It takes a big man to admit a mistake, and I will. Get on up there, little Ed, and tell them it was your fault.

Here's a question that's bugged me for all eternity: is time travel possible, even in theory?—Jan K., Baltimore, Maryland

Cecil's gut feeling on this question was no, based on the following logic: if it were possible, the people of the future would have done it; and if they did, why haven't they shown up yet? But then I thought: come on, is this a century *you'd* want to come back to?

The possibilities of deductive reasoning thus having been pretty much exhausted, I consulted the Straight Dope Science Advisory Board. While the question is far from settled, a few optimists do think time travel may be possible. In fact, a widely noted paper was published a few years ago proposing a hypothetical time machine. The machine requires some outrageous theoretical leaps, though, and the technology is totally beyond our present capabilities. So don't start making plans to visit the Pleistocene era just yet.

The centerpiece of the hypothetical time machine, which was proposed by physicists Kip Thorne, Michael Morris, and Ulvi Yurtsever, is something called a "wormhole." A wormhole is a place where the space-time continuum is so warped it basically doubles back on itself, creating a cosmic shortcut. (Think of it as a tunnel between two points on an apple, the surface of the apple being the ordinary space-time continuum.) Up till now the only known way a wormhole could be created was inside a black hole. But these wormholes were of a cheesy quality and tended to collapse too quickly to be usable. Also, since they're in black holes, once you get in you can't get out.

That's where we get to Great Leap #1. Thorne et al. propose (rather cavalierly, as we shall see) that a black hole–less wormhole could simply be plucked from the "quantum foam." The quantum foam is the microlevel of the universe beneath which things are so small we can't observe them. Since we have no idea what's going on down there, there's no reason to think the usual laws of physics apply. So Thorne and friends say, hey, let's assume that at quantum level, freestanding wormholes exist. Fine, it's a free country. But then they say, now let's assume the holes can be enlarged to usable size. How? God knows. But theoretical physicists pride themselves in not getting hung up on details.

Then we get to Great Leap #2. To keep your enlarged wormhole from collapsing, you need to brace it with special weird materials that would give it negative mass and energy. Only problem is, physicists aren't so sure you can have negative mass and energy, except under exotic circumstances. No problem. With a few deft equations, Thorne and company calmly suggest circumstances don't get much more exotic than this. Negative M&E it is.

All right, suppose we have our stable wormhole, with the two mouths located near each other. While keeping Mouth A stationary, we accelerate Mouth B to near the speed of light, then bring it back to its starting point. (Don't ask how we do this; it's Great Leap #3.) According to the Theory of Special Relativity, this causes Mouth B to age less than Mouth A. Mouth B may thus be said to have been yanked into the future. (Take my word for it.) By traveling through the wormhole from Mouth A to Mouth B we travel forward in time, and by going from B to A we travel backward.

Thornean time travel has its limitations. You can use a wormhole to travel into the future and back, but you can't travel into the past. Furthermore, you won't necessarily get those time travel paradoxes so beloved of sci-fi writers. (You know: if you went back in time and killed your grandmother, you would never have been born, but if you weren't born, you couldn't have killed your grandmother, and so you *would* have been born . . . you get the idea.)

"Causality violation," as it's called, would totally kibosh our current understanding of how the universe works, and a lot of physicists hope desperately that it can be shown to be impossible. In fact, if no way can be gotten around it, a lot of them have half a mind to rule out the possibility of time travel altogether. Physicists can be pretty wild and crazy sometimes, as the above wormhole exercise shows. But other times they're no fun at all.

Since people living close to the poles are moving much more slowly than people living at the equator, isn't it true that a person near the pole will age faster than someone at the equator due to the effects of the theory of relativity?—Jim U., Washington, D.C.

Ordinarily I don't have time for this kind of thing, but I couldn't find a magazine in the john this morning. As near as I can figure, people age the same at the pole and at the equator, mainly because of relativistic effects that cancel each other out.

Here's how it works:

1. Due to the rotation of the earth, people at the equator are moving at about 1,000 miles an hour, while those at the poles are more or less stationary.
2. Special relativity tells us that for any inertial (i.e., nonaccelerating) observer, moving objects seem to age more slowly.
3. Objects at the equator of a rotating sphere are *not* inertial, since they undergo continual acceleration toward the center of the

earth. If they didn't, they would fly off on a straight line into space. (Think about it.)

4. Ergo, a person at the pole may legitimately consider that a person at the equator is aging more slowly, but not vice versa. (This may seem like an odd way of putting it, but the theoretical physicists out there will know what I mean.) However:

5. The earth bulges at the equator due to centrifugal force.

6. The pull of gravity decreases the farther you get from the center of the earth.

7. General (as opposed to special) relativity tells us the farther you are from the point of max gravity (i.e., the center of the earth), the more quickly you age. Thus you age faster on a mountaintop than in a valley (which serves all those rich croutons in Beverly Hills right).

8. Therefore, since people at the equator are farther from the center of the earth, they age faster.

9. The special relativistic effect in #4 exactly cancels the general relativistic effect in #8. In other words, people at the pole and at the equator age at the same rate. Exactly what you would have guessed if you had an IQ of 1! But at least we're right for the right reason.

How does one suck in a piece of spaghetti? Think about it. How one sucks milk through a straw is easy. The lowered pressure in the mouth due to sucking causes the air pressure over the milk to force the liquid up. But if one pushes on the end of a piece of spaghetti it just buckles. The mouth is closed and sealed over the sides of the spaghetti, so passing air doesn't drag it along. Somehow the air very close to the mouth must obliquely communicate a force along the length, and it's far from clear how it's possible.—Berg [I guess; kind of scrawled], El Cerrito, California

You're thinking, this is the lamest question Cecil has ever answered. However, this is because you lack an appreciation of the scientific issues. I blame myself.

It took me a while to get the regulars on the Usenet newsgroup sci.physics to focus on this, too. Apart from the one lamer who said the partial vacuum inside your mouth exerted a positive force that pulled the spaghetti in, most reasoned as follows:

1. Air pressure is customarily conceived of as acting perpendicularly to the surface on which it bears. In other words, it presses straight down.
2. Air pressure at any point on the side of a strand of spaghetti is exactly counteracted by the air pressure on the opposite side.
3. The one place where the air pressure is not counteracted is on the end of the spaghetti. The pressure on the outside end is much greater than the pressure on the inside (mouth) end.
4. Therefore, the force on the spaghetti is equal to outside air pressure minus the pressure inside your mouth times the cross section of the spaghetti.

You're not getting this, I said. I know *how much* pressure is exerted. What I want to know is *where* it's exerted, since it seems pretty obvious that literally pressing on the end of a strand of limp spaghetti doesn't do jack.

What do we care where it's exerted? said the sci.physics regulars. We are scientists. We deal in the world of quantifiable effects. It is enough to know that the air bears somewhere, and that the pressure differential in aggregate is some mathematically determinable amount, as a consequence whereof the spaghetti is sucked, or rather forced, into your mouth.

Freaking gearheads, I said. Screw the mathematics. I want to know, *what is actually happening at the level of individual particles?*

"Heisenberg tells us . . . ," the sci.physics types began.

Screw Heisenberg, I replied.

Finally a few of the scientific types conceded that the question had a certain practical interest. After some discussion we concluded that whereas it is customary to think of air as pressing straight down, most individual air particles, in fact, strike the surface of the spaghetti obliquely. Those particles striking the spaghetti close to the point where it entered the mouth, and whose vector had some inward-pushing component, would force it in. Exactly how close to the mouth the particles would have to hit would of course depend on whether the spaghetti was *al dente* or boiled to within an inch of its life. You want to take it up with the sci.physics crowd, be my guest.

Sucking Up

Mama mia, Cecil! The sci.physics crowd's pathetic shot at explaining how anyone can suck up spaghetti makes one wonder why our tax dollars are still subsidizing hopeless efforts at science education. We might as well be funding pictures of naked thermocouples.

These wonks have missed the point entirely. Spaghetti sucking is not merely a function of the difference in pressure between the outside of the mouth and the inside. You can easily recognize this using a simple thought experiment. Imagine that a physicist—Erwin Schroedinger will do as an example—places the end of a strand of cooked spaghetti in his mouth. Then, instead of sucking, imagine that he turns on a pump that rapidly increases the air pressure surrounding his head.

The air-pressure differential will, according to probability, crush Schroedinger's skull like an eggshell long before it neatly forces the limp spaghetti through his pursed lips. (I encourage any sci.physics wonks who doubt this to try the experiment at home.) Ergo, it's not just air pressure.

A closer approximation to the right answer is that the spaghetti strand has its own density and cohesion. When you suck, the difference in density between the spaghetti strand and the air inside your mouth pulls the molecules on the surface of the spaghetti into your mouth; because the spaghetti's cohesion holds it together, the rest of the spaghetti is pulled in, too. But then, I'm sure you knew that all along.—Harry Doakes, Portland, Oregon

When will I learn? I thought the spaghetti question, while not without interest, was too esoteric and useless to get much reaction, forgetting that giving the Teeming Millions a question that's esoteric and useless is like throwing the piranhas raw meat. I got rants about spaghetti sucking from every unemployed Ph.D. in North America, plus a few who aren't unemployed but who—how shall I put this?—probably ought to keep their résumés up-to-date. A sampling of alternative theories, starting with yours:

- *When you suck, there is a difference in density between the spaghetti strand and the air inside your mouth."*

  I never suck, although I have my off days. What does "a difference in density" have to do with it? There is a difference in density if the stuff just lies there on the freaking table. We're talking about spaghetti, not an ideal gas.
- *"Spaghetti isn't a solid (although one can use air pressure differential to pull a round solid into the mouth, but at nowhere near the spectacular rate at which spaghetti can be sucked, as it were) but a starchy gel and so subject to physical laws that govern both solids and liquids. When subjected to a pressure differential, the spaghetti strand necks down slightly and . . ." (Brian).*

  OK, the spaghetti isn't solid but mushy. So what? You can suck solid things, too. Cecil has been . . . well, I was about to say Cecil has been sucking various cylindrical objects, but I recognize that a certain element will find this comical. Let us pause while the lads get it out of their systems. Very well. By process of experiment, we learn that the speed at which something can be sucked depends very little on whether it's solid or spongy—mostly it's a matter of its weight relative to its cross section. I therefore feel entitled to ignore the fluidic aspects of the situation.

- *"The air pressure around the spagetti causes an internal pressure in the spagetti. At the interface between outside and inside your lips, the internal pressure of the spagetti drops; the spagetti flows down this pressure gradient" (Bruce Kline).*

  Bruce. It's "spaghetti." Quite a few people persuaded themselves that spaghetti exhibits characteristics of flow and that it somehow extrudes into your mouth. But this could not result in motion of the spaghetti without loss of structural integrity or at least permanent deformation, which does not occur, and in any case would be slow. This is spaghetti, not lava.

- *"I'm going with the dragging-it-along theory, wherein the seal of the lips around the strand is not perfect but allows some air or, more probably, a thin layer of spaghetti sauce to be sucked in, dragging the strand along with it" (J. Ebert).*

  First thing I thought of. First thing I rejected. The sauce acts as a lubricant, sure. However, from our experiments with nonpasta above, we conclude that an extremely thin film of spit is sufficient to facilitate sucking. Given the minute amount of fluid and the minimal cross section it presents, it's implausible to suggest that the sauce or whatever is the sole or even the primary medium of propulsion.

- *Cecil must be really desperate if he's consulting the noodleheads on Usenet.*

  Not at all. Cecil loves the noodleheads on Usenet. It's like consulting the regulars at the local bar. The quality of advice is easily as good, and you don't have to stand for the price of drinks.

Everybody knows 0 degrees on the Celsius scale is the freezing point of water and 100 degrees is the boiling point. On the Fahrenheit scale, however, freezing is 32 degrees and boiling 212. How on earth were these numbers arrived at? Do 0 and 100 degrees Fahrenheit mean anything?—Leslie, Montreal, Quebec

Researchers have gone to their graves trying to figure out what old man Fahrenheit was up to, Leslie. Here's the story as well as I can piece it together:

Daniel Gabriel Fahrenheit (1686–1736) was a German instrument maker who invented the first practical mercury thermometer. Casting about for a suitable scale for his device, he visited the Danish astronomer Ole Romer, who had devised a system of his own. As it turned out, it was a case of the blind leading the blind.

Romer had decided that the boiling point of water should be 60 degrees, which at least had the strength of numerological tradition behind it (60 minutes in an hour, right?). But zero was totally arbitrary, the main consideration apparently being that it should be colder than it ever got in Denmark. (Romer didn't like using negative numbers in his weather logbook.) In addition to the boiling point of water, the landmarks on Romer's scale were the freezing point of water, $7\frac{1}{2}$ degrees, and body temperature, $22\frac{1}{2}$ degrees.

D.G., simple soul that he was, thought this cockeyed system was the soul of elegance. He made one useful change: to get rid of the fractions, he multiplied Romer's degrees by 4, giving him 30 for the freezing point and 90 for body temperature. Then, for reasons nobody has ever been able to fathom, he multiplied all the numbers by 16/15, making 32 freezing and 96 body temperature. Boiling point for the time being he ignored altogether.

By and by Fahrenheit got ready to present his scale to London's Royal Society, the scientific big leagues of the day. It dawned on him that it was going to look a little strange having the zero on his scale just sort of hanging off the end, so to speak. So he cooked up the explanation that zero was the temperature of a mix of ice, water, and ammonium chloride.

At some point Fahrenheit figured out that the boiling point of water came in at 212 degrees. Over time this replaced body temp as the upper landmark on his scale. Meanwhile, as more precise measurements were made, body temperature had to be adjusted to 98.6 degrees.

In short, 100 means nothing at all on the Fahrenheit scale, 96 used to mean something but doesn't anymore, and 0 is colder than it ever gets in Denmark. Brilliant. Lest we get too down on Fahrenheit, though, consider Anders Celsius (1701–1744), who devised the centigrade scale (0 to 100). Everybody agrees Celsius's scale makes more sense than Fahrenheit's. Trouble is, the original Celsius scale had 100 for freezing, 0 for boiling. In other words, it was *upside down*. (The numbers were reversed after Celsius's death.) You look back at these guys, sometimes you don't know whether to laugh or cry.

From The Message Board

Subj: Please stand up!
From: TamBlonde

Once we go to heaven (assuming we do) and we have been wid-owed, who is our real spouse who will dwell with us for eternity—the first person we married (who died before us), or our second, third, fourth, etc.? Do we have a choice? What if they don't want us?

From: MIKE834404

If we're talking about heaven then it's gotta be the most recent spouse. If I was ever paired up in the afterlife with my ex-wife I'd have to be in hell.

From: Jaz Beau

Remember, the vow is "UNTIL DEATH do us part." So marriages end at death.

Presumably, in heaven we will know and love everyone there (and be known and loved) so much that what you have experienced in the deepest, most meaningful relationship you have ever had on earth will be revealed as only a tiny part of what you experience in heaven. It's a nice idea, anyway.

Here's one reference I found by searching the Bible on AOL for "marriage" from 22 Matthew, 23–30:

"The same day came to him the Sadducees, which say that there is no resurrection, and asked him, saying, Master, Moses said, If a man die, having no children, his brother shall marry his wife, and raise up seed unto his brother.

"Now there were with us seven brethren: and the first, when he had married a wife, deceased, and, having no issue, left his wife unto his brother: Likewise the second also, and the third, unto the seventh. And last of all the woman died also.

"Therefore in the resurrection whose wife shall she be of the seven? for they all had her.

"Jesus answered and said unto them, Ye do err, not knowing the scriptures, nor the power of God. For in the resurrection they neither marry, nor are given in marriage, but are as the angels of God in heaven."

From: Maartenvdg

After three wives here on earth, what makes you think your father's concept of heaven includes any spouse? Perhaps a large-screen TV and a never-empty cooler would do just fine.

Subj: Misunderstood song lyrics
From: LilethSC

I have a list of stupid things people thought were titles and lyrics to songs. For no good reason, I would love to hear some more. Does anyone out there have any? (Please, only real ones.)

From: Tom Arwood

I used to think "dirty deeds, done dirt cheap" was "dirty deeds, dunder jeep." Which left me wondering what a dunder jeep was.

From: SuesZ

This isn't a song, but a Chinese-American writer (I forget who) had a real cute story about learning the Pledge of Allegiance as a child, and getting the words all garbled up. She thought the last line was "with little tea and just rice for all."

I thought it was "one nation under guard," which made sense because we were at war with Vietnam, but why were we "invisible"?

From: CKDextHavn

There's also the line in "God Bless America" about "through the night, with a light, from a bulb."

From: BayBeary

Creedence Clearwater Revival ("There's a Bad Moon on the Rise"): "There's a bathroom on the right."

From: Iemmolo

When I was eight I thought the Rolling Stones's lyric "I don't wanna be your beast of burden" was "your pizza's burning."

From: JKFabian

Just saw an interview with Jon Cryer (*Pretty in Pink*, Fox TV's

Partners) where he said that he thought Steve Miller's lyric "Big old jet airliner" was "Big old Chad had a light on."

From: CHEVYCAMEO

All these responses and none listing Tom Petty's "I Was Barney Rubble" ("I Was Born A Rebel")? D'OH!!!

From: WildBabe4J

Tom Petty, "You don't have to limp like a referee."

From: Film Esq

Almost ashamed to admit this, but until about three years ago (when I was 28), I thought the tag line from the refrain of "Groovin' on a Sunday Afternoon" was, "It would be ecstasy, you and me and Leslie." One day it dawned on me that "and Leslie" was a (badly) syncopated "endlessly."

From: Nootcheez

"Return To Sender." As a child, I mistakenly thought Elvis was singing "Return To Simba." This made perfect sense to me at the time. If you remember the lyrics, they go, "address unknown." Of course it's unknown; he lives in the jungle!

From: Trindy T

I used to think "only the lonely can play" was "only the lonely get laid."

From: Editeers

Love is a nose but you better not pick it?

Chapter **12**

Why?

I read this as a tagline on the Internet, but it's still a good question: why did kamikaze pilots wear helmets?—Matt McCullar, Arlington, Texas

To keep their ears warm, goofball. As anyone acquainted with aviation or basic physics knows, the pilot's helmet has never been intended to provide protection against a crash. If the plane encounters the landscape too abruptly you're sausage no matter what you're wearing. The leather or cloth head covering worn by WWII aviators was a holdover from open cockpit days, when you needed protection against the wind and rain.

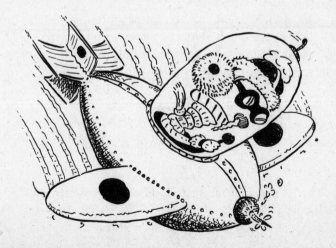

Closed cockpits had come into general use by WWII, but in the early years at least it was customary to take off and land with the canopy open, apparently (Cecil hears differing stories on this point) in the ill-founded hope that you'd be able to get clear of the plane if it nosed in while you were near the ground. Pilots also wore helmets because they held radio earphones but most of all—military bureaucracy being what it was—because regulations required it. When jets came in most air forces switched to the hardened "brain bucket" in use today, but the purpose of this was merely to protect a fighter pilot's head from being bashed against the canopy during high-speed maneuvering, not to save him in the event of a crash. Similarly, the kamikaze pilot's helmet merely helped him complete the trip, not survive it.

Why are there 360 degrees in a circle?—Listener, NPR

Cecil's assistant, little Ed, got this question the other day on a radio talk show and predictably had no clue. However, from long experience we have learned that when in doubt, blame it on the Babylonians. Sure enough, when we looked up "degree" in our *Oxford English Dictionary*, we read, "this division of the circle is very ancient, and appears to have been originally applied to the circle of the Zodiac, a *degree* being the space or distance travelled by the sun each day according to ancient Babylonian and Egyptian computation."

But wait, you say. The year has 365 days, not 360. We seem to be five degrees short.

Well, yeah. Standards of scientific measurement in those days were a little more relaxed. Besides, do you think your experience of trigonometry would have been significantly enhanced if the number of degrees in a right angle had been 91¼?

Why does the United States Surgeon General appear in a military uniform? Have they always done so? Is it because they are leading the nation's battle against disease, smokers, and ill health in general?—Jon Komatsu, Pearl City, Hawaii

The surgeon general wears a uniform because the organization of which he or she is the chief, the U.S. Public Health Service, is a uniformed service. So are mail carriers, you may say, but the postmaster

general doesn't get to dress like Horatio Hornblower. The difference is that the PHS began as the Marine Hospital Service, which was organized along military lines in 1870 to minister to merchant sailors. The members were (and still are) given military-style commissions and naval-style ranks, the idea being that they were a mobile force ready to be thrown into the fray wherever germs raised their ugly if invisible heads. One supposes the fact that MHS doctors often served alongside regular military personnel (e.g., in military camps during wars) and sometimes had to order them around also argued for ranks and uniforms. The Marine Hospital Service was reorganized as the Public Health Service in 1912 and transferred to what is now the Department of Health and Human Services, but the military trappings remain.

Some PHS officers today do lead a semimilitary-type existence, serving tours of duty on Indian reservations or in prisons and the like. But many others are longtime medical researchers at federal labs who joined the PHS rather than the civil service mainly because of the attractive retirement benefits. (You can leave with a nice pension after just 20 years.) Uniforms had fallen into disuse until C. Everett Koop was appointed surgeon general by Ronald Reagan. Koop conceived of his post as a bully pulpit and thought the uniform (the SG is the equivalent of a three-star admiral and has a similar uniform) would get people to take him more seriously. Instead, at least at the outset, it got them to take him for an airline steward, and Koop good-naturedly hoisted a few bags into the overhead bins for fellow passengers.

Eventually, though, Koop's considerable personal presence enabled him to put the uniform thing over, so much so that he decided all commissioned PHS personnel should start wearing them. This rankled the troops and Koop's successor, Joycelyn Elders, did not insist that they be worn. But one gathers they are seen more commonly on PHS officers than they used to be. The whole thing may incline us civilian scoffers to make jokes about swords and epaulets and crossed-hypodermic insignias. But Koop et al. have spoken out forcefully on such public health issues as AIDS and smoking, and if uniforms help get the message across, why not?

Why does the Ku Klux Klan burn crosses when they claim to be such gung-ho Christians? I've heard this comes from a Scottish ritual of some sort, but I shudder to think that a downhome American tradition like the Klan has actually been a subversive plot by wily Scotsmen.—Anonymous, Madison, Wisconsin

The Scottish apparently originated cross-burning, but it was your friends in the mass media who helped sell the idea to the KKK— media being somewhat broadly construed here to include novelists and filmmakers. You think media complicity in the more disreputable aspects of pop culture is a recent phenomenon? Uh-uh. Try 1810.

Eighteen-ten was the year the Scottish romantic writer Sir Walter Scott, a great admirer of ancient Scottish traditions, first brought the "fiery cross" to modern attention in his poem *The Lady of the Lake*. In the poem the cross is set ablaze on the hilltops to summon the Scottish clans. Scott's work was especially popular in the American South, where much of the populace was of Scotch-Irish extraction.

The original Ku Klux Klan, which was founded in 1866 and disbanded in the early 1870s, didn't burn crosses, but that didn't stop author Thomas Dixon from saying they did in his pro-KKK novel *The Clansman* (1905). "The Fiery Cross of old Scotland's hills!" a character in the book announces. "In olden times when the Chieftain of our people summoned the clan on an errand of life and death, the Fiery Cross, extinguished in sacrificial blood, was sent by swift courier from village to village."

Though it had done well enough on its own, *The Clansman* didn't become a national phenomenon until Dixon sold the movie rights to the pioneer filmmaker D.W. Griffith, who used it to make his ground-

breaking film *The Birth of a Nation*. In a dramatic scene, the movie's hero rears up his horse and brandishes a flaming cross to summon the Klans to drive out the black oppressors (!) and their northern white allies who controlled the South during Reconstruction. Meanwhile the movie theater's orchestra (remember, this was the silent era) struck up Wagner's "The Ride of the Valkyries." Southern white audiences generally went nuts at this point, clapping and cheering.

Knowing a good idea when he saw one, William J. Simmons, the founder of the Klan in its second incarnation (1915–1944), cobbled together a cross and burned it at a meeting of the newly established Knights of the Ku Klux Klan on Thanksgiving night, 1915, on Stone Mountain near Atlanta. Flaming crosses have been a Klan trademark ever since.

There's just one problem: the fiery cross of Scottish legend wasn't the upright Roman cross commonly used by the Klan. Rather it was the X-shaped cross of St. Andrew. St. Andrew is the patron saint of Scotland, and an X-shaped cross probably was a lot easier to make a signal bonfire out of. But nobody ever said the Klan's big attraction was its meticulous sense of detail.

Where does the name Ku Klux Klan come from? It seems the men who founded the original Klan were tossing out ideas for a name when somebody came up with *kukloi*, plural of the Greek *kuklos*, "circle." Somebody else came up with the bright idea of twisting *kuklos* into Ku Klux. Klan was added later for alliteration, and they spelled it with a K rather than a C so as not to confuse the rank and file.

Burning Issues

I just read your column on the Scottish origin of cross-burning by the Ku Klux Klan and would like to make a few clarifications. While I do not believe it was your intention, your article seems to imply that Scots were a bunch of bloodthirsty cross-burners. This is not the case at all. The flames were never doused in "sacrificial blood"; rather, each family representative would cast a torch into the fire to announce they had arrived. The flames went out on their own when the timbers had been consumed. This tradition is still performed at the Grandfather Mountain, North Carolina, Scottish Festival every July.

Granted, people of Scottish and Irish descent settled mostly in the southern United States, which explains much of the violence in the history of that region (see Celtic Origins in Southern Violence, *Dr. John Pancake, University of Alabama). However, I can assure you that there is not now, nor has there ever been any connection between the highland clans of Scotland and the KKK.—William Speir, Jr., Plano, Texas*

Why do people, before opening a carbonated drink that has been shaken, tap the top of the can with their finger so that it doesn't explode upon opening?' I have always laughed at this. After lengthy arguments, we even performed a semiscientific experiment by shaking a drink and opening it with and without tapping the top, but with no solid scientific conclusion. We would like to know what you, in your infinite wisdom, think of this.—Benjie Balser, Dallas, Texas

This is not a problem that requires infinite wisdom, Benj. This is a problem that requires enough neural organization to qualify as a vertebrate, apparently a stretch for some folks these days.

First I called the folks at Coke central in Atlanta. I did this in the interest of thoroughness, in case Coke physicists had discovered quantum mechanical aspects of beverage carbonation that had previously eluded the notice of science. However, they didn't return my calls. There are two possible explanations for this: 1) everybody was out in the plant stamping out souvenir Olympic bottles, or 2) Cecil's message was a little too detailed. This is an inherent risk in my business. If you tell some low-level gatekeeper type you have a question about poultry, you actually may get through. Tell them you want to know which end of the egg comes out of the chicken first, and they'll have security trace the call.

No matter. First let's consider the matter from a theoretical perspective. Carbonation is produced by forcing carbon dioxide into solution with H_2O under pressure. Shake up the can and you create thousands of micro-size bubbles. Each bubble offers a tiny surface where CO_2 can rapidly come out of solution, creating the potential for explosive fizzing should you open the can prematurely. Wait a while though, and the bubbles will float to the top of the can and disappear, and eventually all will be as before.

But suppose you're the impatient type. You tap the can. What, pray tell, is this supposed to accomplish? Are we going to noodge the tiny bubbles to the surface faster, after the manner of herding cows? Are we going to maybe dislodge a few bubbles that have stuck to the sides of the can? Maybe we are, but the difference is slight. Open that baby and you're still going to get a faceful of froth.

We confirmed this to our satisfaction out in the Straight Dope Back Yard of Science with a half-dozen cans of pop. OK, so I didn't replicate my results 50,000 times. I figure if extraordinary claims demand extraordinary evidence, stupid claims demand . . . well, something a little less rigorous.

I should tell you that when I had little Ed broach this issue recently on the Usenet he heard from a science teacher, among others, who insisted tapping the can really did reduce fizzing and bragged about a

classroom demonstration he did to make just this point. No wonder today's youth are going to the dogs. But to be sure, I called up physicist Jearl Walker, who's written about the physics of beverage carbonation in *Scientific American*. Jearl, you'll remember, is the guy who used to plunge his hand into a vat of molten lead as a classroom demonstration of the Leidenfrost effect. This makes him either a madman or a genius—in either case, somebody you want to listen to with respect.

Jearl had heard similar claims about the efficacy of tapping and had a similar reaction: these guys are nuts. He said he could only attribute the persistence of the practice to the same suppressed macho ethic that makes people tap the ends of their cigarettes before lighting up.

If you want a real solution, try this. It's an implacable fact that a warm can of pop that's all shook up will fizz more than a shaken cold can. If you absolutely must pop the top on that jug of Jolt, stick it in the fridge first. You'll chill the contents and chill the carbonation, too, an inevitable consequence of increased gas solubility and Charles's law.

Tap Dancing, Part One

You missed the most obvious explanation for tapping on a soda can: tapping takes time, and with the passage of time the CO_2 goes back into solution.—Jonathan Cook, via the Internet

You raise a legitimate point, a sufficiently rare occurrence in these parts that I went right out to the Back Yard of Science to do another experiment. I got two cans of Coke Classic at room temp and shook them each vigorously 60 times. Setting both on the pavement, I opened one immediately and got a good-size gusher of froth. Then I waited 60 seconds and opened the other one. There was no gushing to speak of. Mind you, I had done no tapping.

So you may well be right that what tapping chiefly does is kill time, an issue to which I perhaps gave inadequate attention in my original column. But that doesn't change my main point, which is that tapping per se doesn't do squat.

In your column about tapping Coke cans to reduce fizzing, you said people did this because of "the same suppressed macho ethic that makes people tap the ends of their cigarettes before lighting up." Have you never smoked? As an occasional smoker, I learned as a teen the importance of "packing" one's cigarettes before smoking. "Packing" is the process of compressing the tobacco toward the filter end, ensuring smooth burning. Unpacked cigarettes may burn unevenly, which can cause the cherry, or lit portion, to fall off. This process is usually accomplished by tapping the unopened pack repeatedly on the filter end, but an alternative method is to tap an individual cigarette before striking. (I use my watch face as the striking surface.)—Paul Krieg, via the Internet

I don't believe this. Next you'll be telling me you bury knots at crossroads to get rid of warts.

In a halfhearted attempt to be scientific I bought a pack of cigarettes. I tapped a couple and compared them with some untapped samples. The difference was slight.

Not being a smoker and having no desire to start for the sake of something this ridiculous, I didn't light up to see what practical result my tapping may have had. But I did call up a couple of major tobacco companies, and I also had this question posted to the Usenet. The result, if we eliminate certain extraneous data points, was unanimous agreement that I was right. The most anyone could offer by way of an excuse for this practice was that it may be a throwback to the days of hand-rolled cigarettes.

The best reply came from Bill Penrose of Aurora, Illinois:

"The reason people tap cigarettes is because Humphrey Bogart did it. It is one of the rich vocabulary of gestures that cigarettes allow you to make:

"1. Tapping cigarettes on end: Suave, sophisticated.

"2. Throwing cigarettes on ground and grinding it out: I'm about to do something significant.

"3. Blowing smoke in someone's face: (If a man) Let's take it out in the parking lot. (If a woman) How fast can you get your clothes off?

"4. Holding smoke a long time and exhaling through nose: I'm thinking real hard.

"5. Blowing smoke out through ears: I have defective eustachian tubes.

"6. Going to sleep with cigarette in mouth: In the next scene the firemen will be putting out the fire.

"7. Lighting one cigarette from another: (If a war movie) You can share my foxhole anytime. (Between a woman and a man) We can share oxygen tents.

"8. Quitting a three-pack-a-day habit overnight: My doctor just discovered a tumor the size of a cantaloupe.

"My $0.02."

Tap Dancing, Part Two

Master Cecil,

For years I have enjoyed your columns, and have always accepted what you write as "The Truth," or as close to the truth as is generally possible. However, I have now lost faith in your ability to ferret out the Straight Dope.

Throughout the unfortunate years when I was a tobacco consumer, about 40 percent of the smokers that I encountered tapped either individual cigarettes or the entire pack before opening. Your sample population must be woefully biased against smokers. Also, it really does make a significant difference in the arrangement of the tobacco. There is sufficient momentum to further pack the tobacco—up to several mm is typical. And the result IS a more consistent burn of the coffin nail.

Please reaffirm my faith by some great stunt of mental prowess, like solving the problem of voter apathy in a democracy.

In despair,—Karl Yoder

I bow to your superior intellect on most subjects. At risk of feeling the sting of your wit I must disagree with the pack/no pack conclusion. Perhaps you should let me conduct the experiment. I notice a great difference in the cigarettes I've used to test this. I can produce evidence supporting Paul's earlier claim concerning his teen smoking experience. Dying of cancer sucks but at least my cherry will stay put.—John P. Davis

You are still missing the point. One taps a cigarette to compact the tobacco. This restricts airflow in the cigarette. The tobacco burns slower and thus (trust me) tastes better.—Pat

Cecil, Cecil, Cecil . . . I smoke Marlboro "Regular King Size in a box" cigarettes, and although I was not around when the custom of packing one's smokes sprang forth, I have, in the last 20 years of smoking, noticed a definite advantage (albeit dubious, as you'll see) to doing so. I'm in the habit of packing the filter end of a new pack against the back of my weak hand using five sharp smacks, then rotating the pack on a horizontal axis 180 degrees and repeating. The tobacco mixture is drawn down into the cigarette roughly 3/8". If I fail to do this, my smokes definitely don't last as long (that's the dubious benefit . . . I should be smoking less, not more). Cecil, even though the amount of tobacco is the same whether packed or not, the cigarette simply burns more slowly when packed more tightly.—Jonathan M. Finch

Am I the only survivor from the 1950s? In those days, no one wanted filter cigarettes. Cigarettes with no filter were routinely tapped on a thumbnail or watch crystal. Tapping produced two benefits: fewer shreds of tobacco would would come out in your mouth from the tapped end, and the other end had 2 or 3mm of empty paper tube for good ignition.—Howard in Venice

I can't believe no one could explain this to you! As a former smoker, I don't recommend the habit, but I do have some experience to share. You are right, tapping makes little difference in whether the cigarette

holds together or not. However, with a filtered cigarette, there is a dif-
ference in the "draw," a difference I could notice when I smoked. I
preferred the draw on a tapped cigarette. The practice probably
started with unfiltered cigarettes, where it has a very practical pur-
pose. With unfiltereds, you tap the end you light, packing the tobacco
in the other end a good 1 to 2 millimeters from the end, and causing
loose bits to fly out the end. This gives you a slightly recessed end to
place in your mouth, allowing you to puff to your heart's discontent
without getting a mouth full of tobacco. Since I started with unfiltered
Camels, I can attest to the difference between a tapped and untapped
cigarette. It only takes a few episodes of spitting out little bits of to-
bacco, trying to dislodge it from under tongue and between teeth, to
learn the practical purpose of tapping.

Sometimes there is no substitute for experience, Cecil.—Martin Co-
hen, Ph.D.

As a former smoker I can definitely say that tapping the "lighting"
end of the cigarette loosens the tobacco and makes it easier to light in
the wind.—SBruner785

Thanks for the letters, which represent only a fraction of the response we got. While I happily concede that you folks smoke (or
smoked) and I don't, I feel obliged to point out that we now have at
least six more or less independent theories on what cigarette tapping is
supposed to accomplish:

1. It keeps the cherry from falling off.
2. The cigarette burns slower and thus tastes better.
3. The cigarette burns slower and thus lasts longer.
4. It kept tobacco bits out of your mouth in the 1950s (if you tapped
   the end you lit).
5. It makes the cigarette easier to light by exposing more paper (if
   you tap the end you put in your mouth).
6. It makes the cigarette easier to light by loosening the tobacco (if
   you tap the end you light).

In my experience this usually means:

7. We don't know why we're doing this, but by God there must be some reason, and sooner or later we're going to figure out what it is.

A Few Additional Thoughts, Using The Term Loosely

Did you also know that having "tapped" or "packed" your cigarettes will help in keeping them lit in the rain?—Bessa Mae

On the subject of tapping cigarettes: we all know they are bad, so we spank their little butts before smoking them.—Roadtrash

The Chesterfields-in-Casablanca legend needs a slight bit of filler-outer detail, to wit: by the time a pack of real Chesties got to Casablanca, they were so stale & full of weevils you would have had to pack it down to stun the weevils & prevent your getting a mouthful of fire, tobacco crumbs, & conscious weevils on your first hit.—KarlSnake

Even Jove nods.
I believe the reason your test didn't produce any results is that being a nonsmoker, you simply opened a fresh pack and tapped a few. In fact, freshly opened cigarettes are usually "fully packed."
However, [a pack of cigarettes] bouncing around in one's pocket, especially after a few smokes are removed, gradually loosens the tobacco. As another correspondent has noted, this is especially true of nonfilters, like the kind that killed Bogie. While the issue of loose strands in the mouth is not a problem with filters, tapping does produce a smoother burning, cherry-retaining smoke.
Carry a half full pack around for a few days, then repeat the tap test. Not only will it enlighten you on this issue, but you'll also experience the thrill of being a pariah when people see the pack in your pocket. For most dramatic results, I recommend Luckies or Camel straights.
Yours in undiminished admiration,—J.C. Custer

Yes, but for the full effect, shouldn't I also get a tattoo?

A packed cigarette can be "flicked better," allowing you to keep the burning ember short without having to snub part of it off in the ashtray.

And, of course, my favorite observation: A packed cigarette is easier to light for the kinda "trashed" girl in the bar that just bummed one from you. This is because the newly created "little paper end" will catch fire before the tobacco. Invariably, in my experience, half-drunk people tend to lean forward and stick the business end of the cigarette into your match while breathing out of their nose if the cigarette doesn't light instantaneously. More often than not, either the butt snuffs the flame or the breath does. If the little paper end flares up, they invariably draw on the cigarette and pull back slightly from it, thinking it's lit. Following the withdrawing butt with the match at this point for another half second ensures that it is evenly lit.—Jak Matrix

I'm 33 and I've been smoking since I was 16. In all those years the only thing I've seen accomplished by "packing" cigarettes is the attention drawn to the teenager who is doing it. It seems like an action that tries to convey the message, "HAH! I'm a cool, smoking kid and I don't care who knows it!" Stand outside any convenience store on a summer day and the sounds of "packing" are so loud, you'd think someone was putting a roof up somewhere.—Michael Kelly

Those in the know understand the importance of clandestine signaling to indicate to fellow CSU (Cigarette Smoker's Underground) members of the presence of evil nonsmokers, legislative do-gooders, and aliens from Zendarr who want the Sacred Weed for their journey home where it is easily converted to pzarkxs or purple wyrtlsdes. If you notice cigarette tapping but don't understand it it may be time to report back to your commandant.

Long live the CSU!!—Telslave

Oh.

OK, in addition to the reasons summarized previously, we now have the following hypotheses on what cigarette tapping accomplishes:

8. Easier to light cig bummed by tipsy bimbo.
9. Flicks better.

10. Easier to keep lit in rain.
11. Stuns weevils, keeps away aliens, etc.

You know, I was never able to get the cigarette people to return my calls about this. Betcha I know why. They've been reading this god-blessit thread.

From The Message Board

Subj: The sound of one hand clapping
From: Diviv
Cecil, you could have answered this question if you had done your homework [*The Straight Dope*, page 49]. By asking, say, one million people you would have found someone like myself who can clap with one hand. By vigorously shaking my left hand my fingers flop repeatedly on my palm and make a very audible sound. It is my one and only talent.

From: Jojo5star
<<It is my one and only talent.>>
Be sure to visit us again when you get back from your World Tour.

Chapter 13

Intimate Affairs

Is it true that Isaac Newton was a virgin?—Hoping there are other ways to assure scientific greatness, Douglas Leonard, Department of Astronomy, UC Berkeley

Of course he was a virgin. Once upon a time, so was Madonna. What's tragic is that he may have *died* a virgin. Not that this is all that unusual. You met many electrical engineers? But mathematicians are probably the worst that way. How the math gene perpetuates itself is one of the mysteries of our age.

Admittedly this is an area where it is unwise to make blanket state-

ments. (Sorry.) It's not like they had the guy under constant surveillance. As one of my high school classmates unwisely asked at the lunch table one day, "What, technically, is the definition of a virgin?"

Still, having thus fenced out the boundaries of the knowable, we can say that, with the possible exception of one teenage friendship (there is no sign that it became physical), Isaac Newton apparently formed no romantic attachments during his 84 years of life. Furthermore, he was so straitlaced it seems unlikely he availed himself of, how shall I say, commercial outlets.

The penalty of genius, you are thinking. Not necessarily. Richard Feynman, one of the legendary minds of our time, was quite the bon vivant, and . . . well, I dare not even speak of myself.

Newton, in contrast, was walking proof that one path to immortality, assuming you have the requisite endowment of brains, is to obsess. Ninety percent of what he obsessed about—alchemy, biblical prophecy, and religious disputations were among his lifelong passions—was rubbish. The other 10 percent, the stuff he did for laughs, I suppose we might say, involved taking six thousand years of disjointed fumbling and making it into a science. Two sciences, actually, physics and to a large extent mathematics.

Too bad Newton didn't have the benefit of modern management consultants. "Ike," they would say, "if you chucked the alchemy and prophecy thing you could produce all the scientific achievements that will earn you glory and still leave most of the day for wine, women, and song."

Didn't happen, but let's have some respect. One biographer credits him with "discovering gravitation," and where would we be without that?

I've climbed the highest mountains, searched the darkest depths of the public library and even asked my mother. Still I come up with a blank. So here's my question: have you ever looked at your zipper? I mean really looked? On 90 percent of them there are the letters YKK. Please tell me what YKK means so I can again know inner peace.—Ken Green, Chicago

It means Yoshida Kogyo Kabushikikaisha. Feeling peaceful? Didn't think so. See if the following bonus info helps. YKK translated means

Yoshida Industries Limited. Tadao Yoshida is the Japanese tycoon who founded the company in 1934 and built it into "the foremost manufacturer of closures [zippers, mostly] in the world," the company's annual report notes. It's unfortunate that YKK is not better known, but face it, a zipper isn't exactly the ideal billboard; the only time you get close enough to read the lettering, typically your mind is on other things.

Your idea of a zipper factory might be a couple guys named Izzy and Mort (or the equivalent in Japanese) in some crummy loft in the garment district. Little do you know—this is a mighty industry here. We're talking 54 plants and 114 sales offices in 40 countries with a total of 25,000 employees. (Hey, *everybody* needs zippers.) We're talking mammoth production lines, giant automatic weaving machines, and barrel oscillation plating equipment. (I don't know what it is either, but it looks impressive in the pictures.) We're talking heavy-duty R&D, as dedicated YKK scientists strive to perfect the zippers of tomorrow. Also the aluminum building materials of tomorrow, YKK having diversified thereinto a while back.

Tadao Yoshida's genius was to understand the poetry of zipper manufacture. The company's charmingly loopy brochures explain that the YKK philosophy is "the Cycle of Goodness." Says here, "the concept means that no one prospers unless he renders profit or benefit to others. . . . The people of YKK have dedicated themselves to manufacturing perfection—delivering goods and services that benefit their customers and society as well as their company and their own personal lives. . . . [They are dedicated] to the continued enhancement of everyday life for citizens throughout the U.S.A."

OK, it's just zippers, but Yoshida's idea is, they might as well be great zippers. One more reason why the Japanese are kicking Occidental butt in the fields of commerce.

What do the Queen's Guards or the Black Watch or whatever really wear under those kilts? And if the answer is nothing, like my boss claims, would the desire to follow such pure tradition really result in inspections at the lineup by sergeants or officers with mirrors attached to their shoes to ensure compliance? I could buy the naked bit, but am sure the inspections part (can you just picture a foot thrust between a guard's legs?) is just some weird man thing. Please tell me the truth.—Yvonne Walton, Londonderry, New Hampshire

You'll want to sit down for this, Yvonne. Just make sure you're not sitting directly across from a kilt-clad Scot. Apparently they don't wear anything under there, or at least they're not supposed to. I know because I posted this to the net (soc.culture.celtic) and got numerous replies such as the following: "Me wears the scotty-skirt and I can assure you that correctly there is nowt unner it. However, we twentieth-century derivatives feel the caul a bit and so unless it's a formal

occasion, I actually (NO! No! I can't admit anything . . . not in writing anyway!)"

You're thinking: so what does one weirdo prove? Nowt, I suppose, but when you hear from half a dozen weirdos you have to figure something's up. Here's another. "It is actually true. Underpants or whatever are strictly out. Which reminds me of an old story. American lady: Is anything worn under the kilt? Scotsman: No, madam. I can assure you it's all in perfect condition." Are these guys a laff riot or what?

One more. "Traditionally Scots do not wear anything under their kilts, but the shirts (known as a blouse) have a long tail that [may] be tied between the legs. There are many 'standard' answers a kilt wearer could give you when you ask them [The Question], [including] 'The Glory of God' or in the case of a female questioner, 'Would you care to look for yourself?' . . . As for what I wear under my kilt, 'I Gird my Loins with the Holy Spirit.' "

Enough already. But what about the inspections? Another net denizen writes: "The stories you mentioned have some basis in reality, as I have seen a swagger stick equipped with a mirror for just that purpose." I am willing—nay, eager—to believe that said swagger stick was manufactured as a joke. I mean, come on, at least gynecologists do their exams indoors.

And Now This Closing Thought

The real question is, why do Scotsmen wear kilts at all? Answer: Sheep can hear zippers.—*John S., Birmingham, Alabama*

According to the attached article, AIDS activists are concerned about unsafe sex at a gathering of eunuchs in India. Could you please elaborate on what sexual abilities eunuchs have?—*F.T., Danbury, Connecticut*

F.T. encloses the following item from Chuck Shepherd's "News of the Weird" feature: "In April, an AIDS activist organization in Madras, India, made a public plea that eunuchs convening for their annual festival near the city later in the month use condoms during their wild celebration. Many, but fewer than half, of the country's 400,000 eunuchs retain their penises, and Community Action Network estimated that 10,000 sex acts would take place at the close of the 15-day gathering. An AIDS activist said that because most eunuchs were recruited by force, they are 'angry' and show little sexual restraint."

A bizarre story made even more bizarre by a mistranslation: the festival in question is not a gathering of eunuchs, strictly speaking, but of *hijras,* as they are called in India. Hijras are men who live as women, or to put it another way, transsexuals with religion, being devotees of the mother goddess Bahuchara Mata. Many but not all have been castrated—voluntarily for the most part, although there have been reports over the years of hijras who were forcibly emasculated. A few are hermaphrodites—that is, born with both male and female plumbing, typically underdeveloped. Some hijras, or perhaps we should say parahijras, are normally endowed homosexual men who just like the hijra lifestyle.

The lifestyle is the thing, see. "What makes hijras hijras is not biology or anatomy but culture," says Arvind Kumar, editor of San Jose, California-based *India Currents* magazine, which has run stories on hijras. "Most hijras cross-dress, i.e., wear women's clothing, makeup, etc. Their public behavior and mannerisms are high camp, highly exaggerated feminine gestures, but they make no effort to mask their male voices. Most hijras are good singers and dancers and entertainers. Their presence at weddings is thought to bring good luck.

"There is not a birth in the country that goes unmonitored by the local hijra community—they visit the house and demand to examine

the newborn. In the old days it is said that if the baby's genitals were malformed, parents would not want to raise the child and the hijras would immediately take it away and raise it as their own.

"The coming of the British to India saw the downfall of the hijra community. [During Muslim rule of India hijras were harem guards and court entertainers and many enjoyed privileged status.] The British viewed them as freaks to be shunned, an attitude that prevails among westernized urban Indians. Today hijras are made fun of and avoided, but there is much greater tolerance of them in rural areas."

But there's more to being a hijra than flaming for the yokels. While they support themselves to an extent by begging, their major source of income apparently is prostitution, for which purpose they are in much demand. Hijras are invariably the passive partner, taking their customers anally or between the thighs.

Although not all who call themselves hijras are eunuchs, many hijras say you cannot be a true hijra until you have been castrated. (I rely here on the research of anthropologist Serena Nanda.) The highly ritualized operation is done without anesthetic. Two quick cuts are made, severing both testicles and penis. A stick is inserted to keep the urethra open for purposes of urination. No attempt is made to stanch the bleeding or stitch the wound, which is treated with hot sesame oil to prevent infection. Despite all this, one veteran castrator claims that out of 1,000 patients he lost only one.

The number of hijras is uncertain. One researcher puts it at 50,000; a recent press account of the annual hijra festival says 200,000. Fifty thousand people showed up at the festival, of whom 10,000 were hijras. It was the 40,000 nonhijras (and the nonemasculated faux hijras) who needed the condoms the AIDS activists were urging upon them. Sex among the hijras isn't completely inexplicable, but it's still pretty weird.

Cute introductions be damned. Has anyone ever had sex in space? Go ahead, tell me the NASA folks themselves never wanted to know what it would be like, or whether it would even be possible.

According to my 1995 copy of The World Almanac, *U.S. shuttle crews have enjoyed mixed company since 1983, and a married couple flew on* Endeavor's *September 1992 mission. The almanac also shows— and I'm not suggesting anything—that the human race has been launching at least two at a time since 1964.*

How many weeks cooped up in a spacecraft can anyone take before boredom, isolation, stress, and la différence *set in? (Oops—pardon my heterocentrism.) Heck, it wouldn't surprise me if astronauts did it strictly out of scientific curiosity.*

I suppose a less scrupulous inquirer, in an attempt to bolster popular belief in clandestine space boffs, might point out that a U.S. senator and a U.S. congressman have flown shuttle missions. Rest assured I would never stoop so low.

Please tell me our space program is still a pioneer of science, paving our way toward a happy life among the stars. I know long-term space travel isn't exactly around the corner, but don't we want to know whether future space workers will be able to have normal or near-normal existences during long stretches in free fall? Is there any reason to believe zero G would hinder reproduction? I mean, if sperm couldn't tell up from down . . .

So anyway, Cecil, has one of our finest chuckled and said, "The things I do for my country"?—Bill St. John, Wahiawa, Hawaii

You know, Caller ID is starting to be a real hindrance in my line of work. I don't know for a fact that they have a sign taped by the NASA switchboard saying, "No calls from C. Adams. Dude be *wack*." But it does seem like it takes a lot longer than it used to for them to pick up the phone.

Be that as it may, we did succeed in speaking to Mike. At a loss for a subtle way to broach the topic, we pretty much blurted it out: "Mike! Sex in space! Hosing amongst the asteroids! Fact or fantasy?" (Actually, I didn't say "hosing amongst the asteroids." But I should have.)

There was a pause. "Not in the U.S. program," said Mike at last. "It's highly unlikely it would even be attempted in the space shuttle. You have five to seven astronauts on a mission. You can't turn around without bumping into someone."

Wouldn't stop some people I know. Still, this was what I expected to hear. Then Mike made a strategic error. "The astronauts are considered to be on duty 24 hours a day," he said. "I don't think they would think of such an activity as professional."

Professional! C'mon, Mike, I read *The Right Stuff*. These guys were test pilots! At age 19 they were buzzing the tower! Most of them would consider it their solemn duty to, you know, push the envelope. I mean, how would you guys on the ground know? It's not like they'd leave the electrodes on.

Mike didn't have a good answer for this. He also declined to venture an opinion about what those wacky Russkies had been up to. On the question of whether deep-space sex was even possible, he was agnostic. "There's so much about microgravity we don't know," he said. "They have trouble maintaining plant growth . . ."

But, Mike, that's just it! I said. It's our scientific duty to advance the frontiers of knowledge! (The same general line of BS occurs to everyone who raises this issue.)

"Sounds like you're volunteering," Mike said.

Mike, I said, you send me up, I'll do my best for my country. I'd even bring my own Lava Lamp. (I love this job, I really do.) Then I hung up. I figured my FBI file was fat enough already.

So, not the most definitive answer I ever gave. I mean, to be blunt, who said you needed two people for sex? But there are limits to what even Cecil can hope to know.

Sex In Space, Continued

Re your column on sex in space, I don't know if this helps, but I found a report at monkey.hooked.net/m/chuck/sexshuttle.html. It seems pretty authentic, i.e., none of the sophomoric gags that usually indicate a hoax. Dunno if this helps.—Andy Blau, Toronto, Ontario

Yes, this definitely sounds like the real thing. The report, which purports to be a scientific account of attempts to determine the feasibility of sex at zero G, is posted on a Web site entitled "Chuck's Weird World." You just know this has got to be a major depository of official government documents. The report is right next to the supposed radio transcript of the last moments of the *Challenger* astronauts (Oh, look! The shuttle blew up! We are falling into the ocean! I am so bummed!), which we've previously determined to be a hoax. Also on the page I see Chuck has a picture of what is allegedly Kurt Cobain's head after he blew his brains out. Pretty yucky. Where people come up with this stuff I don't want to know.

Still. We're nothing if not thorough here at the Straight Dope. I called NASA back. My friend Mike was not in. Or rather Mike didn't answer his phone. Told you I was having problems with Caller ID. So I talked to James instead. I swear I could *hear* this guy's eyes roll. James repeated the standard line, namely that nobody in the U.S. program had ever had sex in space, and they certainly hadn't conducted experiments on it, and the nearest thing he could think of to a sex experiment that they *had* conducted was one time when they sent up some fish embryos—but even those were fertilized before the flight, and anyway it's not like anybody's going to make big money selling videos of humping fish. (I know you didn't ask about videos, but I expect to see them show up on Chuck's Weird World any day. Also, to forestall any further mailings on this subject, I've already heard the joke about "Ride Sally Ride.")

So now you're saying, another massive government cover-up. Absolutely. Tell me this quote from the "report" doesn't sound authentic: "The number of married couples currently involved in proposals for long-term projects on the U.S. space station has grown considerably in recent years. This raises the serious question of how such couples will be able to carry out normal marital relations without the aid of gravity." Yeah, like they're going to explode if they can't wait till they get back. My idea: send up couples with small children. They're already used to the celibate life.

Back to the report. Ten, ah, reproductive modalities were allegedly

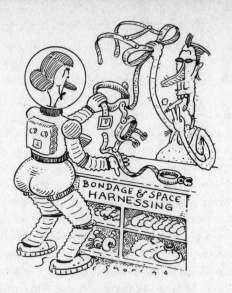

BONDAGE & SPACE HARNESSING

tried. These involved 1) an elastic belt holding the partners together, 2) an inflatable tunnel, and 3) various, how shall we say, grips. All had their drawbacks. "It was difficult to obtain the necessary thrusting motion," blah, blah, blah. Right. Give me ten minutes and some Velcro, and I bet you I'd figure something out.

Oh, yeah. At the end of the report is this incredible line of baloney about partnerless subjects who were provided with a "manipulator" connected to a "two-hidden-layer back-error propagation neural network" for use as a "unisexual device." You say this doesn't reflect any of the "sophomoric gags that usually indicate a hoax," Andy, and in this you are undoubtedly right. Show me the sophomore who can spell "propagation." Then again, looking at the situation in its totality, you can't deny there's some satisfaction in thinking, my tax dollars at work.

Sex In Space, Continued
(Absolute Last Time We Write About This)

Regarding the recent discussion of sex in space, I have here the book Liftoff *by Michael Collins, the Apollo 11 command module pilot. On page 191 he discusses various medical concerns on these long missions. Seems the NASA doctors were concerned that the crew, presumably remaining celibate during their month or two in space, might develop "infected prostate glands that could lead to urinary tract infections." Collins goes on to report that one doctor suggested the crew masturbate regularly, but that at least one crew member ignored this advice. Keep pressing, Cecil. The future of manned space flight may hang in the balance.—Jason Catan, via AOL*

Now, Jason. What Collins says is, "One doctor advised regular masturbation, advice [Skylab crew member] Joe [Kerwin] ignored." He doesn't say other crew members *didn't* ignore it. On the next page he writes, "There was no sex on Skylab," and still further along, in a discussion of the recreational possibilities of space, he says, "And lovemaking! I don't think any astronauts have yet been privileged to sample the ultimate use of weightlessness." It is clear from the context he's talking about sex involving two parties, not masturbation. But if you think I'm calling NASA to ask about this again, you're nuts.

First, an (elderly) joke.

A Harvard man and a Yale man are at the urinal. They finish and zip up. The Harvard man proceeds to the sink to wash his hands, while the Yale man immediately makes for the exit.

The Harvard man says, "At Hah-vahd they teach us to wash our hands after we urinate."

The Yale man replies, "At Yale they teach us not to piss on our hands."

My question: why is it customary for males to wash their hands after urination? I never do, which shocks and disgusts some of my guy friends. I bathe daily and wear fresh underpants, so how does my penis get dirty? It's not like I dig a ditch with it. However, my hands might get dirty from daily activities. Is it not more sensible then to wash my hands before touching my clean penis? Is posturination hand washing a throwback to the bad old days, when sex was "dirty" and so, by extension, were sex organs? I'm serious about this. Please advise.—Tom Sharpley, Los Angeles

Good (if elderly) joke. Common (but stupid) attitude. Rank (but important) topic. Some facts:

1. The purpose of washing is not to get pee off your hands.
2. No amount of washing will make you clean.
3. You have to do it anyway.

I've said this before: your boxer-shorts region—from belly button to midthigh—is crawling with germs known as coliform bacteria. These bacteria originated in your intestine, and some of them are deadly. Remember punji stakes? They were sharpened sticks that the Vietcong concealed point up along trails and daubed with excrement. If you stepped on one you had a good chance of contracting a fatal infection. Similarly, an otherwise not-so-serious gunshot or knife injury could kill you if it perforated the intestine and allowed coliform bacteria to spread around your abdomen.

But you know this (or at least you ought to). What you may not know is that washing will not make the coliform bacteria go away. They're holed up in the pores of your skin and nothing short of sandblasting—certainly not your morning shower—is going to get them out. Showering merely gets rid of the ones that have strayed onto the surface. The bacteria won't do much harm if they stay put, but when

you urinate your fingers come in contact with Mister P. long enough for the coliform bacteria in your pores to hop aboard. Your fingers subsequently touch lots of other infectible items. If you don't wash your hands with soap and water (soap gets rid of the skin oil that the bacteria stick to) . . . hello, Typhoid Mary.

It now dawns on you: jeez, if merely touching my privates is enough to transmit bacteria, it doesn't matter if I pee or not! Just so. Urine itself is actually fairly sterile. Cecil has read reports of it being used during wartime in poor countries as—I'm not making this up—a sort of battlefield Bactine. (U.S. doctors generally blanch at this.) The lesson to draw from this, however, is not that you can go forth dripping (yuck), but rather that just because you *didn't* pee on your fingers doesn't mean you can skip washing up.

Watch What You Eat

After reading your column on hand washing after urination, I'm certain I'm going to die—that is, if coliform bacteria are as bad as you say. My girlfriend and I often share the pleasures of fellatio and cunnilingus. Heck, one night I even got up the nerve to perform (ahem) analingus. But what about the dread coliform bacteria? I'm certain some of these bacteria came in contact with our mouths at some time. Yet I have never been sick due to these forms of sexual gratification. Do we just swallow it and put it back where it came from (our intestines) or what? Please don't tell me I have to refrain from yet another fun thing to do.—Matt Hostetler, via the Internet; similarly from Peter Montgomery, Don Martin, Bubba the Salty Dog, Dr. Dormammu, J. Moore, Parker Trudeau, Joe Mantango, David Reid

Nothing like causing a national panic. Now I know why Pat Buchanan likes to run for president. Mrs. Adams had the same thought you guys did, probably at about the same point during the evening. "Babe," I said, "you think sex is *safe*? Let me tell you about sexually transmitted diseases." Not the most romantic line I ever used. But the truth is you can catch lots of bugs via oral sex. Many of them are transmitted by, or have their transmission facilitated by, coliform or other fecal bacteria or, for that matter, fecal viruses. There's no point in stopping now though. You can catch most of the same germs from intercourse, kissing, or simply holding hands.

For example, a common complaint among women is urinary-tract

2·2·96

infection, which is often caused by sexually transmitted fecal bacteria. Research suggests these bacteria travel to the entrance of the vagina, get shoved in by the penis during intercourse, and then migrate to the bladder. In other words, the guy helps infect the woman with her own germs. (Doctors—male ones usually—blame this on the "woefully short" female urethra.) It seems likely oral sex could accomplish the same thing, but for a given infection there's no way to tell.

It's rare that a specific sexual practice is associated with spreading germs, but there are exceptions. About 20 years ago clinicians began noticing what has come to be called "gay bowel syndrome," a collection of intestinal and rectal complaints that frequently plague gay men. Many of these illnesses stem from infection by fecal bacteria following anal sex—specifically, anal intercourse, analingus, and fellatio following anal intercourse. Some heterosexual couples (estimates range from 5 to 27 percent) also engage in anal sex, and they're at risk, too.

The question is how much risk. The answer is probably not much, unless they're unusually out there sexually. A key factor in gay bowel syndrome and in the spread of STDs generally is multiple sex partners, which exponentially increases your exposure to infection. In contrast, monogamous couples, whether gay or straight, soon achieve "homeostasis"—they've swapped germs, didn't come down with anything, and thereafter coexist in a state of microbial equilibrium. That's not to say they're germ-free; they may simply be "asymptomatic carriers" of some bug that doesn't make them sick but that might lay low an outsider. Granted, the danger isn't very great, but it exists. I was just reading in the *Harvard Medical School Health Letter* about a 51-year-old guy who learned that hepatitis C had destroyed his liver. He'd had no previous symptoms, but the kicker is that he'd contracted hepatitis C 46 years before. Hepatitis C isn't transmitted by fecal bacteria; my point is that just because you don't think you have anything doesn't mean you don't. Thus the apparent paradox: you can frolic with your honey all you want, but you still have to wash your hands after using the pot.

We're Doomed

Mindful of our discussion about the importance of washing one's hands after going to the bathroom and recalling my comment that urine itself, being fairly sterile, is not the problem, a reader sent me a clipping from the March/April 1996 *Yoga Journal*.

Here's the headline:

> DRINK TO YOUR HEALTH: WEALTHY FRENCH WOMEN BATHED IN IT, CHINESE DOCTORS USED IT TO SOOTHE SORE THROATS, AND NOW YOU—ALL SQUEAMISHNESS ASIDE—CAN DRINK IT TO CURE WHAT AILS YOU.

Guess what "it" is.

You guessed right.

I'm serious.

I quote author Blake More:

"Odds are you're among the 27 million Americans who recycle. . . . Would you be willing to take the act of recycling a step further and internally honor your bodily home, if it meant you'd have more energy, a stronger immune system, and an ageless complexion? Of course you would."

Welcome to urine therapy.

All it takes, says Blake, is eight ounces a day.

Blake first heard about UT from a naturopath in Japan. Of course she had to try it—wouldn't you? Four years later, she reports, "I'm a

different person. I'm more in tune with my body's needs and functions, and no longer anemic or hypoglycemic. I rarely get colds, haven't had the flu in years, and the yeast infection that had long been plaguing me is gone. . . . I now feel healthy and strong." Only problem is gargling with those little deodorant blocks.

She goes on to give a long list of diseases, including many related to AIDS, that urine therapy will supposedly alleviate. The list includes everything from gangrene to hair loss to malaria. Sure.

While I don't suppose there's any danger urine therapy will become the next macarena, I did take the precaution of checking out the concept with University of Chicago kidney specialist Dr. John Asplin. He thought urine consumption in moderate quantities was probably harmless.

The stuff *is* fairly sterile, and if you do happen to have a urinary-tract infection or something, well, you've already got whatever germs you're consuming. (Former Indian prime minister Moraji Desai, a daily urine drinker, lived to be 99.)

On the other hand, Asplin said, UT isn't likely to do you much good, either. Listen to your body. Your body is saying, "I just got *rid* of this stuff, granola-brain. Are you *nuts*?"

But if you want to try it, be my guest. Just don't eat any asparagus first.

What causes a person to shiver uncontrollably following urination (i.e., "piss shiver")? My friends and I have wrestled with this for years even to the point of consulting medical authorities (they didn't know either). We currently have two theories. One is the Rapid Heat Loss Theory, which states that an uncontrollable shiver passes over the body following the rapid loss of several ounces of 98.6-degree liquid. This theory seems to have good face validity but as far as we can tell females do not experience piss shiver, which puts a hole in that idea. Our second theory is the Mini-Orgasm Theory, which states that a man's penis is used for two major activities: urination and sexual activity. When a man urinates, the two functions cross briefly and he experiences a mini-orgasm that causes his body to shiver uncontrollably. Is either one of these correct, or is there a third theory we haven't thought of? Please help, Cecil.—Patrick Cormack, Dallas, Texas

I know I promised I wouldn't answer this disgusting question, but my will is weak. Besides, the subject has been debated on alt.fan.cecil-

adams off and on for weeks, and even though no firm conclusions have been arrived at (par for the course on the net), the least I can do is give an interim report. We've made progress on one front: someone came up with an impressive-sounding name. Peter H. M. Brooks proposes *post-micturition convulsion syndrome*, or PMCS. Sure beats "piss shiver." Maybe now we can apply for a big federal grant.

The following key facts have also been unearthed:

1. Women—some, anyway—also experience PCMS.
2. That's it.

Theory productivity has been a little better. Here's what we've got so far:

- Heat loss due to several ounces of warm fluid leaving the body. Maybe, but then why don't we experience it during defecation, vomiting, etc.?
- Heat loss due to exposure of the nether regions. Not likely; as one netter points out, babies snugly clothed in diapers may be observed to experience PMCS.
- It's caused by the passage of spermatozoa into the urinary canal. Guess that explains why it happens to women.
- It dates back to precivilization days when men hadn't learned to do their own shaking. Attributed to George Carlin. What a comedian.
- It's all the fault of the parasympathetic nervous system. The

parasympathetic nervous system is up there with the Babylonians as the default explanation for anything you can't think of a good reason for (e.g., photic sneeze reflex, closing your eyes when you sneeze), but I throw it in for the sake of completeness. Your mini-orgasm theory sounds like a baroque version of this.

End of transmission. Lame, I know, but what are you going to do? Cecil can't figure out everything. I'd convene a special session of the Straight Dope Science Advisory Board, but they're still sleeping it off from our last symposium. Contributions from the Teeming Millions cordially invited.

From The Message Board

Subj: Re: barbers' bottles
From: LAZQX
What is the blue liquid in barbers' bottles? No, not margarita, the stuff on the shelf.

From: LilethSC
Do you mean the stuff that the combs are floating in? It's called Barbicide, which is not murdering your barber, but is a disinfectant.

From: FW Lev
I thought Barbicide was giving Barbie a nice, new tutu of firecrackers. (Did this as a kid; did not use a magnifying glass on ants.)

From: LynnBodoni
Go ahead, put the bimbo out of her misery. You have to wonder where she gets the money for all those clothes . . . I mean, she never keeps a job for very long.

From: LTControls
Not to mention all those pink sports cars. Makes you wonder what's *really* going on in Barbie's Dream House.

Miscellany

Perhaps you can help. Being someone born with very different hair, I am often perplexed at why things are the way they are. That's why I read your column—to find out things that no one else could answer. For example:

1. *Why is it that two wrongs don't make a right, but three rights make a left?*
2. *If it's a penny for your thoughts, why does everyone put their two cents in?*
3. *How come it's a pair of pants, but only one bra?*

4. When the guy invented cottage cheese, how did he know it was done?
5. Why do we play at a recital and recite at a play?
6. If olive oil comes from olives, where does baby oil come from?
7. If vegetarians eat vegetables, why do humanitarians eat?
8. Why are there locks on the doors of 24-hour convenience stores?
9. Why are boxing rings square?
10. If pro and con are opposites, is Congress the opposite of progress?

If you could help out this straight dope, I would be in debt. If you can't, I'll still be in debt and frustrated besides. Inquisitively yours,— Vince Vance, Dallas

You must be a riot at family reunions, Vince. In the fullness of time I will deal with your, ah, metaquestions. But first I want to get to the bottom of this stumper: if you call up a bike company to ask if their business goes in cycles, do they refer you to a spokesman?

I'm thinking of renouncing my U.S. citizenship as a political protest. Where do I go to do this? What are the legal ramifications?—Doug, Auburn, Massachusetts

You're going to protest by renouncing your citizenship? I'm disappointed. Whatever happened to going to the U.S. embassy and setting yourself on fire?

But OK, I understand, it's the '90s. And you probably read in the papers about this guy Terry Nichols, Timothy McVeigh's codefendant in the Oklahoma City bombing, who supposedly renounced his citizenship in 1992. You're thinking, "Wow, hanging around with future mass murderers while working as a farmhand and selling army surplus. What a cool lifestyle!"

Whatever butters your bagel, pal. But you have to do it right. You probably have the idea that renouncing U.S. citizenship consists of going down to the town square, post office (the "all services" window, maybe?), or other public place and announcing, "The United States sucks. I quit."

Wrongo, Benedict Arnold–breath. The process is actually pretty complicated, and for good reason. Renouncing your citizenship is

irrevocable, the political equivalent of a sex-change operation. While the powers that be are willing to make the big slice if that's what you really want, they don't want you waking up next morning and going, "Oh, @#$%!!"

Here's the procedure:

1. Leave the country. There is no procedure for renouncing your citizenship while still physically present in the United States. The government has the idea that if you're mad enough to renounce your citizenship you probably don't want to keep living here (although most militia types seem to want to stick around, presumably to keep their disgust fresh). Also, frankly, most of the 800 or so people who renounce their U.S. citizenship each year aren't protestors but rather are cases of "dual citizenship" who haven't lived in the United States for a long time. What typically happens is that someone is born in the United States to non-U.S. parents, who later return to their native land. Such a person is automatically a U.S. citizen but has a claim to his parents' nationality also. While dual citizenship is usually not illegal—the United States "tolerates" it—it can complicate your life, notably in connection

with taxes. So many people choose one or the other on reaching adulthood.

2. Apply for citizenship somewhere else. Strictly speaking, this is optional, in the sense that it's optional to put on the parachute before you jump out of the plane. But if you're a stateless person living abroad and you get in a jam with the local authorities, or you want to get a passport to travel to yet another country (or back to this one), you're up fecal matter creek.

3. Go to a U.S. embassy or consulate and tell them you want to renounce your citizenship. Often they'll try to talk you out of it, tell you to come back after you've slept it off, etc. Persist. Eventually they'll have you sign an oath of renunciation, an affidavit affirming the oath, and a "statement of understanding," which basically asks you if you're sure you know what you're doing. You also have to supply certain tax-related info and turn in your passport. The consular officer overseeing the proceedings must sign an attestation saying that in his opinion you're not off your nut. The papers will then be forwarded to the U.S. State Department, which in the fullness of time will issue you a Certificate of Loss of Nationality. You're officially un-American. Lotsa luck.

One of many things to consider before you take this rash step is the kind of company you'll be keeping. Setting aside cases of dual nationality, emigration, etc., people who renounce their citizenship typically are war criminals (who do it under the baleful eye of a judge to avoid the expense of a deportation hearing), the aforementioned militia members, and billionaire fat cats who do it to avoid U.S. taxes (although the feds are tightening up on this—that's why they ask renunciants for tax info). My guess is you're not going to want to get together with these guys in some kind of support group.

One last data point you might find interesting. In 1991 a survey asked two thousand U.S. citizens, "What are you willing to do for $10 million?" Twenty-five percent of this very classy group said they'd abandon their families; 23 percent said they'd become a prostitute for a week. Only 16 percent said they'd renounce their U.S. citizenship.

Un-American Activities

I couldn't believe you wrote that the United States "tolerates" dual citizenship, and that people born in the United States to foreign parents are merely encouraged to choose their citizenship. The United States emphatically does not recognize dual citizenship, and those with foreign-born parents are allowed dual citizenship only until adulthood, when they are required to choose. I learned this in eighth-grade civics class, but I seem to be the only person that remembers it.

I had an aquaintance who had trouble managing her dual U.S.-Israeli citizenship. As I remember it, she was trying to use her dual-citizenship status to avoid serving time in the Israeli army. Unfortunately, the United States wouldn't back her up since we don't recognize dual citizenship. She had to either serve in the Israeli army (which meant, I'm pretty sure, renouncing her U.S. citizenship since the United States doesn't allow citizens to serve in foreign armed forces) or give up her Israeli citizenship.—Janet Miller, Oakland, California

Janet and my assistant little Ed exchanged a few notes about this. We tried to explain that the United States *tolerates* dual citizenship

but doesn't officially *recognize* it. Janet found this policy unacceptably ambiguous and blamed *us* for allowing it to persist. You've probably met people like this.

Anyway, we went back and confirmed the following:

1. Cecil was of course right. Persons with dual citizenship are encouraged but not required to choose one over the other on reaching adulthood. Troubled by this, Janet? Deal with it.
2. Serving in another country's armed forces is not, in itself, illegal. You can't aid the enemy, of course, but what with the fall of communism and all, "enemies" is such an outmoded concept. Also, you can't serve as a commissioned or noncommissioned officer.
3. If you're a dual citizen of the United States and Israel and you get an Israeli draft notice, your choices are either to serve or to renounce your Israeli citizenship. U.S. policy in the event an Israeli/American attempts to weasel out of her obligations is to explain the above and go, "poor baby."

Another thing. I said you had to leave the country to renounce your citizenship, which is true. However, maybe you can get back in. Here's the story from Jose Diaz of Puerto Rico:

"A number of our more radical separatists have initiated a movement to renounce U.S. citizenship. So far there's no stampede, but we have learned you *can* renounce citizenship formally and stay within the system, as in the case of [separatist leader] Juan Mari Bras. How? Simple.

"1. Travel to a country with which the United States has liberal entry/exit policies, i.e., where all that is needed to enter/exit is a birth certificate.

"2. Renounce citizenship in the U.S. embassy there.

"3. Do not indicate what citizenship you'll be acquiring.

"4. Get back to United States soil with your birth certificate.

"5. Wait for the State Department to issue your certificate of loss of nationality without noticing you did not truly emigrate anywhere.

"6. Have a local court rule that you have an underlying 'natural' nationality that entitles you to live on U.S. soil without being a citizen.

"This [last thing] is obviously the tricky part. Essentially what the local court said was, Puerto Ricans became U.S. citizens in 1917, but

U.S. rule over Puerto Rico started in 1899, so for 18 years the Puerto Rican people existed as noncitizen U.S. 'subjects' or 'nationals.' This 'colonial nationality,' as it were, was never formally repealed when U.S. citizenship was extended to us; therefore Mr. Mari Bras, in renouncing his citizenship, reverts to the condition of a noncitizen living under U.S. rule.

"This theory would only be useful to people such as Puerto Rican nationalists or members of Native American tribes recognized by the United States as 'sovereign nations,' who can claim some 'natural' nationality apart from the U.S. citizenship."

If only it were that simple, Jose. I have another note here citing various legal authorities (e.g., *ex parte Knowles,* 1855) to show that you can be 1) a citizen of a state without being 2) a citizen of the United States. As you may suspect, this is a prelude to the claim that 3) you can renounce your U.S. citizenship, stay in the United States, and legally avoid federal income tax. I am not about to investigate this because I figure anybody trying to prove you don't have to pay income tax is, ipso facto, wack. But if things get a little rocky during your next IRS audit and it's either this or jail, be my guest.

What does Alice B. Toklas have to do with Alice B. Toklas brownies, anyway?—Judy Prisoc, Chicago

About as much as she had to do with *The Autobiography of Alice B. Toklas*—which is to say, not much. The 1933 "autobiography" was actually written by Gertrude Stein, Toklas's lifelong companion and one of the legendary figures of the Parisian literary scene in the first half of the twentieth century. Similarly, the recipe for marijuana-laced brownies (actually it was a brownielike hashish fudge) that appeared in the 1954 *Alice B. Toklas Cook Book* wasn't Toklas's own but rather that of a wiseacre painter friend named Brion Gysin.

It all started when Alice signed a contract with Harper's to write a cookbook in 1952. She was a pretty fair cook, but what Harper really hoped to get (and what by and large it got) was not so much recipes as tales of Toklas's life with Gertrude Stein, who had died in 1946.

With the deadline only a few months away, Toklas, then in her mid-70s, found herself half a book shy. So she began soliciting recipes from

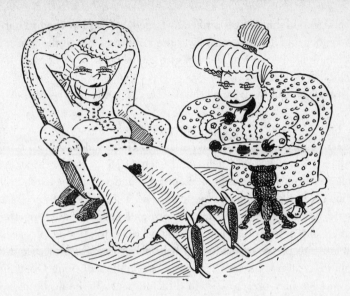

her artsy friends. Gysin came up with "Haschich Fudge, which anyone could whip up on a rainy day." By way of introduction he gushed, "This is the food of Paradise . . . it might provide an entertaining refreshment for a Ladies' Bridge Club or a chapter meeting of the DAR. . . . Euphoria and brilliant storms of laughter; ecstatic reveries and extensions of one's personality on several simultaneous planes are to be complacently expected. Almost anything Saint Theresa did, you can do better." The active ingredient in the fudge was what Gysin called "canibus sativa," more familiarly known as marijuana.

Alice, unfamiliar with "canibus" (at least as spelled by Gysin) and lacking the time to test the recipes, stuck her friend's contribution into her manuscript and sent it off to the publisher. The editors at Harper's spotted the suspicious ingredient and held the recipe out, but the publisher of the British edition didn't. The press promptly went nuts. Tittered *Time*: "The late Poetess Gertrude *(Tender Buttons)* Stein and her constant companion and autobiographee, Alice B. Toklas, used to have gay old times together in the kitchen. Some of the unique delicacies that were whipped up will soon be cataloged . . . in a wildly epicurean tome . . . which is already causing excited talk on both sides of the Atlantic. Perhaps the most gone concoction (and also possibly a clue to some of Gertrude's less earthly lines) was her hashish fudge."

Alice, a believer to the end in her friend's genius, was incensed that anyone should think it was artificially fueled. Still, as her friend Thornton Wilder told her, the recipe was the publicity stunt of the year and the expurgated American version of the cookbook received wide and generally respectful notice.

Just so you can see what all the fuss was about, here's the recipe:

"Take 1 teaspoon black peppercorns, 1 whole nutmeg, 4 average sticks of cinnamon, 1 teaspoon coriander. These should all be pulverized in a mortar. About a handful each of stone dates, dried figs, shelled almonds and peanuts: chop these and mix them together. A bunch of *canibus sativa* can be pulverized. This along with the spices should be dusted over the mixed fruit and nuts, kneaded together. About a cup of sugar dissolved in a big pat of butter. Rolled into a cake and cut into pieces or made into balls about the size of a walnut, it should be eaten with care. Two pieces are quite sufficient. Obtaining the *canibus* may present certain difficulties. . . . It should be picked and dried as soon as it has gone to seed and while the plant is still green."

Cecil must sternly advise that you shouldn't try this at home. If you do anyway, it hardly seems necessary to add, "Bon appétit."

If a tree falls in the woods and there is no living creature to hear it, is there a sound?—Julie Bosselman, Houston

People often ask me my secret. I tell them it's that I still remember how to open a dictionary. According to the (a) definition in my *American Heritage*, sound is vibration carried through a suitable medium in a frequency range capable of being heard by the human ear. It doesn't say the sound actually has to be heard. So according to (a), yes, there's a sound. The (c) definition says a sound is the sensation generated in the organs of hearing by the aforesaid vibration. So according to (c), no, there isn't a sound. Not the most definite answer in the world, you may think, but in view of the fact that this is obviously a matter of definition, certainly definitive.

Since she was a child, my mother has had something my family calls "perfect pitch": give her the name of a note—E flat, for instance—and she can hum it perfectly every time. Though the women in our family (for six generations!) have had a definite musical talent, we know of no one else who has this knack. What is this thing, anyway? How did she get it? And what can she do with it?—Elisabeth E., Chicago

Perfect pitch, to hear musicians who don't have it describe it, is a little like being able to make your ears wiggle—a cute stunt, but without much practical value. Others, however, say that having it is like going to color TV from black-and-white. Having looked into the question I am inclined to the latter view. I spoke to several individuals with perfect pitch and although they were all pretty nonchalant about it, I found at least some of them could do things that were the musical equivalent of a 360-degree slam dunk.

Perfect pitch, also called absolute pitch, has to be distinguished from perfect *relative* pitch—that is, the ability to sing or play accurately given a starting note. Relative pitch obviously is useful to professional musicians; most have it, and to a large extent it can be learned.

Absolute pitch is a different story. It's the ability to sing in tune with some previously memorized standard, for which reason some prefer the term "pitch memory." Contrary to wide impression, you're not born with it, but it does seem to be something you have to learn early. One perfectly pitched singer I spoke to had begun his musical training at age four.

Perfect pitch includes two separate skills: the ability to name a tone

once heard, and the ability to sing a named tone on command. A good singer without perfect pitch can approximate the latter skill because it depends in part on the kinesthetic (muscle) sense—i.e., how the sound feels in your head as you sing it. But we'll assume your mom wasn't faking it.

The terms absolute and perfect pitch misleadingly suggest you're somehow in tune with the basic hum of the universe. Alas, the mundane truth is that typically your reference standard is, as one authority puts it, "the pitch of your mother's piano." God help you if she didn't have that baby in tune.

Perfect pitch is a mixed blessing for musicians. Some claim it adds a new dimension to music, with each note having a character all its own. For just that reason, however, some with perfect pitch find transposing a piece to a different key disorienting—like "seeing purple grass," one writer says—because the feel of the new key is so different.

People with perfect pitch are often called upon by choirmasters and such to be human pitch-pipes. But if you arrive late for practice and the rest of the chorus is singing a quarter tone flat, you may find the experience excruciating. What's worse, as you age, your eardrums lose their elasticity and everything you hear goes a bit sharp. Most people don't notice the change, but for those with perfect pitch, nothing sounds right anymore.

The people with perfect pitch I spoke to pooh-poohed the new-dimension-of-music angle, but some of them were clearly being too modest. One University of Chicago music professor said he could conjure up an entire orchestral piece in his mind strictly from having read the sheet music. To him it was like reading a book. There were pieces he'd enjoyed for years before he'd physically heard them played. Snatches of seen-but-not-heard music would float into his mind the way we might remember an advertising jingle. He didn't own a stereo and didn't need one. He had an experience of music most people would never know.

Some have found other uses for perfect pitch. You may recall the "phone phreaks," the protohackers who used to delight in copping free calls from Ma Bell. One storied hacker was a blind kid named Joe Engressia. Most phreaks needed elaborate equipment to create the precisely pitched Touch-Tones necessary to operate the switching equipment. Not Engressia. Blessed with perfect pitch, he could whistle them.

Could you please provide detailed definitions of the terms "drawn and quartered" and "keelhauling"? The former conjures up images of having cartoons drawn on one's body before being pelted with pocket change. The latter could refer to being bound to the underside of a ship, boat, barge, whatever. My daughter's Disney movie (Peter Pan) *refers to both—didn't they think kids would eventually have access to the Internet?—Ted Jankowski, via the Internet*

We'd all better brush up on this stuff—if they're bringing back the chain gang, can keelhauling be far behind? Not that the latter is a realistic possibility if they nab you for jaywalking in Omaha. Keelhauling was meted out to sailors for minor infractions at sea. Typically the victim was tied to a rope looped beneath the vessel, thrown overboard, and then dragged under the keel and up the other side. Since the keel was usually encrusted with barnacles and other crud the guy's hide would be scraped raw and he'd think twice about doing whatever it was he'd gotten keelhauled for again. Sometimes they heaped chains and such on him to add injury to insult.

"Keelhauling" crops up in your Hollywood pirate's conversation about as often as "shiver me timbers," but as far as I can tell it was officially enacted as a punishment only by the Dutch. The earliest official

mention of keelhauling seems to be a Dutch ordinance of 1560 and the practice wasn't formally abolished until 1853. If you ever play shuffleboard on a Dutch cruise ship, my advice is: don't cheat.

Drawing and quartering is another punishment mentioned in kids' movies only because nobody realizes what's involved. The statutory punishment for treason in England from 1283 to 1867, D&Q was a multimedia form of execution. First the prisoner was drawn to the place of execution on a hurdle, a type of sledge. (Originally he was merely dragged behind a horse.) Then he was hanged. Cut down while still alive, he was disemboweled and his entrails burned before his eyes. (Some references, such as the *Encyclopaedia Britannica*, say this step, and not dragging behind a horse, is what is meant by "drawn," but actual sentences of execution don't support this view.)

Finally the condemned was beheaded and his body cut into quarters, one arm or leg to a quarter. How exactly the quartering was to be accomplished was not always specified, but on at least some occasions horses were hitched to each of the victim's limbs and spurred in four directions. An assistant with a sword or cleaver was sometimes assigned to make a starter cut and ease the strain on the animals. The remains were often put on display as a warning to others. Nothing like the good old days, eh? Just don't anybody mention this to Newt.

A Job Well Done

In your column you suggest that the Encyclopaedia Britannica *entry "drawing and quartering" is incorrect in interpreting the term "drawing" to refer to the prisoner's disembowelment.*

Although David M. Walker's The Oxford Companion to Law *agrees with the* Britannica *interpretation, we found your interpretation favored by several sources, including the* Oxford English Dictionary *as well as Sir Frederick Pollock and Frederick William Maitland's* The History of English Law Before the Time of Edward I. *It is clear that in this context "drawing" is more correctly understood as referring to the act of dragging the prisoner to the place of execution, and the entry will be amended at the earliest opportunity.*

Thank you for bringing the matter to our attention.—Peter Meyerhoff, assistant editor, Encyclopaedia Britannica

Glad to be of service. Anything else I can help you with, just let me know.

In the sixth grade, and many times since, I've heard it claimed that you can double over a piece of paper seven times but never eight, no matter what the paper's size. Since, as a sixth-grader, I could fold the paper in half seven times without difficulty, I felt certain an Arnold Schwarzenegger could do eight. Why not? Is there something inherent in the mathematics of doubling? Some physical limitation? Or is it simply that the eighth doubling takes more strength than most people have—meaning a sufficiently powerful machine could do it eight times?—S.E., New York

My friend Pablo and I heard this story in sixth grade, too, and we had the same thought that everybody who hears it has: "Gosh, what if you had a piece of paper a mile square and one atom thick? Couldn't you fold *that* in half eight times?" Not having access to paper of these specifications at the time, we were unable to put our conjecture to the test.

Unbeknownst to us, however, powerful economic forces were working on our behalf. It has long been the aim of the plastics industry to

produce sheeting so thin it only has one side, and today that aim has very nearly been achieved. We were able to purchase a plastic drop cloth measuring three yards by four yards and having a thickness of just 0.4 of a mil—that is, 4/10,000ths of an inch. This did not quite achieve the experimental standard we had dreamt of in sixth grade, and of course it meant substituting plastic for paper, with God knows what intramolecular consequences. However, we figured it was the best we could do for 59 cents, the drop cloth's price. Besides, we could use it when we painted the closet.

We thereupon embarked upon our experimental regimen. Mrs. Adams agreed to substitute for Pablo, who, having long since lit out for the territory, was no longer available to perform the vital scientific function of holding up the other end. Since Mrs. Adams invariably wants to zig when I want to zag, our progress was initially rocky, but eventually we got our act together and proceeded with the folding. Result: not eight, not nine, but *ten* doublings.

Granted, on the tenth fold the finished package was a little bulbous due to trapped air. (We could have popped the bubbles with a needle but didn't, out of a vague sense that it would be cheating.) The fact remained that we had easily surpassed seven folds. Vindication at last.

This summer I'm taking the family on vacation to Rwanda and Uganda. There's just one thing that's bothering me—what happens when I leave Rwanda where they drive on the right and enter Uganda where they drive on the left?—Anonymous

You're going to Rwanda and Uganda, two of the globe's most infamous localities, and the main thing you're worried about is switching sides of the road? Man, I'm not having you buy the groceries for *my* fallout shelter.

Initially I dismissed this question as being too dumb to bother with. However, I got a note from Robert Teeter of San Jose, California, who had wondered about it himself. Robert sent along an article on the subject he had obtained via ftp ('netters know what I'm talking about and everybody else can rest assured they're not missing much) from ftp.cc.umanitoba.ca/rec-travel/general/drive_which_side. Guess what: this question *was* too dumb to bother with. See for yourself.

"BORDER CROSSINGS. . . . This is not such a great puzzle as it might seem. Here are a few stories from people who have accomplished this mystifying feat.

" 'It was not a problem at the only border I have been to like this (Zaire to Uganda). The traffic was slow and there was very little of it. There was just a sign reminding you to swap sides.'

" 'The border crossing from China (where they drive on the right) to Pakistan (where they drive on the left) merely has a sign at the side of the road that says "Entering Pakistan, Drive Left" and for those going the other way "Entering China, Drive Right." '

" 'Usually you don't drive straight through a border post. The only place I've crossed a land border where the side of the road for driving changes is between Afghanistan and Pakistan. We drove into a car park (using the right-hand side) and after the border formalities, drove out using the left-hand side.' "

So there you have it: they put up a sign telling you to change sides. Who'd have thought it? But for those who found this a real stumper, I'm glad we got things cleared up at last.

Switching Sides, Continued

Regarding what to do when traveling between countries that drive on opposite sides of the road: I once knew a Norwegian who was a student at Oslo U. When he drove home the road passed several times in and out of Sweden, which until around 1965 drove on the left, while Norway drove on the right. The border was and is unguarded and in many places unmarked. The road was fairly narrow and there was a tendency to drive down the middle especially late at night when there was virtually no traffic. Now picture this: you are driving down this road, probably half asleep, you don't know and don't much care which country you are in, and suddenly you see a truck bearing down on you. What do you do?—Michael Barr, Montreal

From The Message Board

Subj: St. Peter's Basilica
From: Blewick

I have a friend who has a cross made of wood supposedly from a door in St. Peter's Basilica. It was said that this door is only opened once every 100 years. Please tell me what is behind the door, and why it is kept closed. Thanks.

From: Bermuda999

St. Peter's Basilica in Vatican City is one of the most visited shrines in the world. It is the second-largest Christian church in the world. It is built on the site of a fourth-century basilica that is believed to enclose the tomb of St. Peter, the founder of the church.

Despite [the church] being so open to pilgrims and tourists, there is one room behind and under the main altar that remains locked and is only opened every 100 years (at the beginning of each millennium; the next opening is scheduled for January 1, 2001). Contained within the walls of this secret shrine are some of the most wonderful treasures in the world. The contents are a closely held secret, but a partial list of contents has been assembled from information obtained by previous visitors:

> Item 121—John Dillinger's penis (broken)
> Item 124—The original recipe for Mrs. Field's chocolate chip cookies
> Item 131—Unretouched photos of the Loch Ness monster, from several locations on shore
> Item 132—The Sphinx's nose (several V-8 stains noted)
> Item 133—Michael Jackson's nose
> Item 134—Michael Jackson's testicles
> Item 146—The Shroud of Turin
> Item 147—The Pillowcase of Turin
> Item 148—The Washcloth of Turin
> Item 166—The Ten Commandments Stone Tablets (second edition)
> Item 167—The Ten Commandments Abridged Edition (paperback)
> Item 171—Jimmy Carter's Attack Bunny (stuffed)
> Item 173—The Chupacabra
> Item 174—A goat (sucked)

Item 180—Quantrill's Skull

Item 184—An elevator surveillance videotape of Lionel Richie, Reggie Jackson, and Eddie Murphy saying "Hit the floor" or "Sit, lady" and then a white woman complying by sitting on the floor of the elevator

Item 187—Walt Disney

Item 183—The "Good Times" virus

Item 189—"Blue Star" blotter acid

Item 191—A dead skin diver (impaled on a branch and burned to a crisp)

Item 193—Jimmy Hoffa

Item 195—The original recipe for Coca-Cola

Item 210—A copy of the original words to "Louie Louie"

Item 211—D.B. Cooper

Item 213—A New York City sewer alligator (stuffed)

Item 214—A videotape of the episode of the *Newlywed Game* in which the husband's response to "What was the strangest place you have made love" was, "That'd be the butt, Bob."

Item 219—A videotape of the *Tonight Show* in which Johnny Carson said he'd pet guest Zsa Zsa Gabor's pussy if she'd move her cat.

Item 221—A Civil War bullet that ripped through a soldier's testicles, continued on through the abdomen of a virgin and impregnated her

Item 224—A kidney stolen from a guy found on a Central Park bench

Item 229—Richard Gere's gerbil (shaved)

Item 236—A screaming lobster

Item 237—A Mexican rat that resembles a dog

Item 238—A JATO car (front end crushed)

Item 241—The Pompatus of Love

Item 243—Noah's Ark

Item 244—The Lost Ark of the Covenant

Item 245—The Golden Fleece

Item 246—The Holy Grail

Item 247—A photograph of Cecil Adams

Item 248—Cecil Adams

Item 666—The third word ending in "gry"

Admittance to the once-a-century ceremony is granted only to those holding special Tootsie Pop wrappers containing a Chief Shooting Star emblem.

From: TUBADIVA
Bermuda, I want you to have my baby!

#1

Questions You Shouldn't Even THINK About Sending In

1. Why do we need a hot water heater? If it's hot it doesn't need to be heated.
2. How can we have jumbo shrimp?
3. Why isn't phonetic spelled the way it sounds?
4. Why do our noses run and our feet smell?
5. Why does quicksand work slowly?
6. Why are boxing rings square?
7. Why, when lights are out, they are invisible, but when the stars are out, they are visible?
8. Why do we call them apartments when they are all together?
9. If cows laughed, would milk come out of their noses?
10. Why does Denny's have locks on the door if it's open 24 hours?
11. Why do ships carry cargoes and cars carry shipments?
12. When will a building actually become a built?

#2

The Straight Dope FAQ (Frequently Asked Questions)

1. Who is Cecil Adams?
Cecil Adams is the world's most intelligent human being. We know this because: 1) he knows everything, and 2) he is never wrong.

2. How do we know that Cecil knows everything and is never wrong?
Because he said so, and he would never lie to us.

3. No, really.
Listen, read the columns. Soon you will agree this is no ordinary man.

4. What do you mean, "columns"? You're telling me the world's smartest human being works for the newspapers?
We all gotta eat. Yes, Cecil works for the newspapers. His syndicated weekly column, the "Straight Dope," presently appears in more than 30 newspapers throughout the United States and Canada. Ballantine

has published three collections of his work, a Straight Dope TV show appeared on the Arts & Entertainment cable network in fall 1996, and we'll be starting on the biopic as soon as we can line up Sly Stallone.

5. *You're making this up.*
All right, the Sly Stallone part we made up. But the other stuff is real.

6. *How come I've never seen the Straight Dope in print?*
You've got to start reading better newspapers. For a list of subscribers, visit one of our online sites and find the page entitled, "Newspapers That Carry the Straight Dope."

For a description of Cecil's previous three books, go to the main screen of our America Online site and click on "Buy Stuff." (This is a subliminal hint.) You will be taken to the Straight Dope store. Or go to your local bookstore. Naturally, if you have not been reading the Straight Dope up till now, we urge you to buy all Cecil's books immediately. This will enable you to make up for the wasted years.

7. *How does the Straight Dope newspaper column work?*
People ask questions. Cecil answers them. It is not a complex concept.

8. *Questions about what?*
Anything. Cecil knows all. Naturally, since he does not want to put his readers to sleep, he does not tell all. (We leave that to movie stars.) He prefers to confine his attention to questions that are interesting and funny, or sometimes just interesting. However, stupid but funny also has a pretty good shot.

9. *Isn't that what Ann Landers does?*
No, no, no. Advice columnists just try to get you through the day. Cecil is trying to eradicate world ignorance. He deals strictly with factual questions. Questions you've always wanted to know the answers to. Questions like: What are the real lyrics to "Louie Louie"? When they execute a guy by lethal injection, do they swab off his arm first? How do the astronauts go to the bathroom in space?

We wanted to make that last one the title of one of the Straight

Dope books, but Ballantine wouldn't go for it. They also wouldn't go for: "THE STRAIGHT DOPE—Third Book of Revelations." Said it was too long to fit on the computers. Sure. We say they were scared of the religious right.

10. Has there ever been a question Cecil couldn't answer?

Yeah, like he'd admit it. But it can honestly be said no question Cecil has seriously pursued has remained beyond his grasp. Admittedly some took longer than others. He got pretty frustrated trying to figure out how they got the M's on M&M's, because Mars, the manufacturer, refused to cooperate. Stonewalled us for years. It got to where we were about to put a guy over the wall.

Luckily, just then Mars hired Hans to run the PR department. Hans believed in freedom of information and had a cool accent to boot. He explained the whole thing. Not that he was telling Cecil anything he didn't already know. Nobody ever does.

Some questions, it must be conceded, lie beyond the veil of things known. For example, while Cecil did his best, he was never able to conduct a systematic search for the Vatican porn collection (i.e., to prove there wasn't one). Also, we do not feel the last word has been written about the phenomenon of piss shiver. Although when we said as much to the management of the *Chicago Reader*, they said, "Wanna bet?"

Just thought of another great book title Ballantine rejected. "Straight Dope 3-D." Suggested by our friend Robert. He's such a card.

11. Has there ever been a question Cecil WOULDN'T answer?

Well, let's see. He discussed the calorie content of sperm. That was pretty out there. He also dealt in a grave and educational manner with the issue of why fecal matter is brown. Actually the question didn't say "fecal matter." But we don't want to get termed (terminated, for you newbies) by the AOL RoboCensors.

Then there was the matter of the gerbils. And placenta stew. No question, we are definitely advancing the frontiers of civic discourse.

But you asked if there was ever a question Cecil refused to answer on grounds other than that it was inane (see Appendix 1). Can't think of one, but we'll say this: if you ever come up with a question that Cecil won't touch, you'd better turn yourself in to the police.

12. How did the Straight Dope come to be?

It all started in February 1973, in the *Chicago Reader*, now a titan of alternative journalism but then . . . well, a skinny titan. The column appeared without fuss or fanfare. This was Cecil's preference. He wanted to start off small and then expand. Just like the universe.

13. Did Cecil have a vast army of assistants to help him with his research?

No. On occasion he called his brother-in-law. He has also had the assistance of an editor, generally a feckless youth, plus an illustrator. For many years now the illustrator has been Slug Signorino, a legend in his own right. Someday we are going to write about Slug, too. We'd do it now, except the court locked up the psychiatric notes.

About those editors. The first was Mike Lenehan. Mike was not feckless. Mike had fecks to beat the band. It may truthfully be said that Mike was something of a father figure to Cecil, who was then of tender years himself. Mike took the young genius under his wing, nurtured his gift, and made him what he is today. Often Mike, who is now executive editor of the *Chicago Reader*, looks back and thinks: Lord, this is all my fault.

Even then, you see, Cecil was a handful. In print this evidenced itself as a certain attitude with regard to readers. Our favorite comment remains, "If ignorance were cornflakes, you'd be General Mills." Or: "I'm going to explain this as well as I can, given the limits of my space and your attention span."

But Cecil also took it out on his editor, so much so that after three years Lenehan bailed. The next editor was Dave Kehr. Dave hung in there for two years. At last, broken in spirit, he took to reviewing movies and wound up writing for the New York *Daily News*. It was tragic.

The management at the *Chicago Reader* huddled. This Cecil, they said, he's brilliant, but his insufferable personality is more than any normal person should be asked to bear. The only solution is to assign him an editor who does not have any sense of self to start with.

This explains Ed Zotti. He started off slow and it's been downhill from there. But since 1978 he's kept Cecil, if not happy, at least constructively pissed, cranking out columns once a week. Better that than letter bombs.

Late addendum: Owing to the press of business on our America Online site, Cecil has now hired two additional assistants. They are JKFabian, also known as Message Board Goddess #1, and TUBADIVA, chat host administrator and Message Board Goddess #2.

14. How does Cecil do his thing?

From what we have been able to piece together, Cecil works in fits and starts. First he rummages through the mail looking for mash notes from groupies. Our favorite (no kidding): "Dear Cecil, are you married? If yes, do you fool around?"

Then he looks for enough interesting questions to fill a column. He ruminates for a while. He cleans the oven. Finally he calls over his editor and dictates. This part takes 20 minutes. Then the editor has to check the facts. This can take years. YOU try definitively establishing what the H stands for in Jesus H. Christ. Finally the finished column is produced and turned over to the typesetting department, which inserts random mistakes.

Nah, just kidding. The people at the *Chicago Reader* never goof up. But stuff happens. Like the other day. We start getting grief from residents of a city in which the column appears because Cecil wrote milliMETERS when it was clear from the context that he meant milliLITERS. Well, it went out of HERE saying milliliters. What's more, it went out ELECTRONICALLY, so if we rule out the influence of cosmic rays we must ask the editors of an unnamed newspaper HOW COULD THIS POSSIBLY GET SCREWED UP? Sorry, just needed to get that off our chest. But you get the idea. ·

15. What's Cecil really like?

Only his editors really know. When you ask them, their eyes glaze, their bodies become rigid, and they start to spit. They are struggling to express their joy, we figure. More than that we cannot say.

16. What do we know about Cecil's private life?

Not much. Over the years he has revealed a few details in the column. For example, he is left-handed. That tells you a lot right there. We also know that there is a Mrs. Adams, although, now that we think about it, that could be his mother. Cecil has made reference from time to time to "the little researchers." These may be children. On the other hand, maybe he just hires dwarves on the side.

17. Tell the truth. Has Cecil ever been wrong?

Never. However, certain questionable situations have arisen. Veteran Straight Dope readers may remember that a column once referred to "talking books for the deaf." Very funny. It was a new copyboy's first day on the job. His body has never been found.

18. Are the questions in the column real?

Of course they're real. You think we could make this stuff up?

19. What's the average lag between the time you receive a question and the time the answer appears in print?

Sometime between 15 minutes and never. The longest lag we know of for a question that was actually published was nine years. But that was unusual. If a question is worth answering, we make a genuine effort to do so while the question asker is still alive.

20. Just one more thing. How do you pronounce "FAQ"?

Fakk, that's how. Don't be smart. That's Cecil's job.

The America Online FAQ [Posted to the Usenet newsgroup alt.fan.cecil-adams]

Cecil has asked me to inform the Teeming Millions that the Straight Dope is now available on America Online. This being the net and all, the occasion seems to call for a FAQ.

1. Why are you doing this?
Because they are paying us to. Had anybody sent us a million-dollar donation like we are constantly hinting, maybe we wouldn't. However, one must face the fiscal realities.

2. But AOL people are such lamers.
Come now, lameness is not exactly unknown on the net. It is true that the intellectual level of discussion in many groups, of which a.f.c-a is certainly the foremost example, is higher than what you typically encounter on AOL. For that matter, on some nights, the level of conversation between two guys sharing a Dumpster is higher than

what you get on AOL. This just goes to show you how desperately these people need us. We will teach them. They will learn. Or we'll kill them.

3. *What exactly are you guys doing on AOL?*

We invite you to check it out. AOL has sent everyone in the universe a software disk; no doubt there is one on your desk now. We are at keyword STRAIGHT DOPE. DOPE will also work, I think, but AOL has a thing about bad words, so let's keep that among ourselves.

Anyway, each week we post the current "Straight Dope" column (actually it appears starting on Monday of the week AFTER the week it appears in our subscribing newspapers). There is also a Straight Dope "classic" column (although in Cecil's opinion they're all classics), which changes daily. Each column features artwork by the legendary Slug Signorino. So does the whole area, in fact. The best part is the pulsating brain. We had to slow it down, lest it induce epileptic seizures.

Other features of interest:

SEARCHABLE ARCHIVE. We currently have about 600 previous questions online, some dating back to 1973, e.g., Cecil's infamous discussion of the caloric content of sperm. Eventually we expect to make the sum total of Cecil's life work available online, complete with Slug's artwork, except for the stuff that's been seized by the police.

RECENT COLUMNS. The past few months' worth of columns in date order as they appeared in the newspaper (e.g., multiple questions per file).

CECIL'S HOUSE O' VALUES. Order books, T-shirts, and mugs online! Just like Disneyland!

MESSAGE BOARD. Just like a.f.c-a. Major positive difference: Cecil's lackey Ed Zotti (me) participates on a regular basis. Major negative difference: the message board software totally eats. They are promising this will improve. They are promising Jesus will come again, too.

MESSAGES FROM CECIL. Queries, exhortations, the occasional venting of bile. A lot like the column only without the distraction of facts.

JUNK DRAWER. Our big chance at last to use all the weird stuff the Teeming Millions send us, such as the color photo of the intestinal hairball removed from an 18-year-old woman who sucked on her split ends. This new medium has many exciting possibilities.

Plenty of other good stuff, too. Check it out.

4. Does this mean the end of alt.fan.cecil-adams?

Of course not. The Straight Dope didn't start a.f.c-a, and we wouldn't have the first clue how to stop it if we wanted to, which we don't. We may include a link to a.f.c-a in the SD AOL area, if we can ever figure out how.

5. Will you stop posting columns to a.f.c-a?

The current week's column plus the 51 or so most recent columns are now posted to our Web site at www.straightdope.com.

6. Doesn't this prove Cecil is a capitalist whore who will do anything for money?

Yeah, right, like Michael Jordan does it for free.

7. Is AOL going to make you restrict the Straight Dope's wide ranging subject matter?

The only thing they've given us grief about so far is bad words. Instead you will find such pathetic euphemisms as @#%!! and [doodoo]. However, we imagine you can figure out what Cecil meant.

8. Why should I, a sophisticated net user, want to avail myself of the AOL Straight Dope when I've got a.f.c-a?

Lotta reasons. Easy access to Cecil's current and past work. The active participation of Ed Zotti and, more usefully, his more recently hired assistants JKFabian and TUBADIVA. The chance to put part of your monthly online nickel in Cecil's deserving pocket. Plus—this is no small thing—access to the vast panorama of Slug's art, most of which is now available for the first time since it was originally published in the newspaper. The first time you fire this sucker up, make sure the kids aren't in the room.

9. Anything else you feel we should know?

Are you kidding? Cecil has spent 25 years telling you things he feels you should know. But that's enough for now.

The alt.fan.cecil-adams FAQ [Posted to the Straight Dope site on America Online]

1. What is alt.fan.cecil-adams?

A.f.c-a is a Usenet newsgroup. A newsgroup is basically a message board like the one we have here on the AOL SD. People post messages and other people reply. The Usenet is a collection of thousands of such newsgroups that (mostly) runs over the Internet and is available to pretty much anyone with an Internet hookup anywhere in the world. We have gotten letters from people in Antarctica (honest). It is pretty cool.

2. How can I access a.f.c-a?

You can get it on AOL through keyword: Newsgroups. On a Web browser click around looking for the word "newsgroups." They say these graphical interfaces are intuitive, and by God they'd better be.

3. Did Cecil Adams start a.f.c-a?

No. The Straight Dope has no formal connection with a.f.c-a. It is a spontaneous efflorescence of wit and learning on the part of the Teeming Millions, proving that our many years of selfless labor are finally paying off. Cecil is very proud.

4. Why would I want to participate in a.f.c-a?
Because the discussion is pretty interesting and the people doing the discussing are, with some conspicuous exceptions, pretty smart.

5. Anything you want to tell me before I participate in a.f.c-a?
Many Usenet users think AOLers are hopeless dimbulbs with barely enough brains to find the "on" switch on their computers. Surprise them.

Index

R

S

sun, why it darkens skin but lightens
hair, 128
Sunday. *See* Sabbath
Surgeon General, why military
uniform worn by, 194–196
Swiss army knife, does Swiss army
really use, 158–159
switching sides of road, when
crossing border between
countries, 242–243
sword swallowers, how they do it,
70–72
syphilis, origin of, 102
"systems," for winning at games of
chance, 119–121

T

talcum powder, contamination of by
asbestos, 103–104
Tapp, Mara, 48
tapping: of cigarettes, purpose of,
200–207; of shaken carbonated
beverages to avoid foam
explosion, 198–200
Taylor, David, 82
Taylor, Zachary (U.S. President),
death of due to consumption of
cherries, 30–31
Teeter, Robert, 242
teeth. *See* rabbit
Teflon, how they get it to stick to
pans, 173–174
teller machines. *See* drive-up ATMs
temperature scales (Fahrenheit and
Celsius), 188–189
theologians. *See* angels, how many
can dance on head of
Thomas Brothers map company,
167–168
Thorne, Kip, 181–182
360 degrees in circle, origin of, 194
time travel, theoretical possibility of,
181–183

TM. *See* Transcendental Meditation
toilet seats, why U-shaped in public
restrooms, 6
Toklas, Alice B. *See* Alice B. Toklas
brownies
Tonto (*Lone Ranger* character). See
"kemosabe"
"toxic lady" (Gloria Ramirez),
emergency room chaos caused by,
107–110
TradeNet (laundry ball marketer), 10
Transcendental Meditation,
levitation and other wonders
attributed to, 136–138
tree, sound of, if falls in woods, 236
Trendle, George W. (*Lone Ranger*
originator), 62
Tyler, John, whether was officially
U.S. President, 24

U

UFOs. *See* Area 51
uniform, why worn by Surgeon
General, 194–196
uranium. *See* Fiestaware
urinals, why ice placed in, 130–131
urination: shivering following ("piss
shiver"), 225–227; why males
should wash hands following,
220–221
urine: as disinfectant, 221;
consumption of, as therapy,
223–225

V

vegetable oil, why 100% fat even
though vegetables are low fat, 178
Vespucci, Amerigo. *See* Amerigo
Vespucci
Victorinox (Swiss army knife maker),
158–159
violent mental instability, whether

writing to Straight Dope is sign
of, 122–123

W

Waldseemueller, Martin
(cartographer), 22, 23
Walker, Jearl, 200
washing, of hands, following
urination, 220–221
Washington Post, 176–177
"water cooling" (burn treatment),
92–93
WD-40 (lubricant), as remedy for
joint pain, 129
Weekly World News, 25
Wenger (Swiss army knife maker),
158–159
wife. *See* spouse
WMCA radio, and role in smiley-
face fad, 34–35

women's illnesses. *See* fainting
Wood, Evelyn. *See* speed reading
World War II veterans, and smoking,
97–99

Y

Yeager, Charles, 62
YKK, significance of, on zippers,
209–211
Yoshida, Tadao (zipper mogul),
209–211
Young, Joy, role of in smiley-face
craze, 33
Yurtsever, Ulvi, 181

Z

Zacchini family (human
cannonballs), 70
Zostrix, 129

About The Author

People often ask whether time will mellow Cecil. We wish.